GREEN HOUSE GAS EMISSIONS REPORTING AND MANAGEMENT IN GLOBAL TOP EMITTING COUNTRIES AND COMPANIES

ADVANCES IN ENVIRONMENTAL ACCOUNTING & MANAGEMENT

Series Editor: Venancio Tauringana

Recent volumes:

Volume 10: Environmental Sustainability and Agenda 2030, 2022

Volume 9: Environmentalism and NGO Accountability, 2020

Volume 8: Environmental Reporting and Management in Africa, 2019

Volume 7: Sustainability Accounting: Education, Regulation, Reporting and Stakeholders, 2018

Volume 6: Social and Environmental Accounting in Brazil, 2017

Volume 5: Accounting for the Environment: More Talk and Little Progress, 2014

Volume 4: Sustainability, Environmental Performance and Disclosures, 2010

Volume 3: Environmental Accounting: Commitment or Propaganda, 2006

Volume 2: Advances in Environmental Accounting and Management, 2003

Volume 1: Advances in Environmental Accounting and Management, 2000

ADVANCES IN ENVIRONMENTAL ACCOUNTING &
MANAGEMENT   VOLUME 11

GREEN HOUSE GAS EMISSIONS REPORTING AND MANAGEMENT IN GLOBAL TOP EMITTING COUNTRIES AND COMPANIES

EDITED BY

VENANCIO TAURINGANA
University of Southampton, UK

And

OLAYINKA MOSES
Victoria University of Wellington, New Zealand

United Kingdom – North America – Japan
India – Malaysia – China

Emerald Publishing Limited
Howard House, Wagon Lane, Bingley BD16 1WA, UK

First edition 2023

Reprints and permissions service
Contact: permissions@emeraldinsight.com

British Library Cataloguing in Publication Data
A catalogue record for this book is available from the British Library

ISBN: 978-1-80262-884-5 (Print)
ISBN: 978-1-80262-883-8 (Online)
ISBN: 978-1-80262-885-2 (Epub)

ISSN: 1479-3598 (Series)

Printed and bound by CPI Group (UK) Ltd, Croydon, CR0 4YY

ISOQAR certified
Management System,
awarded to Emerald
for adherence to
Environmental
standard
ISO 14001:2004.

ISOQAR
REGISTERED
Certificate Number 1985
ISO 14001

INVESTOR IN PEOPLE

CONTENTS

List of Reviewers   *vii*

About the Contributors   *ix*

**Greenhouse Gas Reporting and Management in Top Emitting
Countries and Companies**   *1*
Venancio Tauringana and Olayinka Moses

**Greenhouse Gas Emissions Research in Top-Ranked Journals: A
Meta-Analysis**   *11*
*Emmanuel Eduche Michael, Joy Nankyer Dabel-Moses, Dare
John Olateju, Ikoojo David Emmanuel and Vincent Edache
Michael*

**Impact of State Ownership on Greenhouse Gas Emissions
Disclosures in China**   *29*
Zhifeng Chen, Yixiao Liu, Yuanyuan Hu and Longyao Zhang

**Corporate Governance and Greenhouse Gas Disclosures: Evidence
From the United States**   *51*
*Juma Bananuka (RIP), Pendo Shukrani Kasoga and Zainabu
Tumwebaze*

**Board Interlocks and Carbon Emissions Performance: Empirical
Evidence From India**   *81*
Albert Ochien'g Abang'a and Chipo Simbi

**The Impact of the Paris Climate Change Agreement and Other
Factors on Climate Change Disclosure in South Africa**   *107*
Caitlin Mongie, Gizelle Willows and Shelly Herbert

Social Determinants of Greenhouse Gas Emissions in the Top 100 Developed and Developing Emitting Countries *127*
Venancio Tauringana, Laura Achiro and Babajide Oyewo

Index *159*

LIST OF REVIEWERS

Albert Ochien'g Abang'a	Strathmore University, Kenya
Juma Bananuka (RIP)	Makerere University Business School, Uganda
Marian Chijoke-Mgbame	De Montfort University, United Kingdom
Emmanuel Edache Michael	Victoria University of Wellington, New Zealand
Stephen Nkundabanyana	Makerere University Business School, Uganda
Babajide Oyewo	University of Southampton, United Kingdom

ABOUT THE CONTRIBUTORS

Dr Albert Ochien'g Abang'a is currently an Accounting and Finance Lecturer at Strathmore University Business School, Kenya. He obtained his PhD in Accounting and Finance at Strathmore University in October 2022. His first degree was in Bachelor of Commerce (Accounting option). He also obtained his Master of Commerce (Forensic Accounting) in 2017 from the same University. His areas of interests are sustainability accounting, corporate governance and corporate social responsibility.

Laura Achiro attained her MBA from Heriot-Watt University, Edinburgh, and recently completed her PhD in Business Studies and Management from the University of Southampton (UK). She was later appointed as a Lecturer in Accounting at the University of Southampton. She previously worked in the financial services as a Senior Relationship Manager, Assistant Vice President and Business Credit officer in Corporate and Investment banking at Citibank Uganda. Laura's research interests are so far focussed on ESG (Environmental, Social and Governance).

Dr Zhifeng Chen is a Lecturer in Accounting at the University of Southampton. Her research interests are in corporate social responsibility (CSR), ESG, sustainability, accounting information disclosure and behavioural finance.

Joy Nankyer Dabel-Moses is a Lecturer with the Department of Business Administration, Faculty of Management Sciences, University of Jos, Nigeria. Joy is currently undertaking a PhD programme in Accounting at Massey University, New Zealand. Before commencing her programme, Joy taught Cost and Management Accounting at the Department of Business Administration, University of Jos. Joy is a professional accountant and a member of the Association of National Accountants of Nigeria. Currently Joy's area of research centres around the public sector financial reporting. Joy loves to read and research.

Ikoojo David Emmanuel is a graduate research student at the Nigerian Defence academy (NDA) Kaduna, Nigeria. His professional affiliations include the Institute of Chartered Accountants of Nigeria (ICAN) and the Association of Accountancy Bodies in West Africa (ABWA). He has many years of practical auditing experience. Ikoojo's research interests lie in the area of public sector accounting, corporate financing and internally generated revenues. Ikoojo is a seasonal agriculturist, clean energy advocate and a strong believer in protecting nature.

Shelly Herbert CA(SA) is an Associate Professor at the University of Cape Town. Her research focus is on sustainability and non-financial reporting, including integrated and sustainability reporting.

Dr Yuanyuan Hu is a Senior Lecturer in the School of Accountancy at Massey University, Palmerston North, New Zealand. Yuanyuan's areas of research expertise include corporate social responsibility, corporate governance, executive behaviour, performance management and lean accounting. Yuanyuan publishes in high-quality international journals and is on the referee panel of a wide range of accounting and finance journals.

Pendo Shukrani Kasoga is a Senior Lecturer in the Department of Accounting and Finance at the University of Dodoma, Tanzania. She studied Master of Business Administration at the University of Dar es Salaam. She proceeded with a Doctorate in Business Administration (major microfinance) at the University of Dodoma. She has been working with the University of Dodoma on a full-time basis since September 2007. She has been conducting research, supervising students, publishing articles and offering consultancy services to various public and private organisations. Her major areas of research interest include microfinance, financial services, corporate finance and corporate governance.

Yixiao Liu is a PhD student in Business Studies and Management in the University of Southampton. Her great passion is investigating the corporate sustainable development strategy. Her research focuses on understanding the market attitude for the corporate ESG investment and identifying the long-term value of ESG practice. Identification of market orientation for sustainability may better encourage to incorporate ESG activities into strategies at firm level.

Emmanuel Edache Michael is a Lecturer in Accounting with the Wellington School of Business and Government, Victoria University of Wellington, New Zealand. Emmanuel's teaching experience includes lecturing at the Department of Accounting, University of Jos, Nigeria, and the School of Accounting and Commercial Law at Victoria University of Wellington, New Zealand. As an environmental, social and governance researcher with broad interests in both developing and developed countries, Emmanuel's research focusses on regulatory and practice of environmental, social and governance reporting; corporate investments and financing and capital markets.

Vincent Edache Michael obtained a BSc in Accounting from the University of Jos, Nigeria, in 2014, and an MSc in Accounting and Finance in 2019, from the same University. He is an Associate Member of the Institute of Chartered Accountants of Nigeria (ICAN), where he was granted the much-coveted ICAN Gold Scholarship award upon completing his BSc He is an Audit Manager with Tony Ochei & Co, a firm of Chartered Accountants and Tax Practitioners in Abuja, Nigeria.

Caitlin Mongie completed her Master's at UCT in 2019 and is a registered Charted Accountant (South Africa). She is currently practicing in her role as an Audit Manager for Deloitte for insurance clients.

Olayinka Moses teaches Accounting for Strategy, Performance and Value in the Wellington School of Business and Government, Victoria University of Wellington. Yinka's research overarchingly focusses on environmental and sustainability accounting and accountability and has been published in several journals including *Accounting, Auditing & Accountability Journal*; *Accounting and Finance*; *Journal of Contemporary Accounting & Economics*; *Social and Environmental Accountability Journal*; *Advances in Environmental Accounting & Management*; *Emerging Markets Finance and Trade* among others. Yinka is the Associate Editor for *Advances in Environmental Accounting & Management*. He also serves as a Section Editor for Accounting, Corporate Governance & Business Ethics for *Cogent Business & Management Journal*; and editorial board member for several journals. Yinka is a member of Chartered Accountants Australia and New Zealand, and CPA Australia. He is the Chair of the CPA Australia ESG Committee (New Zealand Division) and an Executive Member of the African Accounting and Finance Association.

Dare John Olateju is a Lecturer in the Department of Banking and Finance, Faculty of Management Sciences, University of Jos, Jos, Nigeria. He is an Associate Member of the Institute of Chartered Accountants of Nigeria (ICAN). Dare is currently pursuing his PhD study at the University of Jos, Nigeria. In addition to his work as a teacher and practitioner, he has published several articles in reputable journals. He has books published to his credit. His research interest is Corporate Social Responsibility, Financial Management and Performance Management.

Babajide Oyewo is currently a Researcher at Southampton Business School, University of Southampton, United Kingdom. He holds academic and professional qualifications in Accounting, Business and Finance. He is a recipient of many awards, including literary prizes in Business communication & Research Methods, and Multi-disciplinary case studies. He is an Associate member of The Chartered Institute of Management Accountants (CIMA, UK), Chartered Global Management Accountants (CGMA, USA), Institute of Chartered Accountants of Nigeria (ICAN) and Chartered Institute of Stockbrokers (CIS). He has published in top-ranked ABS and ABDC journals

Chipo Simbi is an Accounting Lecturer in the Department of Accounting at Rhodes University in South Africa. Chipo holds a Master's in Accounting from the University of Zimbabwe and is currently pursuing her PhD in Accounting at Rhodes University. She is currently researching on capital market consequences of IFRS adoption and the moderating effect of the institutional environment. Chipo's research interest is in financial reporting and capital market behaviour.

Venancio Tauringana is the Head of the Department of Accounting and a Professor of Accounting & Sustainability. He is also the Editor of the *Advances in Environmental Accounting and Management*, Associate Editor of the *Journal of Accounting in Emerging Economies* and Associate Editor of the *South African Journal of Accounting Research*. Ven was President of the African Accounting Association (AAFA) from 2017 to 2019. In 2022, Ven won the Vice-Chancellor Award for Inspiring Leadership at the University of Southampton. He is a Chartered Environmentalist. Ven is also a Global Reporting Initiative (GRI) certified sustainability reporting professional. He leads a project involving undergraduate and postgraduate students training on sustainability reporting and helping SMEs

Dr Gizelle Willows is a Professor at the University of Cape Town. Her research interest lies in behavioural finance, particularly as it relates to personal finance and retirement savings. She is the recipient of multiple best paper awards and leader of the Behavioural Finance and Accounting international research group.

Prof Longyao Zhang is Dean of Finance at College of Finance, Nanjing Agricultural University. His research interests include the rural credit market, fintech, microfinance, bank lending behaviour and financial development.

GREENHOUSE GAS REPORTING AND MANAGEMENT IN TOP EMITTING COUNTRIES AND COMPANIES

Venancio Tauringana and Olayinka Moses

ABSTRACT

This chapter outlines the need for global actions on mitigating greenhouse gas (GHG) emissions and introduces the six chapters contained in this issue. The impact of GHG emissions on the environment undoubtedly exacerbates the consequence of climate change and is not constrained within the borders of the emitting countries and companies. Emitting countries (and companies) export much of the harm created by GHG emissions given that the earth's atmosphere intermixes globally. GHG top emitters are not necessarily the victims of its consequences, since the extent to which each country is affected by adverse weather such as floods depends on the distribution of climate vulnerability rather than jurisdictional emission. Hence, global collective actions are required to find plausible solutions to reduce GHG emissions. This issue consists of one literature review and five empirical chapters. The insight from the literature review highlights the dearth of studies addressing GHG emissions reporting and management in Africa and the Middle East. The first three empirical chapters examine the efficacy of corporate governance in facilitating GHG disclosures and performance in China, the United States and India. The fifth chapter examines the effect of the Paris Agreement on climate change disclosures in South Africa. There is mixed evidence as to how corporate governance affects GHG disclosure, but it is clear that the Paris Agreement had a positive impact on climate change disclosures in South Africa. The sixth chapter examines the social determinants of GHG in top 100 emitting countries and documents evidence that energy use determines the extent of GHG

Green House Gas Emissions Reporting and Management in Global Top Emitting
Countries and Companies
Advances in Environmental Accounting & Management, Volume 11, 1–9
Copyright © 2023 Venancio Tauringana and Olayinka Moses
Published under exclusive licence by Emerald Publishing Limited
ISSN: 1479-3598/doi:10.1108/S1479-359820230000011001

emissions in both developed and developing countries. However, the results show that other social determinants such as urbanisation, literacy and corruption contribute in varying ways to GHG emissions in developing countries. Taken together, the collection of chapters in this issue provides incremental understanding to the effect of GHG emissions and necessary actions that can help in mitigating them.

Keywords: Carbon emissions; China; GHG emission; India; Top emitters; United States

INTRODUCTION

The global effort to reverse the adverse consequences of climate change exacerbated by greenhouse gas (GHG) emissions is intensifying with countries implementing policies aimed at achieving decarbonisation (Bebbington & Unerman, 2018; Moses et al., 2022; Moses & Tauringana, 2022). These efforts have focussed the attention of policymakers on climate-related risks with several companies trying to measure, control and eventually reduce direct and indirect emissions (Choi & Luo, 2021; Johnson et al., 2020; Moses et al., 2019; Tang & Tang, 2019). Consequently, the reporting and management of information about GHG emissions has become relevant to areas of policy and academic discourse aimed at seeking plausible solutions (Bebbington et al., 2017; Bui et al., 2020; Moses et al., 2019). We face increasing global risks linked to GHG emissions and climate change. For example, food shortages, wildfires and respiratory diseases are on the rise consequent of extreme events due, in several respects, to climate change (IPCC, 2014; Tauringana & Chithambo, 2015). Although spatially localised environmental issues such as river or city pollution result in GHG emissions, the most damaging and long-lasting consequence of global climate change is not constrained within the border of the emitting country (IPCC, 2014). By polluting the earth's atmosphere with GHG emissions through fossil fuel combustion, deforestation and agricultural activities, top emitting countries and companies degrade the world's climate system and our common shared resource (Betts, 2008; Stocker et al., 2013). These countries (and companies) export much of the harm created by GHG emissions as the earth's atmosphere intermixes globally. The extent to which there is inequity between GHG emitting countries and countries affected by the resulting climate change depends on the distribution of climate vulnerability.

GHG is the leading contributor to climate change through trapping of heat leading to extreme weather such as droughts and cyclones. The demand for accountability in GHG measurement and management is growing and is an eminent concern. This is because global GHG emissions are not equally created, and actions to address them must consider the idiosyncratic activities and practices of countries and companies. Undoubtedly, the solutions to global emissions are collective in nature (Moses et al., 2020; Moses & Hopper, 2022; Moses & Tauringana, 2022; United Nations, 2015), nonetheless top emitters must demonstrate appropriate commitment relative to the weight of the global burden.

That said, it is somewhat surprising that empirical insights on GHG leading emitters is relatively sparse in the extant literature, despite their significant impact in resetting carbon management practices. However, to succeed in this space, attempts to address excessive GHG emissions must have commitments of leading emitting countries and companies, which is crucial given the magnitude of these emitters in proportion to others. For instance, the combined aggregate GHG emissions of the world's top 10[1] emitting countries from 1970 to 2021 accounted for about 62.4% of total global CO_2 emissions (see Fig. 1).

Relatedly, the Climate Accountability Institute report revealed that the top 20[2] emitting companies in the world collectively generated about 35% of global fossil fuel and cement emissions since 1965 (Climate Accountability Institute, 2020). The emissions jointly produced by the top emitters (i.e. countries and companies) provide a glimpse of their impact on the global environment and, more importantly, the implications they pose for achieving net zero by 2050. Therefore, research that advances our knowledge with regards to extant accountability and management of GHG emissions by top emitting countries at macro level and companies at micro level is vital for global policy formulation and the consequent reduction of global GHG emissions levels.[3] This is what this special issue addresses through the contributions of authors based on empirical insights from the leading GHG emitters.

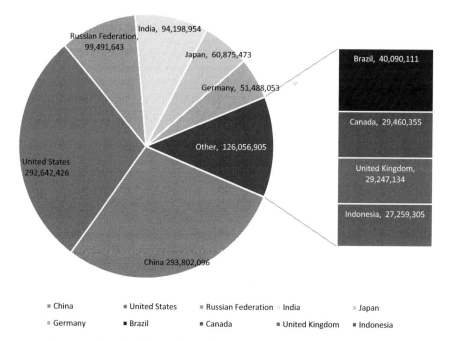

Fig. 1. Top 10 Emitting Countries' CO_2 Emissions in kt (1970–2021).

THE ISSUE

This *Issue* documents new evidence of the extent of GHG emissions reporting and management by governments of top emitting countries and companies alike. Given the magnitude and scale of the problem at hand, we believe that empirical contributions of this nature are crucial towards reducing global temperature and accomplishing a climate-neutral world by 2050. Albeit significant attempts have been made by prior studies to address emission-related issues (Bui et al., 2020; Chithambo & Tauringana, 2014, 2017; Depoers et al., 2016; Johnson et al., 2020; Kim et al., 2015; Moses et al., 2022; Tang & Tang, 2019; Tauringana & Chithambo, 2015), we have limited accounting and environmental management understanding of top emitters' contributions to the problem (solution) of GHG emissions globally. Interestingly, not much has been explored in terms of the specific accounting and environmental management practices of top emitters despite the threat their activities pose to global sustainability (Parvez et al., 2019). Some extant studies have focussed on selected countries (and companies), including those outside the leading emitters (Choi & Luo, 2021; Comyns, 2018; Faisal et al., 2018; Hollindale et al., 2019; Mahmoudian et al., 2021; Moses et al., 2022; Parvez et al., 2019). Advancing the understanding of GHG emissions reporting and management globally in the top emitting countries is important. DEFRA (2009) hints at the existence of a link between environmental measurement, reporting and management as only 'what gets measured gets managed'. Consistent with this view, empirical evidence shows that GHG measurement and reporting are likely to reduce emissions, especially when large emitters proactively manage their environmental impacts (DEFRA, 2010; Tauringana & Chithambo, 2015).

Collectively, the research contained in this issue contributes to extant accounting and environmental management accounting research in several ways. First, it synthesises the research on GHG emissions published in top journals. Second, the issue documents the efficacy of corporate governance mechanisms such as state ownership and board interlocks on GHG disclosures and performance. Third, the issue, for the first time, provides evidence of how the Paris Climate Change Agreement impacted climate change disclosures. Finally, the issue contributes by providing evidence of how social factors determine the extent of GHG emissions.

CONTRIBUTIONS TO THIS SPECIAL ISSUE

The research contained in this volume documents important findings of national and corporate practices of the top jurisdictions and emitting entities. Opening the volume is the work by Michael et al. (2023), in which the authors undertake a structured literature review to investigate GHG reporting practices at firm and country levels. Based on the 75 articles identified, the findings indicate the underrepresentation of Africa and the Middle East and the prevalence of quantitative-based research methods. The chapter recommends more research on

GHG reporting practices in Africa, the Middle East and countries with high annual emissions. Therefore, to an extent, the current issue is timely as it focusses on top emitting countries, as Michael et al. (2023) recommended.

Chen et al. (2023) contribute by investigating how government ownership in China affects the likelihood of a firm disclosing GHG information based on the top 300 listed firms. Relying on the lens of stakeholder–agency theory and using binary logistics regression analysis, the results indicate that there is a negative relationship between state ownership and GHG disclosure. The implication of the findings is that state-owned enterprises are less likely to disclose GHG information. According to the authors, the findings could be a consequence of managerial, political self-interest, economic and policy-oriented decision-making processes and the power differential between the government and state-owned enterprises. Evidence of the likelihood of state-owned enterprises disclosing GHG emissions is particularly useful given that China is the world's highest emitter of GHG.

The contribution by Bananuka et al. (2023) documents how corporate governance variables (board size, non-executive directors, ownership concentrations and insider ownership) affect GHG disclosures in the United States, the second highest emitter of GHG in the world. The study is based on a sample of 168 firms listed on the New York Stock Exchange (NYSE) for the period 2017–2020. The findings suggest that board size has a significant positive impact on GHG disclosure while ownership concentration and insider ownership have a significant negative influence. The percentage of non-executive directors is found to have no significant influence on the extent of GHG emissions.

Abang'a and Simbi (2023) examine the impact of different interlocks in board compositions on carbon emissions performance in India. Using a sample of 63 of top 200 Bombay Stock Exchange (BSE) listed companies for the period 2013–2020, the study shows that CEO and women on board interlocks contribute to GHG reduction, especially in top emitting developing jurisdictions. One likely plausibility could be due to the opportunity that CEOs serving on other boards get to leverage on their experiences to respond to environmental challenges. The study provides us with evidence about women's commitment to environmental issues and their efforts in mitigating carbon emissions akin to their sensitivity and ethical values (Liao et al., 2015; Liu, 2018; Nuber & Velte, 2021). This study, through the lens of resource dependency theory, demonstrates the impact interlocks in boards could have in the journey towards decarbonisation among emitters in the globe, especially in a developing country such as India that accounts for a substantial portion of global GHG emissions.

Despite the Paris Climate Agreement (PCA) being one of the most notable Conference of Parties (COP) in nearly 30 years, there has not been much research that has examined its impact, especially on disclosure. The contribution by Herbert et al. (2023) is, therefore, timely. The chapter's novel aspect compares the disclosure of climate information three years before and two years after the PCA. The noted finding of positive relationship between the PCA and climate change disclosures means that the PCA increased the reporting of climate change information. The chapter is a significant contribution to the literature given that it is the first treaty negotiated in 25 years that envisages all countries participating in climate action and has been adopted by 195 countries. Therefore, the PCA is considered a turning point for climate action, particularly since, under the Kyoto Protocol, only 35 countries were prepared to limit their GHG emissions.

The final contribution in this issue by Tauringana et al. (2023) examines the social determinants of GHG emissions in the top 100 emitting countries. Investigating the determinants of GHG emissions is important because it has policy implications. For example, the finding that fossil fuel use is leading to global warming has already led to policies and, in some cases, legislation aimed at reducing reliance on fossil fuels. Tauringana et al.'s (2023) chapter focusses on social determinants and this is based on the reasoning that most extant studies are focussed on either environmental (energy use) or economic (gross domestic product [GDP]) determinants of GHG emissions. The chapter by Tauringana et al. (2023) also makes an important contribution as it divides the sample of the top 100 into developed and developing countries which yields further insights. The findings for all top 100 countries and developing countries show that urbanisation and corruption are significantly positive and negative determinants of GHG emissions, respectively. Literacy is also a significant positive determinant of GHG emissions in developing countries but not in the top 100 countries. Population is not significant in the top 100, developed and developing countries. The results for the control variables suggest that primary energy consumption is a significant positive determinant of GHG emissions in the top 100, developed and developing countries. However, GDP is not.

CONCLUSION

This issue of *Advances in Environmental Accounting and Management* (AEAM) is dedicated to GHG reporting and management in top emitting countries and companies. GHG emissions reduction is perhaps the greatest challenge that the world is facing today due to the effects of global warming that is mostly attributed to the concentration of GHG in the atmosphere. Overall, the research in the six chapters is based on company and country levels. While the company-based research is limited to the companies in top emitting countries, the countries include both developed (China and the United States) and developing (India and South Africa) ones. For example, out of the six chapters, four chapters (Chen et al., 2023), Bananuka et al. (2023), Abang'a and Simbi (2023), and Herbert et al. (2023) are at the company level and investigate how corporate governance and the signing of the PCA on climate change affected the reporting of GHG or carbon emissions performance. Although mixed, evidence suggests that some corporate governance mechanisms are related to GHG emissions reporting and management.

Of the remaining two chapters, Michael et al.'s (2023) literature review chapter covers GHG reporting and management practices based on micro and macro data. The chapter concludes that more research on GHG needs to be carried out in Africa. This is not a surprise given that most of the countries in Africa are developing and companies are still trying to develop systems that will measure GHG emissions. The last chapter by Tauringana et al. (2023) is at the macro level and examined social determinants of GHG emissions. The interesting feature of the study is that it separately analysed the determinants of GHG emissions from top emitting developed and developing countries. The findings of the chapter suggest that there are differences between the social determinants of GHG in developing and developed countries. However, the finding that energy use is a determinant of GHG emissions in both developed and developing countries suggests that the world needs to come up with policies that will reduce energy use from fossil fuels and encourage the use of renewable sources of energy. Regarding future research, we agree with Michael et al. (2023) that further research needs to be done in Africa and the Middle East to gain a further understanding of GHG reporting and management practices. This is particularly important as the arguments are now shifting to who pays for mitigating the consequences of floods caused by GHG emissions. We conclude that an understanding of GHG reporting, management and determinants is more important than ever and that this issue has started the debate which will hopefully lead to solutions.

NOTES

1. These countries include China, the United States, the Russian Federation, India, Japan, Germany, Brazil, Canada, the United Kingdom and Indonesia (Crippa et al., 2022).
2. The companies include Saudi Aramco, Chevron, Gazprom, ExxonMobil, National Iranian Oil Company, BP, Royal Dutch Shell, Coal India, Pemex, Petróleos de Venezuela, PetroChina, Peabody Energy, ConocoPhillips, Abu Dhabi National Oil Company, Kuwait Petroleum Corporation, Iraq National Oil Company, Total SA, Sonatrach, BHP Billiton and Petrobras.
3. Global GHG reporting and management is a major objective of the Paris Climate Agreement (PCA) 2015 (United Nations, 2015). PCA is a legally binding treaty on climate change adopted by 196 countries in 2015 and entered into force in November 2016. The treaty aims to limit global warming to below 2 but preferably to 1.5 degrees Celsius compared to pre-industrial levels (Comyns, 2018). To achieve this goal, countries have been encouraged to aim to reach global peaking of GHG emissions as soon as possible to achieve a climate-neutral world by 2050.

REFERENCES

Abang'a, A. O., & Simbi, C. (2023). Board interlocks and carbon emissions performance: Empirical evidence from India. *Advances in Environmental Accounting & Management, 11,* 81–106. https://doi.org/10.1108/S1479-359820230000011005

Bananuka, J., Kasoga, P. S., & Tumwebaze, Z. (2023). Corporate governance and greenhouse gas disclosures: evidence from The United States. *Advances in Environmental Accounting & Management, 11,* 51–79. https://doi.org/10.1108/S1479-359820230000011004

Bebbington, J., Russell, S., & Thomson, I. (2017). Accounting and sustainable development: Reflections and propositions. *Critical Perspectives on Accounting, 48,* 21–34. https://doi.org/10.1016/j.cpa.2017.06.002

Bebbington, J., & Unerman, J. (2018). Achieving the United Nations sustainable development goals: An enabling role for accounting research. *Accounting, Auditing & Accountability Journal, 31*(1), 2–24. https://doi.org/10.1108/aaaj-05-2017-2929

Betts, R. (2008). Comparing apples with oranges. *Nature Climate Change, 1*, 7–8. https://doi.org/10. 1038/climate.2007.74

Bui, B., Moses, O., & Houqe, M. N. (2020). Carbon disclosure, emission intensity and cost of equity capital: Multi-country evidence. *Accounting and Finance, 60*, 47–71. November 2018. https://doi.org/10.1111/acfi.12492

Chen, Z., Liu, Y., Hu, Y., & Zhang, L. (2023). Impact of state ownership on greenhouse gas emissions disclosures in China. *Advances in Environmental Accounting & Management, 11*, 29–50. https://doi.org/10.1108/S1479-359820230000011003

Chithambo, L., & Tauringana, V. (2014). Company specific determinants of greenhouse gases disclosures. *Journal of Applied Accounting Research, 15*(3), 323–338. https://doi.org/10.1108/JAAR-11-2013-0087

Chithambo, L., & Tauringana, V. (2017). Corporate governance and greenhouse gas disclosure: A mixed-methods approach. *Corporate Governance, 17*(4), 678–699. https://doi.org/10.1108/CG-10-2016-0202

Choi, B., & Luo, L. (2021). Does the market value greenhouse gas emissions? Evidence from multi-country firm data. *The British Accounting Review, 53*(1), 100909. https://doi.org/10.1016/j.bar.2020.100909

Climate Accountability Institute. (2020). *Carbon majors 2020 dataset*. Carbon Majors. https://climateaccountability.org/carbonmajors.html

Comyns, B. (2018). Climate change reporting and multinational companies: Insights from institutional theory and international business. *Accounting Forum, 42*(1), 65–77. https://doi.org/10.1016/j.accfor.2017.07.003

Crippa, M., Guizzardi, D., Banja, M., Solazzo, E., Muntean, M., Schaaf, E., Pagani, F., Monforti-Ferrario, F., Olivier, J. G. J., Quadrelli, R., Risquez Martin, A., Taghavi-Moharamli, P., Grassi, G., Rossi, S., Oom, D., Branco, A., San-Miguel, J., & Vignati, E. (2022). *CO2 emissions of all world countries*. JRC/IEA/PBL 2022 Report. https://doi.org/10.2760/07904

DEFRA. (2009). *Guidance on how to measure and report your greenhouse gas emissions*. Department for the Environment, Food and Rural Affairs.

DEFRA. (2010). *Review of the contribution of reporting to GHG emission reductions and associated costs and benefits*. Department for the Environment, Food and Rural Affairs.

Depoers, F., Jeanjean, T., & Jérôme, T. (2016). Voluntary disclosure of greenhouse gas emissions: Contrasting the carbon disclosure project and corporate reports. *Journal of Business Ethics, 134*(3), 445–461.

Faisal, F., Andiningtyas, E. D., Achmad, T., Haryanto, H., & Meiranto, W. (2018). The content and determinants of greenhouse gas emission disclosure: Evidence from Indonesian companies. *Corporate Social Responsibility and Environmental Management, 25*(6), 1397–1406. https://doi.org/10.1002/csr.1660

IPCC. (2014). In C. B., Field, V. R., Barros, D. J., Dokken, K. J., Mach, M. D., Mastrandrea, T. E., Bilir, M., Chatterjee, K. L., Ebi, Y. O., Estrada, R. C., Genova, B., Girma, E. S., Kissel, A. N., Levy, S., MacCracken, P. R., Mastrandrea, & L. L., White (Eds.), *Climate change 2014: Impacts, adaptation, and vulnerability. Part A: Global and sectoral aspects*. Cambridge University Press. papers2://publication/uuid/B8BF5043-C873-4AFD-97F9-A630782E590D

Herbert, S., Mongie, C., & Willows, G. (2023). The impact of the Paris climate change agreement and other factors on climate change disclosure in South Africa. *Advances in Environmental Accounting & Management, 11*, 107–125. https://doi.org/10.1108/S1479-359820230000011006

Hollindale, J., Kent, P., Routledge, J., & Chapple, L. (2019). Women on boards and greenhouse gas emission disclosures. *Accounting and Finance, 59*(1), 277–308. https://doi.org/10.1111/acfi.12258

Johnson, J. A., Theis, J., Vitalis, A., & Young, D. (2020). The influence of firms' emissions management strategy disclosures on investors' valuation judgments. *Contemporary Accounting Research, 37*(2), 642–664. https://doi.org/10.1111/1911-3846.12545

Kim, Y.-B., An, H. T., & Kim, J. D. (2015). The effect of carbon risk on the cost of equity capital. *Journal of Cleaner Production, 93*, 279–287. http://linkinghub.elsevier.com/retrieve/pii/S0959652615000104

Liao, L., Luo, L., & Tang, Q. (2015). Gender diversity, board independence, environmental committee and greenhouse gas disclosure. *The British Accounting Review, 47*(4), 409–424. https://doi.org/10.1016/j.bar.2014.01.002

Liu, C. (2018). Are women greener? Corporate gender diversity and environmental violations. *Journal of Corporate Finance, 52*(July), 118–142. https://doi.org/10.1016/j.jcorpfin.2018.08.004

Mahmoudian, F., Lu, J., Yu, D., Nazari, J. A., & Herremans, I. M. (2021). Inter-and intra-organizational stakeholder arrangements in carbon management accounting. *The British Accounting Review, 53*(1), 100933. https://doi.org/10.1016/j.bar.2020.100933

Michael, E. E., Dabel-Moses, J. N., Olateju, D. J., Emmanuel, I. D., & Michael, V. E. (2023). Greenhouse gas emissions research in top-ranked journals: A meta-analysis. *Advances in Environmental Accounting & Management, 11*, 11–27. https://doi.org/10.1108/S1479-359820230000011002

Moses, O., & Hopper, T. (2022). Accounting articles on developing countries in ranked English language journals: A meta-review. *Accounting, Auditing & Accountability Journal*. https://doi.org/10.1108/AAAJ-04-2020-4528

Moses, O., Michael, E. E., & Dabel-Moses, J. N. (2019). A review of environmental management and reporting regulations in Nigeria. *Advances in Environmental Accounting and Management: Environmental Reporting and Management in Africa, 8*, 159–182. https://doi.org/10.1108/s1479-359820190000008007

Moses, O., Mohaimen, F., & Emmanuel, M. (2020). A meta-review of SEAJ: The past and projections for 2020 and beyond. *Social and Environmental Accountability Journal, 40*(1), 1–18. https://doi.org/10.1080/0969160X.2020.1730213

Moses, O., Nnam, I. J., Olaniyan, J. D., & Tariquzzaman, A. T. M. (2022). Sustainable development goals (sdgs): Assessment of implementation progress in Brics and Mint. *Advances in Environmental Accounting and Management, 10*, 11–44. https://doi.org/10.1108/S1479-35982022 0000010002

Moses, O., & Tauringana, V. (2022). Environmental sustainability and the progress towards Agenda 2030. *Advances in Environmental Accounting and Management, 10*, 1–8. https://doi.org/10.1108/S1479-359820220000010001

Nuber, C., & Velte, P. (2021). Board gender diversity and carbon emissions: European evidence on curvilinear relationships and critical mass. *Business Strategy and the Environment, 30*(4), 1958–1992. https://doi.org/10.1002/bse.2727

Parvez, M., Hazelton, J., & James, G. (2019). Greenhouse gas emissions disclosure by cities: The expectation gap. *Sustainability Accounting, Management and Policy Journal, 10*(4), 685–709. https://doi.org/10.1108/SAMPJ-11-2017-0138

Stocker, B. D., Roth, R., Joos, F., Spahni, R., Steinacher, M., Zaehle, S., Bouwman, L., Xu-Ri, & Prentice, I. C. (2013). Multiple greenhouse-gas feedbacks from the land biosphere under future climate change scenarios. *Nature Climate Change, 3*(7), 666–672. https://doi.org/10.1038/nclimate1864

Tang, Q., & Tang, L. M. (2019). Toward a distributed carbon ledger for carbon emissions trading and accounting for corporate carbon management. *Journal of Emerging Technologies in Accounting, 16*(1), 37–46. https://doi.org/10.2308/jeta-52409

Tauringana, V., Achiro, L., & Oyewo, B. (2023). Social determinants of greenhouse gas emissions in the top 100 developed and developing emitting countries. *Advances in Environmental Accounting & Management, 11*, 127–158. https://doi.org/10.1108/S1479-359820230000011007

Tauringana, V., & Chithambo, L. (2015). The effect of DEFRA guidance on greenhouse gas disclosure. *The British Accounting Review, 47*(4), 425–444. https://doi.org/10.1016/j.bar.2014.07.002

United Nations. (2015). *Transforming our World: The 2030 Agenda for sustainable development*. United Nations. https://www.un.org/en/development/desa/population/migration/generalassembly/docs/globalcompact/A_RES_70_1_E.pdf

GREENHOUSE GAS EMISSIONS RESEARCH IN TOP-RANKED JOURNALS: A META-ANALYSIS

Emmanuel Edache Michael, Joy Nankyer Dabel-Moses, Dare John Olateju, Ikoojo David Emmanuel and Vincent Edache Michael

ABSTRACT

In this chapter, we conduct a metadata analysis of articles published in accounting, business and finance journals ranked by Australian Business Dean Council (ABDC), and benchmarked against the Chartered Association of Business Schools (ABS) ranking, that discuss firm- and country-level greenhouse gas (GHG) emission practices and reporting. Number of publications on GHG research, research methods, number of citations and ratio, across countries and continents are some of the topics we cover. We employ a list of articles on accounting, business and finance journals ranked A* and A in the ABDC journal rankings from 2015 to 2022. The study uses a structured literature review to analyse 74 papers on GHG reporting practices at the firm- and country level. Although this line of enquiry is still nascent and developing, the study found underrepresentation of Africa and the Middle East in GHG literature generally. In addition, majority of the articles examined also concentrate on quantitative methods. Most of the articles on GHG research are A-ranked in the ABDC ranking scheme. It was also found that few studies focus on the countries and companies with the highest emissions. While there has been some progress in interrogating GHG across the globe, there is still much room for further research. A key area of future research is exploring the GHG reporting practices in the African and the Middle Eastern sub-regions. There is also a need to examine countries and companies with high emissions.

Green House Gas Emissions Reporting and Management in Global Top Emitting Countries and Companies
Advances in Environmental Accounting & Management, Volume 11, 11–27
Copyright © 2023 Emmanuel Edache Michael, Joy Nankyer Dabel-Moses, Dare John Olateju, Ikoojo David Emmanuel and Vincent Edache Michael
Published under exclusive licence by Emerald Publishing Limited
ISSN: 1479-3598/doi:10.1108/S1479-359820230000011002

A further study needs to explore the benefits of other research methods in addition to quantitative methods, as different research methods could yield different insights that would enhance research-based conclusions.

Keywords: ABDC ranking; ABS ranking; greenhouse gas emission; GHG practices; GHG reporting; meta-analysis

INTRODUCTION

Historically, one of the first scholars to draw global attention to the global warming effects of greenhouse gases (GHGs) may have been Svante Arrhenius (1859–1927) in his 1896 publication (Buha, 2011; Maslin, 2004). As GHGs began to have devastating effects on the world's ecological systems, further publications on GHGs, such as Gilbert Plass (1955) and Schneider & Mesirow (1976), could have arguably cemented Svante's position (Maslin, 2004). At this time, issues on the real threats posed by GHG began to top the economic and developmental policy agenda of various countries' governments and intergovernmental organisations. In particular, the United Nations Environmental Programme (UNEP) and World Meteorological Organisation partnered to form an Intergovernmental Panel on Climate Change (IPCC), which brought together 2,500 peer-reviewed scientific studies in history and experts from over 60 countries from a variety of fields to predict the impact of GHGs based on historical climate models (Enzler, 2018; Khalid et al., 2016). The Brundtland Commission, also known as the World Commission on Environment and Development, was established in 1987 with the sole purpose of directing nations towards sustainable development (World Commission on Environment and Development, 1987). As part of the Kyoto Protocol of 1998, the participating countries were encouraged to reduce their anthropogenic GHG emissions by at least 5% below 1990 levels (Enzler, 2018; Yu & Lee, 2020). The United Nations Global Compact (UNGC), which began in 2000, aims to implement universal sustainability principles (UN Global compact, 2021). These efforts culminated in the 2015 Paris Climate Agreement involving 196 countries as signatories, seeking to reduce global warming below the 2°C target by 2050[1] (United Nations, 2015).

Consequently, ambitious targets- and goals-setting aimed at achieving a carbon-free world – such as achieving *net-zero* carbon emissions world by 2050 – became the order of the day, echoing the fight against GHG emissions. However, there is little knowledge about how top emitting nations and companies disclose and report GHG emissions. Several GHG reporting initiatives have been launched in recent years to encourage businesses and organisations to report their GHG emissions and their plans to reduce them. The idea is that transparency in an organisation's GHG practices and reporting activities should contribute significantly to kerbing the GHG menace. Measurement, reporting and management of GHG emissions can reduce global emissions, especially when large emitting companies and countries take proactive measures (Chithambo et al., 2022; Tauringana, 2021; Tauringana & Moses, 2021).

In 2006 the Global Reporting Initiative (GRI) developed the first reporting standards on GHG and other sustainability matters (GRI, 2020; Worokinasih et al., 2020). The GRI is a global independent standards organisation that helps businesses, governments and other organisations understand and communicate climate change, human rights and corruption impacts. Although various initiatives have been taken to kerb GHG emissions, including GHG reporting initiatives, little is known about the state of GHG reporting and disclosure research in top-rated accounting, business and finance journals especially with regards to top emitting countries and companies. Perhaps the lack of transparent reporting and disclosure by these corporates of their GHG emissions (Haque et al., 2016) may have contributed to this trend. There is a growing need for accounting, business and finance research to illuminate the reporting and management practices of top emitters, in light of their impact on global sustainability (Tauringana & Moses, 2021). This will satisfy the need to know where we are, how close we are and new management techniques in the fight against GHG emissions menace.

Consequently, the study provides a meta-analysis of the research in GHG practices and reporting in top-ranked journals covering accounting, business and finance by asking the following important questions:

(1) In top-ranked journals, what is the number and citation proportion of GHG articles?
(2) Which research methods are used in top-ranked journal publications on GHG?
(3) How are GHG articles distributed across countries and continents?

It would be beneficial to investigate these questions in relation to both country-level and company-level GHG practices and reporting, since these are 'critical for sustaining our ecosystem' (Moses et al., 2019, p. 2).

STUDIES ON GHG REPORTING AND DISCLOSURE RESEARCH

The literature on the practices and reporting of GHG emissions is growing (for example, Borghei et al., 2016, 2018; Chu et al., 2013; Comyns, 2016; Morrone et al., 2022; Rokhmawati, 2021; Svensson et al., 2021; Tariq & Xu, 2022; Yan et al., 2018; Yu & Lee, 2020), yet only few studies consider the top GHG emitting countries and companies. Chu et al. (2013) note that the rate of emission in China alone is at an alarming proportion, suggesting that GHG emission practices and reporting deserve more attention. According to Moses et al. (2022), climate action related to the Sustainable Development Goal 13 (SDG13) is only making marginal progress across most developing countries. Thus, we provide a general overview of prior literature between the period of 2015 and 2022 on general GHG practices in this section. The merit of this review is to highlight what has been done on GHG emissions research since the signing into operation of the 2015

Paris Climate Agreement, with a view to provide potential areas for further research.

The GHG literature can be subdivided into firm- and country-level studies. At the firm level, Giannarakis et al. (2017) employ legitimacy and voluntary disclosure theories to examine whether climate change disclosure is reflective of a firm's environmental performance. Consistent with voluntary disclosure theories and literature, the study found that environmental performance enhances climate change disclosure. Giannarakis et al.'s (2017) study seems to imply that companies would only disclose their carbon-related activities when their environmental performance averages better. Albarrak et al. (2019) found that firms disseminating carbon-related information tend to have a lower cost of equity. This association persists throughout alternative estimations, and environmental disclosures are unaffected. Furthermore, the study suggests that market participants utilise Twitter for disseminating carbon information, in addition to disclosure.

Lewandowski (2017) observes that firms that have better carbon performance also have better financial performance as measured by return on sales. However, Lewandowski (2017) also demonstrates that carbon performance is negatively related to overall firm value (Tobin's Q). They conclude that the negative relationship between carbon performance and firm value could be the reason why companies are yet to fully subscribe to the sustainability movement. It could be contended that the findings by Lewandowski (2017) imply that firm managers view carbon performance in the short term, which may compromise long-term strategies towards sustainable business practices, including the overall sustainability drive which has begun picking up steam across the globe.

In contrast to studies that note some positive link between corporate carbon performance and financial performance, Trumpp and Guenther (2017) report an inverse association between corporate environmental performance (CEP) and corporate financial performance, but this is only observed for companies with low CEP and not for those with high CEP. Similarly, Tuesta et al.'s (2020) findings imply that carbon emission has a negative impact on firms' profitability. According to Yagi and Managi (2018), while the change in total carbon emissions is positive for equity, it has a significant negative impact on the Total Assets Turnover Ratio (TATR) and leverage as well. Eleftheriadis and Anagnostopoulou (2015) found a significant positive relationship between size and increased climate-related disclosures, but no significant relationship between profitability and leverage. Among the factors affecting corporate GHG reduction strategies, Cadez et al. (2019) found that market pressures for reducing GHG emissions, perceived GHG regulatory uncertainty and environmental strategy focus are key.

It has also been suggested in previous studies that companies can achieve carbon management through conscious pragmatic strategies (Tuesta et al., 2020). For instance, companies must design and develop a carbon management accounting (CMA) system (Tuesta et al., 2020). Meschi and Norheim-Hansen (2019) point out that there should be pragmatic guidance focussed on environmental protection and green sustainable energy consumption. In line with this, Hsueh Lily (2019) found that 'participation and effort in voluntary carbon disclosure by global businesses' is a function of the existence of supportive management structures, even though the voluntary carbon disclosure has both costly and beneficial outcomes. Companies' demonstration of participation and efforts could include diversifying their employees and management mass. Thus, Tingbani et al. (2020) explored the impact of gender diversity and environmental committees on GHG voluntary disclosures, utilising a sample of 215 firms listed on the London Stock Exchange, for a period of 2011–2014. Accordingly, firms can legitimise their green credentials by being diverse and open to a mixed-gender governance approach, thus gaining greater trust from a wider range of stakeholders besides shareholders. Tingbani et al. (2020) demonstrate that environmental committees are not effective at enhancing GHG voluntary disclosures, indicating that firms do not need to directly link their disclosure practices and decisions to their governance mechanisms. Ben-Amar and Mcklienny (2015) examine whether companies' boards respond to the Carbon Disclosure Project (CDP) annual questionnaire effectively, as well as the quality of disclosures regarding climate change-related risks and mitigation strategies. It was found that board effectiveness was positively correlated with the decision to answer the CDP questionnaire as well as the quality of the company's carbon disclosure.

Tauringana and Moses (2021) believe that there should be concerted efforts between both the State and companies to control and reduce GHG emissions if the 2050 net-zero target would not become a mirage. Thus, prior literature is also replete with studies that argue that country characteristics may well have significant influence on overall GHG emission practices. As such, Muttakin et al. (2020) contend that countries with donations to political manifestos and party activities have higher carbon emissions than countries without donations. Lazarevic and Martin (2018) consider country regulations' effectiveness in kerbing emission by acknowledging the ineffectiveness of regulations in ensuring sustainability compliance. Tang and Demeritt (2018), however, argue that firms may disclose their carbon activities if there are financial benefits or both social- and country-level regulatory pressures. Muttakin et al. (2020) demonstrate the influence of a country's political system on the level of companies' GHG emissions and found that companies operating in countries with majoritarian electoral systems (MAJ) – where corporations have relatively little influence on election outcomes – emit fewer GHGs than companies in proportional electoral systems. Muttakin et al. (2020), similarly to Muttakin et al. (2020), also confirm the influence of corporate political donations on GHG emission as relates to MAJ and GHG emission intensity indicating that companies utilise political donations to ease environmental regulation from the State. According to Muttakin et al. (2022), carbon emission intensity is inversely associated with companies in countries with strong democratic institutions. Furthermore, they argue that cultures influence companies' environmental practices more than democracies in terms of their strategies. According to Zameer et al. (2021), in addition to customer scrutiny and management environmental awareness, country-level regulatory requirements are crucial to ensuring good environmental practices. Adedoyin et al. (2021) investigate the environmental consequences of economic complexities, air travel and energy use employing panel data covering 119 countries from the World Bank Development database from 1995 to 2016. Low-income, upper middle-income and high-income groups all have high carbon contents because of economic growth. Ultimately, the study concludes that policymakers or concerned authorities in each income group should harness country resources to boost their GDP levels while preventing environmental degradation. Despite Husaini et al.'s (2021) finding that energy subsidies cause significantly higher CO_2 emissions at low oil prices, the value of the subsidy should not cause significantly higher CO_2 emissions at low oil prices.

METHOD AND DATA

We conducted an ordered search of articles published in highly ranked Australian Business Dean Council (ABDC) and Chartered Association of Business Schools (ABS) journals on GHG emission practices and reporting to measure the extent of research on these topics in accounting, business and finance. Consistent with Moses and Hopper (2022), we use Google Scholar[2] by employing a set of key-words in searching for articles published in either A-star or A-ranked journals in the ABDC, which we then benchmarked against the ABS ranking scheme. Following Moses et al. (2020), the study uses Google Scholar citation metrics to gauge the impact of each article and to calculate the ratio of citations to the number of publications a journal has because number of publications in a journal may not equate to overall citations. The study limits the search to the title, the abstract or the keywords of an article. The stringent search criteria are designed to ensure that we focus on highly ranked articles with the greatest visibility and citations, which may indicate how much *quality* attention is devoted to GHG research in accounting, business and finance journals. The search terms we employ are: 'GHG emission', 'GHG accounting', 'Carbon emission', 'Green-house gas', 'CO_2' accounting, 'Climate change' accounting, 'Emission intensity', 'Carbon disclosure', 'Top emitting countries' and 'Top emitting companies'. In total, we obtain 74 articles, consisting of 18 A-star and 56 A-ranked papers.

RESULTS

We examine articles published on GHG emission reporting practices in top-ranked ABDC journals relative to their ABS ranking. Specifically, we focus on all A-star and A-ranked journals covering accounting, business and finance discipline published between the period of 2015 and 2022. Our choice of 2015 as a starting point is so that we have a cut-off from when the Paris Agreement on Climate Change was initiated, which started one of the *real* efforts at attacking the climate change crises. During the period of the study, SDG 2030 was formulated and implemented, which arguably led to a more general commitment to environmental sustainability issues, including GHG emissions.

Number of GHG Papers in Top-Ranked Journals: The Methodology Employed and Google Citations

Table 1 (Fig. 1) reports total number of articles on GHG practices and reporting published in highly ranked ABDC journals in relation to their ABS ranking. In total, there are 74 papers available in 14 journals, including five A-star papers and nine A-ranked papers. It is intended to identify which journals shape the research agenda for GHG emissions.

We note that there are 19 articles on GHG representing about 26% published in five A-star (A*) journals, including the *British Accounting Review* (11), *Journal*

Table 1. Total Number of GHG Articles and Their Relative Ranking in ABDC and ABS.

S/N	ABDC-Ranked Journal	Number of Articles	ABDC Rank	ABS Rank	ISI-IF	Google Citations	Research Methods	
							Qualitative	Quantitative
1	Business Strategy and the Environment	27	A	3	11.28	1,065	2	25
2	British Accounting Review	11	A*	3	5.58	1,371	6	5
3	International Journal of Production Research[a]	9	A	3	8.57	231	3	7
4	Australasian Journal of Environmental Management	6	A	NR	2.08	41	1	5
5	Accounting & Finance	5	A	2	2.94	347	2	3
6	Accounting and Business Research	3	A	3	2.65	45	1	2
7	Journal of Cleaner Production	3	A	2	10.96	355	1	2
8	Journal of Banking & Finance	2	A*	3	3.07	217	1	1
9	Journal of Corporate Finance	2	A*	4	4.86	14	1	1
10	Review of Accounting Studies	2	A*	4	4.19	9	0	2
11	Accounting, Auditing & Accountability Journal	1	A	3	4.89	479	1	0
12	Business and Politics	1	A	2	2.33	19	1	0
13	Meditari Accountancy Research	1	A	1	3.52	55	0	1
14	The Accounting Review	1	A*	4*	4.99	115	0	1
	Total	74						

Note: NR = Not Ranked.
[a]*International Journal of Production Research* includes a paper that employs a mixed-method approach.

Fig. 1.   Number of Articles.

of Banking and Finance (2), *Journal of Corporate Finance* (2), *Review of Accounting Studies* (2), *Accounting, Auditing and Accountability Journal* (1) and *The Accounting Review* (1). However, only one of these journals is highly ranked as four star (4*) in the ABS ranking category, i.e. *The Accounting Review*. The rest are ranked in ABS as 4 and 3, respectively, i.e. *Journal of Corporate Finance, Review of Accounting Studies*, the *British Accounting Review* and *Accounting, Auditing and Accountability Journal*.

The ABDC A-ranked journals category has the highest number of publications in the sample with 55 papers representing about 74% of total publications. The A-ranked journals including *Business Strategy and the Environment* (27), *International Journal of Production Research* (9), *Australasian Journal of Environmental Management* (6), *Accounting & Finance* (5), *Accounting and Business Research* and *Journal of Cleaner Production* all have 3 articles each. *Business and Politics* and *Meditari Accountancy Research* all have 1 publication each. While some of these journals enjoy the top spot in the ABDC ranking classification scheme, at the same time they may be lowly ranked in the ABS ranking list. For instance, *Meditari Accountancy Research* ranked A in ABDC is, however, ranked 1 in ABS. In this context, it is important to note the differences between the two approaches to journal ranking.

The ISI-IF number, Google citations and research methods adopted in the sampled journals are also reported in Table 1. We observe that, the *British Accounting Review* has more Google citations (at 1,371), closely followed by *Business Strategy and the Environment* (at 1,065). The ratio of citations to publications for these two journals (1,371/11 = 125 vs. 1,065/27 = 39) is contrary to what we would expect if we attributed citations to the total number of publications. This highlights the point that highly rated journals could receive more citations irrespective of the total number of publications. For example, even though *Accounting, Auditing & Accountability Journal* has 1 article publication, nevertheless, it leads the entire pack with the highest ratio to total publications (at 479 citations per publication). Similarly, we observe that all highly ranked journals both in the ABDC and ABS ranking categories have the highest combined citations.

As we examine the research methods employed by GHG articles published in the journals sampled, we find 20 qualitative versus 55 quantitative papers. It is important to note that a paper in *International Journal of Production Research* adopted a mixed-method approach and is so double-counted. This finding demonstrates that most of the articles sampled are *Quantitative* papers in orientation (at 72% vs. 28%). *Business Strategy and the Environment* journal with the highest number of publications has the highest number of *Quantitative* papers (at 25 vs. 2). In all, the *British Accounting Review* has more *Qualitatively* inclined articles (at 6 vs. 5).

GHG Articles Spread by Country

By analysing GHG studies by country/countries of focus in terms of countries where empirical evidence was sourced and analysed, we are trying to determine countries' representation in GHG studies. We report this analysis in Table 2. In Panel A, it can be observed that Australia has the highest number of GHG papers (at 4) followed by the United Arab Emirates (UAE) (at 3) for the A* ranking category. Next in this category are Canada, Hong Kong, the United Kingdom and the United States with 2 GHG publications each, representing approximately 11%. France and Germany have 1 GHG publication each, representing approximately 6%. Finally, 1 paper emanates from both the United Kingdom and the United States, respectively.

In the analysis of the A-ranked category (Panel B), we observe that Australia has the highest number of publications with 10 papers representing 17.54%. This is closely followed by China with 9 papers (at approximately 16%). The United Kingdom has 7 papers (at approximately 12%), whereas Germany and the United States share 3 articles each representing approximately 5%. Greece, Japan and Turkey have 2 publications each representing approximately 4%. Finally, Canada, France, India, Iran, Italy, Malaysia, New Zealand and Spain have 1 publication each (at approximately 2%). 10 papers (at approximately 19%) represent articles that focus on multiple countries at the same time.

GHG Articles Spread by Continent

In Table 3 (Fig. 2), we analyse sampled articles by continent. The merit of this analysis is to identify continent(s) with the most articles on GHG reporting practices as this may reflect efforts towards kerbing GHG emissions. We observe that Europe leads the pack with 31 GHG articles representing approximately 41% of the total sampled articles. In Comyns (2016), it is reported that European firms' GHG reporting averages better due to mimetic isomorphism and political and social pressure. Unsurprisingly, most of the initiatives towards controlling

Table 2. GHG Articles Spread by Country.

Nation	Number of Articles	Percentage
Panel A: A* star rank category by countries		
Australia	4	22.22%
UAE	3	16.67%
Canada	2	11.11%
Hong Kong	2	11.11%
United Kingdom	2	11.11%
United States	2	11.11%
France	1	5.56%
United Kingdom and United States	1	5.56%
Germany	1	5.56%
Total	18	100%
Panel B: A rank category by country		
Australia	10	17.54%
China	9	15.79%
United Kingdom	7	12.28%
Germany	3	5.26%
United States	3	5.26%
Greece	2	3.51%
Japan	2	3.51%
Turkey	2	3.51%
Canada	1	1.75%
France	1	1.75%
India	1	1.75%
Iran	1	1.75%
Italy	1	1.75%
Malaysia	1	1.75%
New Zealand	1	1.75%
Spain	1	1.75%
International	10	19.30%
Total	**56**	**100.00%**

emissions were birthed in Europe, even though China in Asia is currently the highest emitter in the world, according to Statista (2021). In contrast, Asia contributes 17 GHG articles (23%) to the sample, while the United States, which predominates the North American continent (and has 8 articles), is the second biggest emitter. Oceania consisting mostly of contributions from Australia and New Zealand has 13 papers (at approximately 17%). The Middle East has the lowest observations with just 1 article (at approximately 1%). International with 4 publications are papers that cut across different continents.

Table 3. Continent and the Total Number of GHG Research in Top-Rated ABDC Ranked Journals.

	Panel A: Continents and Number of GHG Articles		
S/N	Continent	No of Articles	Percentage
1	Asia	17	22.67
2	Europe	31	41.33
3	International[a]	4	5.33
4	Middle East	1	1.33
5	North America	8	10.67
6	Oceania	13	17.33
Total		74	100

[a]International Comprise Studies That Cut Across More Than Continent.

DISCUSSION OF RESULTS

The analysis of the number of GHG papers in top-ranked journals suggests that there is limited research at both country- and firm level on GHG emissions, practices and reporting in elite journals. It could be argued that researchers have no incentive to investigate this area, or that it is just a relatively new and developing field of research. However, it may be concerning that this state of GHG research may threaten the achievement of a carbon-free world by 2050 (Broadstock et al., 2018) and all the other corollaries of sustainability.

One journal that stands out in publication effort is the *Business Strategy and the Environment* with 27 GHG-related articles. This could be caused by the journal's publication target goals as published on the journal's website within Wiley Online Library, and as partially outlined below,

[...] It seeks to provide original contributions that add to the understanding of business strategies for improving the natural (green) environment. It seeks to publish research into

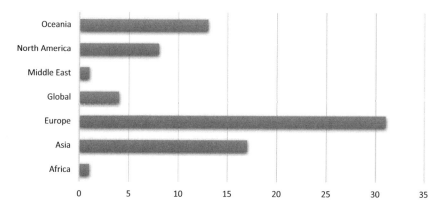

Fig. 2. GHG Article Spread by Continent.

systems and standards, environmental performance, eco-innovation, corporate environmental management tools, organisations and management, particular industry sectors and responses of business to climate change and other contemporary environmental issues. It examines the role of environmental regulation and policy in the business sector and encourages cross-country analysis. Contributions are encouraged which extend the scope of activity from environmental management to sustainability in business.

Business Strategy and the Environment's GHG publication number might suggest that a journal with 'Environment' in its title name should have more papers on GHGs. Thus, when we interrogated further, we observed that this may hardly be the case. For instance, journals such as *Advances in Environmental Accounting & Management* (ranked as B in ABDC and 1 in ABS) with 'Environmental' in its title, as does *Business Strategy and the Environment*, have only one publication on GHG. Overall, this suggests that, in addition to a journal's objective, number of articles published in a particular period matter in terms of publication focus areas. The age of a journal may also indicate number of published articles as it would be expected that older papers should have more GHG-related research. Further, the overall low rate of GHG research publications in top-ranked ABDC and ABS journals may result from companies focussing more on process-oriented GHG performance than actually reducing emissions (Haque, 2017). The results of Broadstock et al. (2018) show that despite GHG reporting and disclosure being argued to have a significant effect on reducing GHG emissions, a wide pattern of non-disclosure exists over time.

Related to number of publications, our findings from the analysis of Google citations suggest that highly ranked articles irrespective of their GHG publication number shape and direct GHG reporting research agenda. Such papers could play a crucial role in achieving GHG targets, such as SDG13 on Climate Action, the Paris Climate Agreement and the 2050 net-zero goal. According to Comyns (2016), reporting serves as an instrument of transparency for informing stakeholders about company plans and actions regarding emissions of GHGs. Overall, the evidence suggests that there are more to do to up the ante on research on GHG emission and GHG reporting by top emitters around the world.

The results of the analysis of the research methods employed by GHG papers are consistent with Moses and Hopper (2022) and Muttakin et al. (2022) who demonstrate that there are more *Quantitative* articles relative to *Qualitative* articles in top-ranked journals. Aside the methods adopted in GHG articles, we also note a general lack of strong theoretical link that could explain the relationship between GHG emission disclosure and reduction in GHG emission. Furthermore, most GHG papers are market-based studies, examining the relationship between emissions reporting and financial performance (See, for instance, Alsaifi et al., 2020; Brouwers et al., 2018; Capece et al., 2017; Lewandowski, 2017; Tuesta et al., 2020).

The analysis of GHG articles spread by country show that Australia has the highest number of total GHG research (at 14), when A* and A-ranked journals are combined. This is closely followed by China with 9 articles. Interestingly, no country from Africa is represented in the sample. Overall, the result demonstrates that developed markets are more committed to the fight against GHG as there are more developed markets GHG research than there are developing markets GHG research. The implication is that richer nations are more likely to commit to sustainability efforts than poor nations who are more worried about their daily needs (Liang & Renneboog, 2017). Rissman et al. (2020) argue that decarbonisation could enhance human and economic development of developing nations. In addition to economic prosperity positively influencing GHG research, Comyns (2016) point out that European companies are associated with high reporting quality owing to mimetic isomorphism, political and social scrutiny and pressure in relation to climate change.

The lower rate of GHG emission in smaller economies could be due to marginalisation of articles publication that emanate from developing countries (Moses & Hopper, 2022). For instance, Wachira and Mathuva (2022) claim that literature on GHG emissions is scanty as researchers have often queried the truthfulness of environmental reporting in Africa. Nevertheless, the various GHG targets as mentioned before may become achievable only when there is a holistic approach to research agendas that incorporates all parts of the world as the fight against climate change is a fight for all.

CONCLUSION AND SUGGESTIONS FOR FUTURE RESEARCH

We conducted a meta-analysis to appraise the nature and extent of research on GHGs around the world in this study. Thus, we note the gaps in the GHG research necessary to achieve a *net-zero* world by 2050. In our meta-review, we found that there is a need for more research in accounting, business and finance, especially in top-rated journals, to examine GHG reporting practices at the national and company levels. Considering the increasing importance of GHG-related climate change, it is important for accounting, business and finance researchers to conduct high-quality investigations to inform in-depth GHG practices and reporting. This would help kerb GHG emission levels and the menace it poses, while working towards achieving a net-zero globe. Although progress has been made to document the development of GHG across the globe, the research area is still nascent and developing. Following our extensive review of GHG-related research in A-star and A-rated ABDC-ranked journals as benchmarked against the ABS ranking scheme, we suggest the following further research areas.

Despite an increase in research in top-rated journals on GHG emission practices and reporting across continents, Africa and the Middle East are areas with potential research opportunities. There is a general underrepresentation of the above continents in the GHG literature in the top-rated papers we examine. A higher journal's ranking is associated with a lower proportion and number of articles from developing countries, according to Moses and Hopper (2022). Only a few of the A-ranked articles focus on developing countries, for instance. The dominance of quantitative methodologies over qualitative approaches is another trend we observe in our analysis. Therefore, GHG research in accounting, business and finance lacks a wide range of methodologies and philosophical perspectives that could enrich research-based conclusions. The study also demonstrates a need for further research into how countries and companies could well align their GHG strategies towards emissions reduction initiatives such as the *net-zero*.

NOTES

1. Countries that sign up to the Paris Agreement agree to monitor, control and eventually reduce GHG emissions in their various countries.
2. Wachira and Mathuva (2022) also use a similar search engine to locate articles for their investigation.

REFERENCES

Adedoyin, F. F., Nwulu, N., & Bekun, F. V. (2021). Environmental degradation, energy consumption and sustainable development: Accounting for the role of economic complexities with evidence from World Bank income clusters. *Business Strategy and the Environment*, 2727–2740. https://doi.org/10.1002/bse.2774

Albarrak, M. S., Elnahass, M., & Salama, A. (2019). The effect of carbon dissemination on cost of equity. *Business Strategy and the Environment*, 1179–1198. https://doi.org/10.1002/bse.2310

Alsaifi, K., Elnahass, M., & Salama, A. (2020). Carbon disclosure and financial performance: UK environmental policy. *Business Strategy and the Environment*, 711–726. https://doi.org/10.1002/bse.2426

Ben-Amar, W., & Mcilkenny, P. (2015). Board effectiveness and the voluntary disclosure of climate change information. *Business Strategy and the Environment*, *719*, 704–719. https://doi.org/10.1002/bse.1840

Borghei, Z., Leung, P., & Guthrie, J. (2016). The nature of voluntary greenhouse gas disclosure – An explanation of the changing rationale Australian evidence. *Meditari Accountancy Research*, *24*(1), 111–133. https://doi.org/10.1108/MEDAR-02-2015-0008

Borghei, Z., Leung, P., & Guthrie, J. (2018). Voluntary greenhouse gas emission disclosure impacts on accounting-based performance: Australian evidence. *Australasian Journal of Environmental Management*, *25*(3), 321–338. https://doi.org/10.1080/14486563.2018.1466204

Broadstock, D. C., Collins, A., Hunt, L. C., & Vergos, K. (2018). Voluntary disclosure, greenhouse gas emissions and business performance: Assessing the first decade of reporting. *British Accounting Review*, *50*(1), 48–59. https://doi.org/10.1016/j.bar.2017.02.002

Brouwers, R., Schoubben, F., & Van Hulle, C. (2018). The influence of carbon cost pass through on the link between carbon emission and corporate financial performance in the context of the European Union emission trading scheme. *Business Strategy and the Environment*, 1422–1436. https://doi.org/10.1002/bse.2193

Buha, A. (2011). *The greenhouse effect*. Toxipedia.

Cadez, S., Czerny, A., & Letmathe, P. (2019). Stakeholder pressures and corporate climate change mitigation strategies. *Business Strategy and the Environment*, 1–14. https://doi.org/10.1002/bse.2070

Capece, G., Di Pillo, F., Gastaldi, M., Levialdi, N., & Miliacca, M. (2017). Examining the effect of managing GHG emissions on business performance. *Business Strategy and the Environment*, *1060*, 1041–1060. https://doi.org/10.1002/bse.1956

Chithambo, L., Tauringana, V., Tingbani, I., & Achiro, L. (2022). Stakeholder pressure and greenhouses gas voluntary disclosures. *Business Strategy and the Environment*, 159–172. https://doi.org/10.1002/bse.2880

Chu, C. I., Chatterjee, B., & Brown, A. (2013). The current status of greenhouse gas reporting by Chinese companies: A test of legitimacy theory. *Managerial Auditing Journal*, *28*(2), 114–139. https://doi.org/10.1108/02686901311284531

Comyns, B. (2016). Determinants of GHG reporting: An analysis of global oil and gas companies. *Journal of Business Ethics, 136*(2), 349–369. https://doi.org/10.1007/s10551-014-2517-9

Eleftheriadis, I. M., & Anagnostopoulou, E. G. (2015). Relationship between corporate climate change disclosures and firm factors. *Business Strategy and the Environment, 789,* 780–789. https://doi. org/10.1002/bse.1845

Enzler, S. M. (2018). History of the greenhouse effect and global warming. *Science, Environmental Climate Change.* https://nanopdf.com/download/history-of-the-greenhouse-effect-and-global-warming-by-sm-enzler_pdf

Giannarakis, G., Zafeiriou, E., & Sariannidis, N. (2017). The impact of carbon performance on climate change disclosure. *Business Strategy and the Environment, 1094,* 1078–1094. https://doi.org/10. 1002/bse.1962

GRI. (2020). *Consolidated set of GRI sustainability reporting standards.*

Haque, F. (2017). The effects of board characteristics and sustainable compensation policy on carbon performance of UK firms. *British Accounting Review, 49*(3), 347–364. https://doi.org/10.1016/j. bar.2017.01.001

Haque, S., Deegan, C., & Inglis, R. (2016). Demand for, and impediments to, the disclosure of information about climate change-related corporate governance practices. *Accounting and Business Research.* https://doi.org/10.1080/00014788.2015.1133276

Hsueh, L. (2019). Opening up the firm: What explains participation and effort in voluntary carbon disclosure by global businesses? An analysis of internal firm factors and dynamics. *Business Strategy and the Environment,* 1302–1322. https://doi.org/10.1002/bse.2317

Husaini, D. H., Lean, H. H., & Ab-rahim, R. (2021). The relationship between energy subsidies, oil prices, and CO2 emissions in selected Asian countries: A panel threshold analysis. *Australasian Journal of Environmental Management.* https://doi.org/10.1080/14486563.2021.1961620

Khalid, R., Khan, M. R., Usman, M., & Yasin, M. W. (2016). Spatiotemporal monitoring for deforestation and forest degradation activities in selected areas of Khyber Pakhtunkhwa (KPK). *International Journal of Geosciences,* 1191–1207. https://doi.org/10.4236/ijg.2016. 710089

Lazarevic, D., & Martin, M. (2018). Life cycle assessment calculative practices in the Swedish biofuel sector: Governing biofuel sustainability by standards and numbers. *Business Strategy and the Environment, 27,* 1558–1568.

Lewandowski, S. (2017). Corporate carbon and financial performance: The role of emission reductions. *Business Strategy and the Environment, 1211,* 1196–1211. https://doi.org/10.1002/bse.1978

Liang, H., & Renneboog, L. (2017). On the foundations of corporate social responsibility. *The Journal of Finance, LXXII*(2), 853–910.

Maslin, M. (2004). *Global warming: A very short introduction.* Oxford University Press.

Meschi, P. X., & Hansen, A. N. (2019). Partner-diversity effects on alliance termination in the early stage of green alliance formation: Empirical evidence from carbon-emission reduction projects in Latin America. *Business Strategy and the Environment,* 250–261. https://doi.org/10.1002/bse. 2362

Morrone, D., Schena, R., Conte, D., Bussoli, C., & Russo, A. (2022). Between saying and doing, in the end there is the cost of capital: Evidence from the energy sector. *Business Strategy and the Environment,* 390–402. https://doi.org/10.1002/bse.2900

Moses, O., & Hopper, T. (2022). Accounting articles on developing countries in ranked English language journals: A meta-review. *Accounting, Auditing & Accountability Journal, 35*(4), 1035–1060. https://doi.org/10.1108/AAAJ-04-2020-4528

Moses, O., Michael, E. E., & Dabel-Moses, J. N. (2019). A review of environmental management and reporting regulations in Nigeria. *Advances in Environmental Accounting & Management, 8,* 159–182.

Moses, O., Mohaimen, F. J., & Emmanuel, M. (2020). A meta-review of SEAJ: The past and projections for 2020 and beyond. *Social and Environmental Accountability Journal.* https://doi.org/ 10.1080/0969160X.2020.1730213

Moses, O., Nnam, Imaobong, J. I., Olaniyan, J. D., & Tariquzzaman, A. T. M. (2022). Sustainable development goals (SDGs): Assessment of implementation progress in BRICS and MINT. *Advances in Environmental Accounting & Management, 10,* 11–44.

Muttakin, M. B., Mihret, D. G., & Rana, T. (2020). Electoral system, corporate political donation, and carbon emission intensity: Cross-country evidence. *Business Strategy and the Environment*, 1767–1779. https://doi.org/10.1002/bse.2714

Muttakin, M. B., Rana, T., & Mihret, D. G. (2022). Democracy, national culture and greenhouse gas emissions: An international study. *Business Strategy and the Environment*, 1–14. https://doi.org/10.1002/bse.3059

Plass, G. N. (1955). The carbon dioxide theory of climate change. *Tellus, VIII*, 140–154.

Rissman, J., Bataille, C., Masanet, E., Aden, N., Morrow, W. R., Zhou, N., Elliott, N., Dell, R., Heeren, N., Huckestein, B., Cresko, J., Miller, S. A., Roy, J., Fennell, P., Cremmins, B., Koch Blank, T., Hone, D., Williams, E. D., de la Rue du Can, S., . . . Helseth, J. (2020). Technologies and policies to decarbonize global industry: Review and assessment of mitigation drivers through 2070. *Applied Energy*, 266. https://doi.org/10.1016/j.apenergy.2020.114848

Rokhmawati, A. (2021). The nexus among green investment, foreign ownership, export, greenhouse gas emissions, and competitiveness. *Energy Strategy Reviews*, 37. https://doi.org/10.1016/j.esr.2021.100679

Schneider, S. H., & Mesirow, L. E. (1976). *The genesis strategy: Climate and global survival*. Plenum Press.

Statista. (2021). Distribution of carbon dioxide emissions worldwide in 2021 by select country. Accessed on January 2023. https://www.statista.com/statistics/271748/the-largest-emitters-of-co2-in-the-world/

Svensson, J., Waisman, H., Vogt-Schilb, A., Bataille, C., Aubert, P. M., Jaramilo-Gil, M., Angulo-Paniagua, J., Arguello, R., Bravo, G., Buira, D., Collado, M., De La Torre Ugarte, D., Delgado, R., Lallana, F., Quiros-Tortos, J., Soria, R., Tovilla, J., & Villamar, D. (2021). A low GHG development pathway design framework for agriculture, forestry and land use. *Energy Strategy Reviews*, 37. https://doi.org/10.1016/j.esr.2021.100683

Tang, S., & Demeritt, D. (2018). Climate change and mandatory carbon reporting: Impacts on business process and performance. *Business Strategy and the Environment*, 27, 437–455.

Tariq, M., & Xu, Y. (2022). Heterogeneous effect of GHG emissions and fossil energy on well-being and income in emerging economies: A critical appraisal of the role of environmental stringency and green energy. *Environmental Science and Pollution Research*. https://doi.org/10.1007/s11356-022-20853-3

Tauringana, V. (2021). *Greenhouse gas emissions reporting and management in global top emitting countries and companies* (pp. 1–4).

Tauringana, V., & Moses, O. (2021). Greenhouse gas emissions reporting and management in global top emitting countries and companies. In *Advances in environmental accounting & management* (pp. 1–4).

Tingbani, I., Chithambo, L., Tauringana, V., & Papanikolaou, N. (2020). Board gender diversity, environmental committee and greenhouse gas voluntary disclosures. *Business Strategy and the Environment*, 29, 2194–2210.

Trumpp, C., & Guenther, T. (2017). Too little or too much? Exploring U-shaped relationships between corporate environmental performance and corporate financial performance. *Business Strategy and the Environment*, 68, 49–68. https://doi.org/10.1002/bse.1900

Tuesta, Y. N., Soler, C. C., & Feliu, V. R. (2020). Carbon management accounting and financial performance: Evidence from the European Union emission trading system. *Business Strategy and the Environment*, 1270–1282. https://doi.org/10.1002/bse.2683

UN Global compact. (2021). UN global compact strategy. https://unglobalcompact.org/library/5869

United Nations. (2015). Paris club agreement. Https://Www.Un.Org/En/Climatechange/Paris-Agreement

Wachira, M. M., & Mathuva, D. M. (2022). Corporate environmental reporting in Sub-Saharan Africa: A literature review and suggestions for further. *Advances in Environmental Accounting & Management*, 10, 159–182. https://doi.org/10.1108/S1479-359820220000010008

World Commission on Environment and Development. (1987). *Report of the World Commission on Environment and Development: Our common future acronyms and note on terminology Chairman's Foreword*. https://sustainabledevelopment.un.org/content/documents/5987our-common-future.pdf

Worokinasih, S., Zaini, M. L. Z., & bin, M. (2020). The mediating role of corporate social responsibility (CSR) disclosure on good corporate governance (GCG) and firm value. A technical note. *Australasian Accounting Business and Finance Journal, 14*(1), 88–96. https://doi.org/10.14453/aabfj.v14i1.9

Yagi, M., & Managi, S. (2018). Decomposition analysis of corporate carbon dioxide and greenhouse gas emissions in Japan: Integrating corporate environmental and financial performances. *Business Strategy and the Environment*, 1476–1492. https://doi.org/10.1002/bse.2206

Yan, J., Su, B., & Liu, Y. (2018). Multiplicative structural decomposition and attribution analysis of carbon emission intensity in China, 2002–2012. *Journal of Cleaner Production, 198*, 195–207. https://doi.org/10.1016/j.jclepro.2018.07.003

Yu, J., & Lee, S. (2020). The impact of greenhouse gas emissions on corporate social responsibility in Korea. *Sustainability*, 1–15. https://doi.org/10.3390/su9071135

Zameer, H., Wang, Y., & Saeed, M. R. (2021). Net-zero emission targets and the role of managerial environmental awareness, customer pressure, and regulatory control toward environmental performance. *Business Strategy and the Environment*, 4223–4236. https://doi.org/10.1002/bse.2866

IMPACT OF STATE OWNERSHIP ON GREENHOUSE GAS EMISSIONS DISCLOSURES IN CHINA

Zhifeng Chen, Yixiao Liu, Yuanyuan Hu and Longyao Zhang

ABSTRACT

Greenhouse gas (GHG) emission has a detrimental impact on climate change. There is an increasing trend for firms to use disclosure to signal stakeholders about its environmental responsibilities and performance in dealing with climate change. China is one of the countries producing the most carbon emissions. Over the last decade, Chinese state-owned enterprises (SOEs) are becoming important players in international trade. However, the existing literature provides limited evidence on how Chinese SOEs influence GHG disclosure. Through the lens of stakeholder–agency theory, this chapter studies the top 300 listed firms to examine the relationship between Chinese SOEs and the likelihood of GHG disclosure. The result suggests a negative relationship between Chinese SOEs and the likelihood of GHG disclosure. This could be explained as a consequence of the managers' political self-interests, economic and policy-oriented decision-making process and the power differentials between the government and SOE managers. This research extends the GHG literature to Chinese SOEs context, providing direct evidence on how state ownership impacts on GHG disclosure.

Keywords: Greenhouse gas (GHG) emission; state-owned enterprise (SOE); GHG disclosure; political self-interest; power differential; decision-making

Green House Gas Emissions Reporting and Management in Global Top Emitting
Countries and Companies
Advances in Environmental Accounting & Management, Volume 11, 29–49
Copyright © 2023 Zhifeng Chen, Yixiao Liu, Yuanyuan Hu and Longyao Zhang
Published under exclusive licence by Emerald Publishing Limited
ISSN: 1479-3598/doi:10.1108/S1479-359820230000011003

INTRODUCTION

It has been widely documented that greenhouse gas (GHG) emission adversely affects climate change, causing globe warming (Depoers et al., 2016), biodiversity degradation (Afrifa et al., 2020), surplus human deaths (the World Health Organisation, 2019) and wildlife loss (Reed et al., 2016). There is an increasing trend that firms use environmental and GHG disclosure to signal their efforts and commitments to their environmental responsibilities and meet stakeholders' environmental requirement. The increasing evidence indicates that stakeholders have a significant influence on environmental and GHG disclosure. For instance, Chithambo et al. (2021) report that shareholders, investors and the community are the most influential stakeholders in GHG disclosure decisions, followed by governments and organisational stakeholders. Kassinis and Vafeas (2006) and Murillo-Luna et al. (2008) indicate that regulatory bodies are the most influential stakeholders in the disclosure decision.

Given the detrimental effect of GHG emission, Chithambo et al. (2021) call for more research on the relationship between stakeholders and GHG disclosure (rather than environmental disclosure in general). They argue that the environmental issues from GHG emissions do not constrain within the emitting countries but threaten the whole world's climate system with long-lasting and damaging consequences. It is because the pollution from GHG emissions is caused through activities such as farming, fossil fuel consumption and deforesting that damage the common resources shared by the world. In the same chapter, Chithambo et al. (2021) report that shareholders, investors and the community are the most influential stakeholders on GHG disclosure decision, followed by governments and organisational stakeholders.

Although the existing literature (such as Chithambo et al., 2021; Kassinis & Vafeas, 2006; Murillo-Luna et al., 2008) provides us with some understanding of how stakeholders influence GHG disclosure, we argue that more attention is required on how state-owned enterprises (SOEs), which have state ownership as a key stakeholder, influence the likelihood of GHG disclosure in the Chinese context. This is due to the following three SOE features: influential global economic force, maximising social value as the ultimate goal, and political intervention and government protections.

First, SOEs have become an influential force in the global economy, driven by the growth of Chinese SOEs (PwC, 2015). SOEs are defined as 'any corporate entity recognised by national law as an enterprise, and in which the state exercises ownership, should be considered as an SOE' (OECD, 2015, p. 14). PwC (2015) reports that SOEs accounted for 23% of firms in Fortune Global 500 in 2014, with Chinese SOEs comprising 14%. Three Chinese SOEs (Sinopec Group, China National Petroleum and State Grid) have ranked in the top 10 since 2010 and contributed 16% of revenue from 114 SOEs in Fortune Global 500 in 2014. The report also indicates that emerging countries such as China have explicitly announced strategies and policies to support SOE growth and are more actively involved in international trade. Second, SOEs have specific social and policy responsibilities (OECD, 2015); thus, SOEs can play an important role in the long-term decarbonisation to deal with climate change

(Prag et al., 2018). The OECD (2015, p. 29) states 'the ultimate purpose of state ownership of enterprises should be to maximise value for society, through an efficient allocation of resources'. PwC (2015, p. 6) further indicates that SOEs should be evaluated on a wider basis of 'how they contribute to societal value creation'. This means SOEs have specific social and policy responsibilities such as environmental responsibilities. Thus, firm-level low-carbon mandates could be used as part of SOE evaluation criteria and to accelerate low-carbon transition (Prag et al., 2018).

Third, Chinese SOEs have their own features. Compared to SOEs in OECD countries, Chinese SOEs have stronger political intervention and government protections from state ownership. Extant literature provides mixed evidence of how political intervention and protection influence environmental disclosure and compliance. Qian and Chen (2021) and Eaton and Kostka (2017) provide evidence of a negative relationship between SOEs and disclosure and compliance, while Li and Zhang (2010) suggest a positive relationship between political intervention and disclosure. Furthermore, limited literature directly focusses on the relationship between state ownership and GHG disclosure among Chinese SOEs. Instead, the existing literature mainly investigates carbon policy (Yang et al., 2021), Carbon Disclosure Project (CDP) and green innovation (Li et al., 2018), environmental disclosure and political connection (Qian & Chen, 2021) and GHG performance at the regional or sector level (Xu et al., 2014).

The primary purpose of this chapter is to directly investigate the relationship between Chinese listed SOEs and the likelihood of GHG disclosure through the lens of stakeholder–agency theory. To test the likelihood of GHG disclosure in SOEs, we examine 300 top-listed firms based on the market capitalisation in 2020 with the data from China Stock Market & Accounting Research Database (CSMAR). The result suggests that SOEs are negatively associated with the likelihood of GHG disclosure. The result also shows that GHG disclosure is significantly positively linked with board independence, but board gender diversity and board size do not have such influence. The findings further indicate a positive relationship between firm size and GHG disclosure, but negative relationships between industry, market-to-book value and GHG disclosure.

This chapter contributes to the literature on GHG disclosure by providing direct evidence on how SOEs influence the likelihood of GHG disclosure in the Chinese context, where such direct evidence is limited. This chapter makes the following contributions to the GHG disclosure literature. First, it contributes to the understanding of GHG disclosure practices in China, the world's biggest carbon emitter. Although the top 10 emitting countries accounted for 66% GHG emissions in 2019 (Climate Accountability Institute, 2020), many GHG studies do not focus on top emitting countries (for example, Chithambo et al., 2021; Haque & Ntim, 2020; Tingbani et al., 2020). DEFRA (2009) suggests 'what gets measured gets managed'. Therefore, it is important to understand GHG practice, including its reporting, measure and management, in the top emitting countries to deal with emission-related issues efficiently. This study investigates GHG disclosure in Chinese listed firms, filling the gap of understudy of GHG in top-tier emitters. Second, this research extends GHG literature by directly focussing on the impact of state ownership. Chinese SOEs have become a significant economic force globally (PwC, 2015). SOEs' senior managers are appointed by the government and hold dual identity – business managers and government officials. The dual identity brings political intervention and government protection in business operations through political self-interests, policy- and economic-oriented decision-making process, and power differentials. Consequently, Chinese state ownership significantly impacts GHG disclosure due to divergent interests between senior managers and stakeholders. However, the existing literature investigates GHG disclosure dominantly from the perspectives of corporate governance (Liao et al., 2015), industrial sector (Xu et al., 2014), disclosure motivation (Li et al., 2019) and environmental legitimacy (Li et al., 2018) and only includes state ownership as a control variable (such as Liao et al., 2018; Yu et al., 2022). Therefore, the governmental influence in SOE operation is relatively understudied in the GHG domain. This research studies GHG disclosure in the light of political intervention and government protection in Chinese SOEs to cast new insights in the GHG literature. Third, this study provides extra empirical evidence of the relationship between Chinese SOEs and GHG disclosure. The environmental issues from GHG emissions threaten the whole world's climate system with a long-lasting consequence (IPCC, 2014) that requires more research to study the issue (Chithambo et al., 2021). In this chapter, we answer the call by examining the relationship between state ownership, an important stakeholder and GHG disclosure as a main effect and provide insights from the perspective of ownership.

The rest of the chapter is organised as follows: Section 'Literature Review and Hypotheses Development' reviews literature related to stakeholder–agency theory and SOEs. Section 'Data Collection and Methodology' develops hypotheses. Section 'Empirical Results' discusses the empirical results. Section 'Conclusion' provides the conclusions.

LITERATURE REVIEW AND
HYPOTHESES DEVELOPMENT

Theoretical Framework

Existing literature uses stakeholder theory (Chithambo et al., 2021), agency theory (Chithambo & Tauringana, 2017; Liao et al., 2018), legitimacy theory (Tingbani et al., 2020) and neo-institutional theory (Haque & Ntim, 2020) to explore and explain the rationale and determinants behind GHG disclosure. Following Hill and Jones (1992) and Tauringana and Chithambo (2015), we use stakeholder–agency theory to investigate the impact of ownership on the likelihood of GHG disclosure in Chinese listed firms.

Stakeholder–agency theory states the firm is a nexus of implicit and explicit contracts between managers and the stakeholders (Hill & Jones, 1992). It generalises the principal–agent relationship to stakeholders–agent relationship. Stakeholders refer to 'any group or individual who can affect or is affected by the achievement of the organisation objectives' (Freeman, 1984, p. 46). Stakeholders provide critical resources to the firm and expect their interests to be satisfied through an exchange relationship (Hill & Jones, 1992; March & Simon, 1958). Through the exchange relationship, stakeholders establish the legitimacy claims against the firm (Hill & Jones, 1992). The claims are priorities by the managers on the basis of stakes on the firms.

Similar to the agency theory, stakeholder–agency theory focusses on divergent interests between stakeholders and managers. For example, Tauringana and Chithambo (2015) indicate that managers have less preference on environmental actions than stakeholders. The divergent interests in the environmental initiatives are due to two reasons: first is the relatively short-term employment contract, compared with the long-term environmental benefits. Environmental performance requires significant investments such as redesign of internal process, establishment of environmental competencies and investment of extra unobservable managerial efforts (King & Lenox, 2002; Marcus & Fremeth, 2009). The initiatives with long-term benefits conflict with the manager's employment interests which are short term mirrored in the employment contract. The second reason is the lack of financial interests from the stakeholders with environmental claims. Other than shareholders, few stakeholders have direct financial interests in a firm. Hence, managers will be less likely to hinge stakeholder's environmental claims to the firm's profit.

Like the agency theory, the stakeholder–agency theory suggests that asymmetric information reduces the effectiveness of governance. The governance structure can serve to monitor managers' behaviours to align managers' actions with stakeholders' interests to reduce stakeholders' utility loss from the divergency (Hill & Jones, 1992). However, the existence of asymmetric information makes it difficult for stakeholders to discover whether the managers act on stakeholders' best interests. In response to asymmetric information, stakeholders tend to collect more information, such as disclosure, to identify whether managers act on their interests (Hill & Jones, 1992). For example, existing research suggests that environmental pressure from various stakeholders to managers is increasing (Chithambo et al., 2021). Based on the mailing survey of FTSE 100 UK listed companies, Chithambo et al. (2021) argue that provider stakeholders, who supply critical resources to the firm, such as shareholders, investors and community, have the most significant influence on managers' GHG decision. This finding is consistent with stakeholder–agency theory that suggests there is a dramatic rise in financial institutions acting as capital providers which have tighter control over management actions. In a similar argument, Huang and Kung (2010) suggest that in response to the divergent environmental interests, managers can use social and environmental discourse to minimise conflicting interests and respond to stakeholders' environmental claims from the firm. The reason could be that the need for continued access to resources controlled by the stakeholders encourages managers to disclose the information required by the stakeholders, including voluntary disclosure (Tauringana & Chithambo, 2015).

However, the stakeholder–agency theory is different from the agency theory in its assumptions. It assumes that the market could be inefficient from a short to medium term and it takes a prolonged period to re-establish the equilibrium. The disequilibrium gives the rise of power differentials between the manager and the stakeholders. Power differentials refer to 'a condition of unequal dependence between the parties to an exchange' (Hill & Jones, 1992, p. 134). Given managers hold the position of making decisions in the firm, they are in the better position than the stakeholders to exploit power differentials in the stakeholder–agent relationship (Hill & Jones, 1992). Thus, managers could take advantage of power differentials to reduce the effectiveness of the existing governance structures and increase management power over the firm's resources. In developing the hypotheses, we discuss how power differentials reduce stakeholders' pressure on GHG disclosure. In response to power exploration, stakeholders may drive the evolution of governance structure to increase the power to further their interests. For example, the board of directors emerges to limit the opportunities that managers act toward their own interests contrary to stakeholders' interests (Fama & Jensen, 1983). Another example of evolution of governance structure is the board diversity (such as gender diversity, non-executive directors), with the purpose to enable the board to serve its responsibilities effectively through balanced skills, experience, independence and knowledge domains (Liao et al., 2015).

State-Owned Enterprises

SOEs can be defined as 'any corporate entity recognised by national law as an enterprise, and in which the state exercises ownership, should be considered as an SOE' (OECD, 2015, p. 14). SOEs have various legal forms depending on factors such as the percentage of state ownership (full, majority and minority), listing or not listing on a stock exchange (listed and non-listed SOEs) and the public administration hierarchy position (owned by central, regional and local governments) (OECD, 2015; PwC, 2015). This chapter focusses on listed Chinese SOEs 'whose shares are publicly traded' (OECD, 2015, p. 16). PwC (2015) suggests three reasons behind state ownership in the business: (1) developing strategic sectors (OECD, 2015), such as national defence and health sectors; (2) boosting the national economy, such as preserving employment and restructuring sunset industries and (3) political and social considerations (OECD, 2015), such as limiting foreign control in domestic economy. Chinese SOEs share similar purposes with SOEs in OECD and G20 countries, such as boosting domestic economy and driving economic growth. However, it is common in China that governmental officials are pointed as senior managers in SOEs (Qian & Chen, 2021). It means SOE managers may have dual identities – business managers and governmental officials (Eaton & Kostka, 2017; Qian & Chen, 2021). The dual identity makes Chinese SOEs different from OECD counterparts in the operation and decision-making process. First, Chinese SOEs are governed with strong political intervention, opposite to the OECD (2015) guideline. The OECD (2015) states 'the government should allow SOEs full operational autonomy to achieve their defined objectives and refrain from intervening in SOE management' (OECD, 2015, p. 34), although 'the ultimate purpose of state ownership of enterprises should be to maximise value for society, through an efficient allocation of resources' (OECD, 2015, p. 29). However, the dual identity in SOEs' managers brings strong political connection to the business which embeds the political intervention in an economic decision through political motivations (Chang & Lin, 2021). On the one hand, SOEs benefit from strong political intervention by securing important resources, such as lower cost of capital (Tsai et al., 2016; Yu & Zheng, 2019), less financial constraints (Chan et al., 2012) and less IPO rejection risk (Bao et al., 2016). On the other hand, political intervention may prevent SOEs performing well in environmental protection and disclosure. This can be explained by stakeholder–agency theory with managers' political self-interests. The performance of SOEs' senior managers is evaluated by the government based on both financial results and policy application without an explicit consideration of environmental protection (Eaton & Kostka, 2017). Therefore, when conflicting interests occurs between financial performance, environmental protection and the policy application, SOE managers may make politically motivated decisions by compliance with policy in the hope to be promoted to a higher administrative rank (Eaton & Kostka, 2017). Thus, the political intervention is amplified by the political motivated decision. In recent years, there is an increasing trend in political intervention in SOEs. In 2015, the Chinese Communist Party (CCP) and state political councils issued a guidance to strengthen the CCP's leadership over SOEs. It is the first time that government guidance requires SOEs to include internal party (CCP) organisations into corporate charters and decision-making processes (Chang & Lin, 2021). This guidance enhances the CCP members' influence in the decision-making process in SOEs. Furthermore, in 2016, President Xi Jinping publicly and explicitly endorsed the guidance, which accelerated the guidance compliance in SOEs. Qian and Chen (2021) find that Chinese SOEs are subject to greater political pressure and scrutiny after 2015 and the disclosure has become a political instrument rather than a reporting requirement.

Second, Chinese SOEs receive great government protection (Eaton & Kostka, 2017; Qian & Chen, 2021). The OECD (2015) emphasises that SOEs' specific social and policy responsibilities need to be mandated and motivated by laws and regulations. The governments should avoid granting special protection to SOEs if the protection is not necessary to achieve SOEs' special responsibilities or obligations. However, Chinese SOEs receive government protection to an extent that SOEs break regulations without significant penalties. Eaton and Kostka (2017) find that Chinese SOEs failed to comply with environmental regulation and were responsible for many serious pollution incidents. They believe that government protection is part of the reasons of the non compliance of regulations. Senior managers in SOEs hold higher governmental administrative ranks (such as head of department or minister) than the officials in the regulation body like environmental bureaucracy. The lower level ranks make it difficult for environmental officials to effectively monitor and punish SOE managers. Furthermore, the government relies on SOEs to provide utilities, taxation as income and employment. This reduces the government's, particularly local government, power as a key stakeholder. When there is conflicting interesting between finance, policy and environmental protection, the government would turn a blind eye to SOE environment protection but profitable projects or activities. The government protection is reinforced by the policy (i.e. go bigger and go stronger) with an aim of developing large SOEs as global players in key sectors. The policy achieved its aim. PwC (2015) indicates that Chinese SOEs account for 14% firms in Forbes Global 500, with three SOEs ranked top 10 since 2010. However, the policy was criticised to promote profitability and policy implementation over environmental protection.

Hypotheses Development

SOE

Tauringana and Chithambo (2015) state that the need to continued access to resources controlled by the stakeholders motivates managers to disclose the information and satisfy the stakeholders' legitimacy claims against the firm. Deegan (2002) proposes 11 CSR disclosure motivations, including the desire to comply with borrowing requirements, meet with community expectations, manage stakeholder groups and forestall efforts to introduce regulations. Chithambo et al. (2021), echoing Deegan (2002), suggest that business managers are forced to disclose more GHG information, to deal with stakeholders' pressure on environmental issues. They state that the shareholders and investors are firms' resource providers; thus, they are among the most influential stakeholders on manager's GHG disclosure decision. Literature (Brammer & Millington, 2005; Chithambo et al., 2021) suggests shareholders have positively changed their attitude towards ethical investments. The positive attitude encourages managers to disclose GHG information without concerning the lack of support from shareholders. However, it may not be applied to Chinese SOEs due to three reasons: managers' political self-interests, policy- and economics-oriented decision-making process, and the power differentials.

First, SOE managers have political self-interests to bring political intervention into business operation. Stakeholder–agency theory assumes there is agent opportunism and self-interests among managers (Hill & Jones, 1992). It raises the issue of divergent interests between the stakeholders and managers. As a result, managers may not act in the stakeholders' interests. Li et al. (2019) provide evidence that Chinese SOEs are less motivated to disclose GHG information due to managers' political self-interests. In their study, Li et al. (2019) report that the senior managers in SOEs are government officials with administrative rank due to the appointment by the government. Their performance is assessed by the government mainly based on economic performance and policy implementation. Managers with outstanding performance are expected to be promoted to a higher administrative rank. Although the Chinese government promotes the voluntary carbon-related disclosure practice in firms, the carbon reduction and carbon performance are not part of SOE managers' performance criteria. Li et al. (2019) report that the performance criteria set out in the document of Comprehensive Assessment and Evaluation Methods for Leading Group and Leaders of the Central Firms have both political and economic performances, with each weighing at 50% in the evaluation. Thus, the carbon reduction and performance are not part of the evaluation criteria. This fails to signal to the managers the importance of environmental issues and GHG disclosure. Thus, to maximise performance to fulfil their political interests or to be promoted to higher administrative rank, the SOE managers prioritise policy influence and government interests over environmental protection in the business operation.

Second, there is a policy- and economics-oriented decision-making process in SOEs due to government protection. In their study focussing on central protectionism on SOEs causing severe pollution incidents, Eaton and Kostka (2017) argue that the central protectionism coupling with the insufficient monitoring mechanism incentive SOEs to violate environmental rules. Their research finds that central protectionism motivated SOE managers to prioritise policy goals (such as achieving a high growth rate, boosting local employment level and maintaining or increasing profitability) on top of other goals, which include environmental protection. Central protectionism provides shelter to the managers by encouraging them to achieve economic growth where economic growth is conflicting with environmental protection. This inclination reflects on managers' promotion criteria in which the environmental performance plays a less important role in the managers' promotion operation.

Eaton and Kostka (2017) also provide evidence with regard to the effect of the dual identity in SOE management as business managers and governmental officials. They indicate that SOE managers hold higher administrative rank than local and environmental officials. This makes it difficult for low-rank officials to monitor SOE managers' environmental initiatives. Thus, administrative rank asymmetry undermines the environmental regulatory enforcement capacity. Therefore, the insufficient regulatory mechanism further amplifies the impact of central protectionism that provides opportunities for SOE managers to ignore environmental protection in decision-making with the consequence of few penalties.

Third, the power differentials in SOEs are not in favour of stakeholders. Chithambo et al. (2021) provide strong evidence that employees are important stakeholders in increasing the likelihood of GHG disclosure. They argue that the employee prefers to work for a firm with a positive environmental image that maintains the legitimacy of continued survival. When a negative environmental event occurred due to the firm's behaviour, employees may cut ties with the firm by terminating employment contract and finding another employer with green credentials. However, this finding may not be applied to Chinese SOEs due to power differentials. Stakeholder–agency theory assumes that the market is inefficient in the short to medium term. The inefficient market provides limited opportunities to the contract parties (stakeholders and managers) to freely enter into and/or exist from existing contract and create power differentials. Chinese SOEs are a large business with tremendous ecological footprint in the local area. It may be the main source of local employment (Eaton & Kostka, 2017). It is not easy for an employee to find another employer once they leave the SOEs; thus, the employee is more dependent on SOEs than SOEs being dependent on the employee. This resource dependency creates a power differential in SOE managers' favour. Therefore, the employee is less likely to threaten to leave SOEs to put pressure on environmental activities. Consequently, the SOEs are less likely to disclose GHG information (Qian & Chen, 2021).

Prior literature (such as Huang & Kung, 2010; Li et al., 2019, Tauringana & Chithambo, 2015) suggests that managers may use environmental disclosure to mitigate the risk of being dismissed from their current position and response to the accountability towards the stakeholder groups. The SOEs are possible to engage with voluntary disclosure due to two reasons: first, SOEs disclose GHG information to the extent that maintains social stability and promotes policy implementation (Bai et al., 2006). Second, it is under increasing pressure to comply with the regulations and policy requirements. However, the long-lasting protectionism and the self-interests still deeply root in the SOEs, and those efforts remain ineffective. Furthermore, the inefficient market and the power differentials in favour of managers will exist for a prolonged period before an efficient market is re-established. Therefore, we hypothesise.

H1. There is a significantly negative relationship between SOEs and the likelihood of GHG disclosure.

DATA COLLECTION AND METHODOLOGY

Sample Selection

Following prior research (Du, 2015; Gong et al., 2021; Liao et al., 2018), we obtain data mainly from CSMAR. CSMAR is a leading research-oriented database, focussing on comprehensive information at firm and market level with regard to finance, CSR, corporate governance, ownership etc. We also collected the data from China Statistical Yearbook and marketisation data.

Our initial sample consists of top 300 A-share listed firms on the Shenzhen or Shanghai stock market based on 2020 market capitalisation. The top 300 firms are chosen because they cover a wide range of industries and comprise both SOEs and non-SOEs. Brammer and Pavelin (2008) state that a selection of large firms in a wide range of industries in the research can provide a comprehensive review of disclosure and reasonable generalisation of results. We selected the year 2020 in our research due to the availability of GHG disclosure information in CSMAR.

Then, we eliminate firms based on following criteria (Du, 2015; Taurignan & Chithambo, 2015): (1) 46 firms which are in banking industry (including banking, insurance and other financial industry) because they are subject to different accounting policies and corporate governance structures (Mangena & Tauringana, 2007); (2) 16 firms which miss the corporate governance information such as the number of woman directors in the board and (3) one firm which is suspended from trading. This left a total sample size of 236.

Model Specification

H1 predicts that SOEs negatively associate with the GHG disclosure. Following prior literature (Du, 2015; Gong et al., 2021; Liao et al., 2018), we used binary logistic regression model to analyse the relationships between SOEs and the likelihood of GHG disclosure in the sampled firms.

$$
\begin{aligned}
\text{GHG\_Disclosure} = {} & \beta_0 + \beta_1 \text{SOE} + \beta_2 \text{GenderDiversity} + \beta_3 \text{BoardIndependence} \\
& + \beta_4 \text{BoardSize} + \beta_5 \text{Duality} + \beta_6 \text{Emission\_Industry} \\
& + \beta_7 \text{FimeSize} + \beta_8 \text{FirmAge} + \beta_9 \text{ROA} \\
& + \beta_{10} \text{Leverage} + \beta_{11} \text{Slack} + \beta_{12} \text{MarketBookVal} \\
& + \beta_{13} \text{Marketization} + \beta_{14} \text{GDP/CAPITA} \\
& + \beta_{15} \text{PopulationDensity}
\end{aligned}
$$

All variables are defined in Table 1.

Dependent Variable

Dependent variable *GHG_disclosure* is a dummy variable.[1] It is equal to 1 if a firm discloses GHG emission information, and zero otherwise.

Table 1. Variable Description.

Variable	Measurement
Dependent variable	
GHG_Disclosure	Dummy variable that is equal to 1 if a firm discloses GHG emission information, and zero otherwise
Independent variable	
SOE	Dummy variable measured as 1 if a firm is a SOE, and zero otherwise
Control variable	
Corporate governance	
GenderDiversity	Percentage of woman directors over total directors in a board
BoardIndependence	Percentage of the independent directors over total board directors
BoardSize	Number of directors in the board
Duality	A dummy variable that is equal to 1 if the CEO and Board chair are different individuals, and zero otherwise
Firm characteristics	
FirmAge	Number of the years since the firm was founded
FirmSize	Natural log of total assets of a firm
ROA	Proxy of a firm's profitability
Leverage	Gearing ratio of total debt to total assets.
Slack	Ratio of cash and equivalents to total assets
MarketBookValue	Ratio of market-to-book value of equity
EmissionIndustry	Dummy variable measured as 1 if a firm is in carbon−intensive industry, and zero otherwise
Local economic development	
GDP/CAPITA	GDP per CAPITA in the region where the firm's headquarters is
PopulationDensity	Number of individuals in each square kilometre in the region where the firm's headquarters is located
Marketisation	Market development levels of provinces where the company headquarters is located

Independent Variables

SOE is a dummy variable measured as 1 if a firm is a SOE, and zero otherwise.

Control Variables

Based on extant literature (Chithambo & Tauringana, 2017; Du, 2015; Gong et al., 2021; Haque & Ntim, 2020; Liao et al., 2018; Tingbani et al., 2020), we used three sets of control variables to capture corporate governance, firm characteristics and local economic development level.

We included four corporate governance control variables: *GenderDiversity, BoardIndenpendence, BoardSize* and *Duality. GenderDiversity* is measured as percentage of woman directors over total directors on a board (Gong et al., 2021; Tingbani et al., 2020). *BoardIndenpendence* is measured as a percentage of the independent directors over total board directors. *BoardSize* is the number of directors on the board. *Duality* is a dummy variable that is equal to 1 if the CEO and board chair are different individuals, and zero otherwise (Chithambo & Tauringana, 2017; Haque & Ntim, 2020; Tingbani et al., 2020).

We also controlled *firmSize, FirmAge, ROA, Leverage, Slack, EmissionIndustry* and *MarketBookValue* as firm characteristics. *FirmSize* is a proxy of firm's visibility and is measured as the natural log of total assets of a firm. High visibility leads to more public scrutiny towards environmental and GHG disclosure (Tingbani et al., 2020); therefore, a large firm has positive association with GHG (Al-Qahtani & Elgharbawy, 2020). *FirmAge* is measured as the number of the years since the firm was founded. Clarkson et al. (2008) stated that compared to younger firms, the older firms have more resources, such as extensive stakeholder network, research centres and enough time, to invest in environmental issues. Therefore, older firms are more likely to disclose the GHG information (Tingbani et al., 2020). *ROA* is the proxy of firm's profitability and calculated as return on assets. *Financial slack* is measured as the ratio of cash and equivalents to total assets (Haque & Ntim, 2020). The firm with high profitability and financial slack likely has resources to invest in environmental and GHG initiatives (Brammer & Pavelin, 2008); thus, a positive association between financial slack, ROA and GHG disclosure is expected. *Leverage* is measured as gearing ratio (Haque & Ntim, 2020). It is expected that firms with high liquidity tend to engage with environmental initiatives due to more resources available to the firm (Tingbani et al., 2020). We also account for the impact of industry in GHG disclosure. *EmissionIndustry* is a dummy variable measured as 1 if a firm is in carbon-intensive industry, and zero otherwise. Freedman and Jaggi (2005) indicate that the carbon-intensive industries disclose more GHG information due to strict environmental regulations. Following Yu et al. (2022) the carbon-intensive industry includes coal mining and dressing; petroleum and natural gas extraction; petroleum, coal and other fuel processing; production and supply of electric power and heat. Haque and Ntim (2020) suggest a positive association between *MarketBookValue* and the carbon performance. The *MarketBookValue* is calculated as the ratio of market-to-book value of equity.

Following the prior research (Du, 2015; Gong et al., 2021), we controlled for local economic development level with *marketisation, GDP/Capita* and *PopulationDensity*. *GDP/CAPITA* measures regional affluence level. It is calculated as GDP per CAPITA in the region where the firm's headquarters is. *PopulationDensity is* measured as the number of individuals in each square kilometre in the region where the firm's headquarters is located. Liu et al. (2017) indicated a significant impact of population density on GHG emission. GDP and population data are from China statistical yearbook 2020. *Marketisation* denotes market development levels in the region where the company headquarters is located and is extracted from Wang et al. (2019).

EMPIRICAL RESULTS

Descriptive Statistics

The descriptive statistics results are presented in Table 2. The data indicate that 43 firms (18.22% of the sample) disclosed GHG information in 2020. There are 104 SOEs, representing 44% of the samples. In terms of board gender diversity, women directors count for 13.67% in an average board size of 11 directors. However, when disaggregated by the ownership, SOEs have 8.82% women directors in the board, much lower than average 13.67% in the samples. A total of 73 SOEs (70% SOEs of the sample) reported having one woman director (30%) or no women directors (40%) out of an average board size of 12 directors.

With regard to board independence, on average four non-executive directors are on a board, presenting 39.21% of the board members. SOEs have a similar percentage at 38.55%. The result also shows a moderate level of duality between the CEO and chair by a mean of 63.56%. The firm age has a wider range from five to 41 years with the mean of 20. Firm size is measured as natural log of the total asset with the mean of 10. Sampled firms have a wide range of variability in profitability (measured by ROA) and the leverage with mean of 35% and 85%, respectively, demonstrating an overall good profitability and the healthy leverage level. On average, sampled firms have financial slack of 5.53% with SOEs having only half of the slack size at 2.58%. The average market-to-book value for the sampled firms is 0.5336. The data suggest that 8% of samples firms are in high emission industry, much lower than 17% in SOEs. The result also shows that sampled firms are located in advanced economic developed regions as means of GDP/CAPITA at 11.47, population density at 6.46 and marketisation at 9.43, all above the national average.

Table 3 shows the correlation between the variables. There is no indication of concern of multicollinearity issue in this study. The result shows the highest correlation coefficient is between firm size and the market-to-book value at 0.78, which is still below the multicollinearity threshold 0.8 (Field, 2009). To further examine the multicollinearity, we run a linear regression to obtain tolerance and VIF as suggested by Field (2009). The tolerance values are greater than 0.1 and the highest VIF value is 3.548, much smaller than 10. The results further confirm that there is no major concern of multicollinearity in the variables.

Table 2. Descriptive Statistics.

	Total Sampled Firms				SOEs				NON–SOEs			
	Minimum	Maximum	Mean	Std. Deviation	Minimum	Maximum	Mean	Std. Deviation	Minimum	Maximum	Mean	Std. Deviation
GHG_Disclosure	0.00	1.00	0.182	0.387	0.00	1.00	0.173	0.380	0.00	1.00	0.189	0.393
SOE	0.00	1.00	0.441	0.498	1.00	1.00	1.000	0.000	0.00	0.00	0.000	0.000
GenderDiversity	0.00	0.60	0.137	0.129	0.00	0.54	0.088	0.101	0.00	0.60	0.175	0.136
Boardindependence	0.23	0.67	0.392	0.083	0.23	0.67	0.385	0.082	0.25	0.67	0.397	0.083
DirectorNumber	5.00	24.00	10.699	3.273	7.00	24.00	12.192	3.703	5.00	17.00	9.523	2.297
Duality	0.00	1.00	0.636	0.482	0.00	1.00	0.808	0.396	0.00	1.00	0.500	0.502
FirmAge	5.00	41.00	19.936	6.145	5.00	41.00	21.221	6.318	5.00	31.00	18.924	5.832
FirmSize	9.15	12.40	10.659	0.673	9.64	12.40	11.046	0.644	9.15	11.73	10.354	0.523
ROA	−0.09	0.35	0.075	0.064	−0.06	0.23	0.056	0.054	−0.09	0.35	0.090	0.068
Leverage	0.02	0.89	0.460	0.193	0.11	0.89	0.515	0.179	0.02	0.85	0.417	0.193
Slack	−0.18	0.64	0.054	0.104	−0.08	0.20	0.026	0.050	−0.18	0.64	0.075	0.128
MarketBookValue	0.03	1.48	0.534	0.365	0.06	1.48	0.723	0.392	0.03	1.13	0.383	0.257
EmissionIndustry	0.00	1.00	0.081	0.273	0.00	1.00	0.173	0.380	0.00	1.00	0.008	0.087
GDP/CAPITA	10.68	12.01	11.480	0.410	10.68	12.01	11.523	0.456	10.73	12.01	11.446	0.368
PopulationDensity	2.74	8.27	6.460	0.995	2.74	8.27	6.525	1.157	2.74	8.27	6.409	0.847
Marketisation	4.43	11.40	9.428	1.776	4.43	11.40	9.258	1.813	4.43	11.40	9.563	1.741

Table 3. Correlation Matrix.

	GHG_Disclosure	SOE	Gender Diversity	Board Independence	BoardSize	FirmAge	FirmSize	ROA	Leverage	Slack	MarketBook Value	Emission Industry	GDP/ CAPITA	Population Density	Marketisation
GHG_Disclosure	1.000														
SOE	-0.021	1.000													
GenderDiversity	-0.044	-0.334 ***	1.000												
BoardIndependene	0.129 **	-0.071	0.015	1.000											
BoardSize	0.007	0.406 ***	-0.082	-0.221 ***	1.000										
FirmAge	0.062	0.186 ***	-0.049	-0.072	0.098	1.000									
FirmSize	0.214 ***	0.511 ***	-0.286 ***	-0.001	0.234 ***	0.109 *	1.000								
ROA	-0.052	-0.257 ***	0.176 ***	0.072	-0.223 ***	0.009	-0.472 ***	1.000							
Leverage	0.114 *	0.252 ***	-0.170 ***	0.006	0.169 ***	0.101	0.615 ***	-0.501 ***	1.000						
Slack	-0.053	-0.237 ***	0.067	-0.007	-0.160 **	-0.253 ***	-0.310 ***	0.106	-0.407 ***	1.000					
MarketBookValue	0.075	0.464 ***	-0.305 ***	-0.094	0.242 ***	0.023	0.781 ***	-0.601 ***	0.505 ***	-0.216 ***	1.000				
EmissionIndustry	0.143 **	0.302 ***	-0.156 **	-0.093	0.304 ***	0.192 ***	-0.045	0.327 ***	-0.151 **	0.140 **	-0.115 *	1.000			
GDP/CAPITA	0.048	0.093	-0.118 *	-0.060	-0.015	-0.186 ***	0.160 **	-0.209 ***	-0.023	0.099	0.191 ***	0.072	1.000		
PopulationDensity	0.074	0.058	-0.153 **	0.009	-0.074	-0.135 **	0.128 **	-0.177 ***	-0.011	0.103	0.123 *	0.045	0.777 ***	1.000	
Marketisation	0.110 *	-0.085	-0.069	0.081	-0.134 **	-0.072	0.063	-0.135 **	-0.004	0.085	0.031	-0.018	0.739 ***	0.752 ***	1.000

Note: *** Significant at 1%; ** Significant at 5%; * Significant at 10%.

Binary Logistic Regression Analysis

Binary logistic regression is used in the data analysis. The dependent variable is a dummy variable, and independent and control variables are categorical (such as SOE, Duality and Industry) or continuous (the remaining variables). Table 4 provides log-likelihood information to assess the fit of the model. The $-2LL$ for the constant-only model and the final model are 225.582 and 192.217, respectively, with the chi-square value of 32.326 at 0.006 significant level. The table suggests that the final model, which includes all the variables, predicts the GHG disclosure significantly more accurately than the constant-only model does.

Table 4 also presents the analysis results on the relationship between SOEs and the likelihood of GHG disclosure. The result indicates that SOEs have a significantly negative impact on the likelihood of GHG disclosure. As a result, *H1* is confirmed. In terms of control variables, the corporate governance variable *BoardIndependence* and firm characteristics variables (*FirmSize, Market-BookValue* and *EmissionIndustry*) significantly impact on GHG disclosure. All other control variables have no significant impact on GHG disclosure. The model explains 21% of the data in the GHG disclosure.

The confirmation that the SOEs are negatively associated with the likelihood of GHG disclosure is consistent with prior studies. For example, Li et al. (2019)

Table 4. Binary Logistic Regression.

	B	S.E.	Wald	df	Sig.	Exp(B)	95% C.I. Lower	Upper
SOE	−1.328 **	0.562	5.595	1	0.018	0.265	0.088	0.796
GenderDiversity	−0.652	1.670	0.152	1	0.696	0.521	0.020	13.762
BoardIndependence	4.122 *	2.169	3.611	1	0.057	61.670	0.879	4,328.227
BoardSize	0.041	0.066	0.380	1	0.538	1.041	0.915	1.185
Duality	0.201	0.418	0.231	1	0.631	1.222	0.539	2.771
FirmAge	0.040	0.033	1.498	1	0.221	1.041	0.976	1.110
FirmSize	1.928 ***	0.545	12.523	1	0.000	6.874	2.363	19.993
ROA	−1.057	4.385	0.058	1	0.810	0.347	0.000	1878.043
Leverage	−0.343	1.492	0.053	1	0.818	0.710	0.038	13.219
Slack	−0.043	2.449	0.000	1	0.986	0.958	0.008	116.403
MarketBookValue	−1.891 *	1.005	3.543	1	0.060	0.151	0.021	1.081
EmissionIndustry	−1.361 **	0.672	4.095	1	0.043	0.256	0.069	0.958
GDP/CAPITA	−0.599	0.957	0.391	1	0.532	0.550	0.084	3.589
PopulationDensity	0.225	0.399	0.320	1	0.572	1.253	0.573	2.737
Marketisation	0.205	0.183	1.255	1	0.263	1.228	0.858	1.757
Constant	−18.723 *	10.290	3.311	1	0.069	0.000		
Model fitness	−2 Log-likelihood (−2 LL)	Chi-square	df	Sig				
Intercept-only (constant)	225.582							
Final	192.217	32.326	15	0.006				

study CDP-surveyed listed firms (mainly top 100 listed firms by market capitalisation) between 2008 and 2016 to examine firm's motivations to respond to CDP survey. They found SOEs are significantly negatively associated with responding to the CDP survey and disclosing GHG information. They explained that carbon reduction and carbon performance enhancement are not part of SOE managers' assessment criteria; thus, the managers are not encouraged to disclose carbon information. In another study of carbon policy on SOEs' performance, Yang et al. (2021) find a significant negative relationship between the carbon policies and SOE operation performance and profitability due to production inefficiency and technical inefficiency. They argue that the compliance with carbon policy comes with the cost of the deterioration of financial performance in SOEs. As a result, the decreased profitability ability restricts SOEs' ability to invest in the environmental issue and GHG disclosure. Li et al. (2018) supports this argument by providing strong evidence that the environmental legitimacy negatively influences the likelihood of GHG disclosure after the Chinese government enforced more stringent environmental regulations.

Among corporate governance variables examined in this study, board independence has a significant positive relationship with GHG disclosure which is consistent with prior literature (such as Liao et al., 2015; Post et al., 2011). It means that increasing the number of non-executive directors improves board efficiency and enhances the likelihood of GHG disclosure (Chithambo & Tauringana, 2017). The results of firm characteristics variables suggest that the firm size has a significant positive relationship with the likelihood of GHG disclosure. This result is supported by prior research, such as Prado-Lorenzo and Garcia-Sanchez (2010) and Berthelot and Robert (2011) that large firms have more resources to invest in GHG disclosure and environmental issues. The results also suggest there is significant negative relationship between the market-to-book value and the likelihood of GHG disclosure which means that the stock market seems to undervalue firms to engage with GHG disclosure. The negative coefficient with regard to heavy emission industry means that firms in those industries less likely disclose GHG information. This result contradicts prior literature which found a significant positive relationship (Ben-Amar et al., 2017). One of the reasons could be that heavy emission firms tend to be SOEs, as shown in descriptive analysis in Table 2. Therefore, those firms are under the government protection (Eaton & Kostka, 2017) and the managers are not encouraged to invest in the environmental issues and engage with GHG disclosure (Eaton & Kostka, 2017; Li et al., 2019).

CONCLUSION

This chapter has investigated the relationship between Chinese SOEs and the likelihood of GHG disclosure. The study examines Chinese listed firms with a model of the likelihood of GHG disclosure as the dependent variable, state ownership as the independent variable and corporate governance, firm characteristics and local economic development as control variables. The finding reveals that compared to private companies, SOEs are less likely to disclose GHG information. It also indicates that the board independence has positive significant impact on the likelihood of GHG disclosure, although board gender diversity and the board size do not matter in the model. Furthermore, the results suggest that the high emission industry and market-to-book value negatively significantly associate with the GHG disclosure.

Our research contributes to the literature by extending GHG literature in Chinese context, focussing on state ownership in GHG disclosure, and providing direct evidence on the relationship between the state ownership and the likelihood of GHG disclosure in Chinese context. The result also suggests that the policy-maker may clearly incorporate environmental protection and GHG disclosure as part of the SOE managers' performance evaluation criteria to change managers' behaviour and reduce the stakeholder–agency issues with regard to GHG information.

The limitations in this study include: first, we don't separate different levels of state ownership in SOEs. There are three levels of state ownership: central, region and local government. Further research can separate SOEs based on the ownership level to further investigate the impact of different levels of ownership on the likelihood of GHG disclosure. Second, our research only focusses on top 300 firms. It means the samples are large firms. Given that firm size matters in the disclosure, the future research can investigate how different sizes of SOEs influence the likelihood of GHG disclosure.

ACKNOWLEDGEMENT

This research was funded by the Confucius Institute (University of Southampton) project 2021 funding.

NOTE

1. The coding is based on the item 'GHGEmission' in CSMAR carbon neutrality research database. *GHG_disclosure* is coded as 1 if there is an amount of GHG emission in the CSMAR, otherwise it is 0. The data source of Carbon Neutrality research database are from the People's Bank of China, Shanghai Environment and Energy Exchange, China Energy Statistical Yearbook, China Statistical Yearbook on Environment, Annual Reports, Social Responsibility Reports and Environmental Reports of Listed Companies, Announcements of Fund Management Companies, Institute of Public and Environmental Affairs, Annual Reports of Banks etc.

REFERENCES

Afrifa, G. A., Tingbani, I., Yamoah, F., & Appiah, G. (2020). Innovation input, governance and climate change: Evidence from emerging countries. *Technological Forecasting and Social Change, 161.* https://doi.org/10.1016/j.techfore.2020.120256

Al-Qahtani, M., & Elgharbawy, A. (2020). The effect of board diversity on disclosure and management of greenhouse gas information: Evidence from the United Kingdom. *Journal of Enterprise Information Management, 33*(6), 1557–1579. https://doi.org/10.1108/JEIM-08-2019-0247

Bai, C.-E., Lu, J., & Tao, Z. (2006). The multitask theory of state enterprise reform: Empirical evidence from China. *The American Economic Review, 96*(2), 353–357. https://search.ebscohost.com/login.aspx?direct=true&db=edsjsr&AN=edsjsr.30034672&site=eds-live

Bao, X., Johan, S., & Kutsuna, K. (2016). Do political connections matter in accessing capital markets? Evidence from China. *Emerging Markets Review, 29*, 24–41. https://doi.org/10.1016/j.ememar.2016.08.009

Ben-Amar, W., Chang, M., & McIlkenny, P. (2017). Board gender diversity and corporate response to sustainability initiatives: Evidence from the carbon disclosure project. *Journal of Business Ethics, 142*(2), 369–383. https://search.ebscohost.com/login.aspx?direct=true&db=edsjsr&AN=edsjsr.44253321&site=eds-live

Berthelot, S., & Robert, A.-M. (2011). Climate change disclosures: An examination of Canadian oil and gas firms. *Issues in Social & Environmental Accounting, 5*(1/2), 106–123. https://doi.org/10.22164/isea.v5i2.61

Brammer, S., & Millington, A. (2005). Corporate reputation and philanthropy: An empirical analysis. *Journal of Business Ethics, 61*(1), 29–44. https://doi.org/10.1007/s10551-005-7443-4

Brammer, S., & Pavelin, S. (2008). Factors influencing the quality of corporate environmental disclosure. *Business Strategy and the Environment, 17*(2), 120–136. (John Wiley & Sons, Inc). https://doi.org/10.1002/bse.506

Chan, K. S., Dang, V. Q. T., & Yan, I. K. M. (2012). Chinese firms' political connection, ownership, and financing constraints. *Economics Letters, 115*(2), 164–167. https://doi.org/10.1016/j.econlet.2011.12.008. https://search.ebscohost.com/login.aspx?direct=true&db=ecn&AN=1292864&site=eds-live

Chang, Y.-c., & Lin, L. Y.-H. (2021). Do state-owned enterprises have worse corporate governance? An empirical study of corporate practices in China. *European Business Organization Law Review.* https://doi.org/10.1007/s40804-021-00223-1

Chithambo, L., & Tauringana, V. (2017). Corporate governance and greenhouse gas disclosure: A mixed-methods approach. *Corporate Governance: The International Journal of Business in Society, 17*(4), 678–699. https://doi.org/10.1108/CG-10-2016-0202

Chithambo, L., Tauringana, V., Tingbani, I., & Achiro, L. (2021). Stakeholder pressure and greenhouses gas voluntary disclosures. *Business Strategy and the Environment.* https://doi.org/10.1002/bse.2880

Clarkson, P. M., Li, Y., Richardson, G. D., & Vasvari, F. P. (2008). Revisiting the relation between environmental performance and environmental disclosure: An empirical analysis. *Accounting, Organizations and Society, 33*(4), 303–327. https://doi.org/10.1016/j.aos.2007.05.003

Climate Accountability Institute. (2020). Carbon majors 2020 dataset. Carbon Jajors. https://climateaccountility.org/carbonmajors.html

Deegan, C. (2002). Introduction: The legitimising effect of social and environmental disclosures – A theoretical foundation. *Accounting, Auditing & Accountability Journal, 15*(3), 282–311. https://doi.org/10.1108/09513570210435852

DEFRA. (2009). *Guidance on how to measure and report your grenhouse gas emission.* Department for the Environment, Food and Rural Affairs.

Depoers, F., Jeanjean, T., & Jérôme, T. (2016). Voluntary disclosure of greenhouse gas emissions: Contrasting the carbon disclosure project and corporate reports. *Journal of Business Ethics, 134*(3), 445–461. https://search.ebscohost.com/login.aspx?direct=true&db=edsjsr&AN=edsjsr.24703782&site=eds-live

Du, X. (2015). Does confucianism reduce minority shareholder expropriation? Evidence from China. *Journal of Business Ethics, 132*(4), 661–716. https://search.ebscohost.com/login.aspx?direct=true&db=edsjsr&AN=edsjsr.24703557&site=eds-live

Eaton, S., & Kostka, G. (2017). Central protectionism in China: The central SOE problem in environmental governance. *China Quarterly, 2017*(231), 685–704. https://search.ebscohost.com/login.aspx?direct=true&db=edshol&AN=edshol.hein.journals.chnaquar2017.79&site=eds-live

Fama, E. F., & Michael, J. (1983). Separation of ownership and control. *The Journal of Law and Economics, 26*(2). https://doi.org/10.1086/467037

Field, A. (2009). *Discovering statistics using SPSS* (3rd ed.): Sage Publishers.

IPCC. (2014). In C. B. Field, V. R. Barros, D. J. Dokken, K. J. Mach, M. D. Mastrandrea, T. E. Bilir, M. Chatterjee, K. L. Ebi, Y. O. Estrada, R. C. Genova, B. Girma, E. S. Kissel, A. N. Levy, S. MacCracken, P. R. Mastrandrea, & L. L. White (Eds.), *Climate change 20140: Impacts, adaptation, and vulnerability. Part A: Global and sectoral aspects. Contribution of working group II to the fifth assessment report of the intergovernmental panel on climat change.* Cambridge University Press. Paper2://publication/uuid/B8BF5043-C873-4AFD-97F9-A630782E590D

Freedman, M., & Jaggi, B. (2005). Global warming, commitment to the Kyoto protocol, and accounting disclosures by the largest global public firms from polluting industries. *International Journal of Accounting, 40*(3), 215–232. https://doi.org/10.1016/j.intacc.2005.06.004

Freeman, E. (1984). *Strategic management: A stakeholder approach.* Pitman Press.

Gong, M., Zhang, Z., Jia, M., & Walls, J. L. (2021). Does having a critical mass of women on the board result in more corporate environmental actions? Evidence from China. *Group & Organization Management, 46*(6), 1106–1144. https://doi.org/10.1177/1059601121998892

Haque, F., & Ntim, C. G. (2020). Executive compensation, sustainable compensation policy, carbon performance and market value. *British Journal of Management, 31*(3), 525–546. https://doi.org/10.1111/1467-8551.12395

Hill, C. W., & Jones, T. (1992). Stakeholder-agency theory. *Journal of Management Studies, 29*, 2. https://onlinelibrary.wiley.com/doi/10.1111/j.1467-6486.1992.tb00657.x

Huang, C.-L., & Kung, F.-H. (2010). Drivers of environmental disclosure and stakeholder expectation: Evidence from Taiwan. *Journal of Business Ethics, 96*(3), 435–451. https://search.ebscohost.com/login.aspx?direct=true&db=edsjsr&AN=edsjsr.40863834&site=eds-live

Kassinis, G., & Vafeas, N. (2006). Stakeholder pressures and environmental performance. *Academy of Management Journal, 49*(1), 145–159. https://doi.org/10.5465/AMJ.2006.20785799

King, A., & Lenox, M. (2002). Exploring the locus of profitable pollution reduction. *Management Science, 48*(2), 289–299. https://search.ebscohost.com/login.aspx?direct=true&db=edsjsr&AN=edsjsr.822664&site=eds-live

Liao, L., Lin, T., & Zhang, Y. (2018). Corporate board and corporate social responsibility assurance: Evidence from China. *Journal of Business Ethics, 150*(1), 211–225. https://search.ebscohost.com/login.aspx?direct=true&db=edsjsr&AN=edsjsr.45022560&site=eds-live

Liao, L., Luo, L., & Tang, Q. (2015). Gender diversity, board independence, environmental committee and greenhouse gas disclosure. *The British Accounting Review, 47*(4), 409–424. https://doi.org/10.1016/j.bar.2014.01.002

Li, H., Fu, S., Chen, Z., Shi, J., Yang, Z., & Li, Z. (2019). The motivations of Chinese firms in response to the carbon disclosure project. *Environmental Science and Pollution Research, 26*(27), 27792–27807. https://doi.org/10.1007/s11356-019-05975-5

Li, D., Huang, M., Ren, S., Chen, X., & Ning, L. (2018). Environmental legitimacy, green innovation, and corporate carbon disclosure: Evidence from CDP China 100. *Journal of Business Ethics, 150*(4), 1089–1104. https://doi.org/10.2307/45022617

Liu, Y., Gao, C., & Lu, Y. (2017). The impact of urbanization on GHG emissions in China: The role of population density. *Journal of Cleaner Production, 157*, 299–309. https://doi.org/10.1016/j.jclepro.2017.04.138

Li, W., & Zhang, R. (2010). Corporate social responsibility, ownership structure, and political interference: Evidence from China. *Journal of Business Ethics, 96*(4), 631–645. https://search.ebscohost.com/login.aspx?direct=true&db=edsjsr&AN=edsjsr.29789741&site=eds-live

Mangena, M., & Tauringana, V. (2007). Corporate compliance with non-mandatory statements of best practice: The case of the ASB statement on interim reports. *European Accounting Review, 16*(2), 399–427. https://doi.org/10.1080/09638180701391014

March, J. G., & Simon, H. A. (1958). *Organization.* Wiley.

Marcus, A. A., & Fremeth, A. R. (2009). Green management matters regardless. *Academy of Management Perspectives, 23*(3), 17–26. https://doi.org/10.5465/AMP.2009.43479261

Murillo-Luna, J. L., Garcés-Ayerbe, C., & Rivera-Torres, P. (2008). Why do patterns of environmental response differ? A stakeholders' pressure approach. *Strategic Management Journal, 29*(11), 1225–1240. https://doi.org/10.1002/smj.711

OECD. (2015). *Guidelines on corporate governance of state-owned enterprises* (2015 ed.). https://www.oecd.org/publications/oecd-guidelines-on-corporate-governance-of-state-owned-enterprises-2015-9789264244160-en.htm

Post, C., Rahman, N., & Rubow, E. (2011). Green governance: Boards of directors' composition and environmental corporate social responsibility. *Business & Society, 50*(1), 189–223. https://doi.org/10.1177/0007650310394642

Prado-Lorenzo, J.-M., & Garcia-Sanchez, I.-M. (2010). The role of the board of directors in disseminating relevant information on greenhouse gases. *Journal of Business Ethics, 97*(3), 391–424. https://search.ebscohost.com/login.aspx?direct=true&db=edsjsr&AN=edsjsr.40929462&site=eds-live

Prag, A., Röttgers, D., & Scherrer, I. (2018). *State-owned enterprises and the low-carbon transition* (pp. 1–57). OECD Environment Working Papers (129/130). https://doi.org/10.1787/06ff826b-en

PwC. (2015). State-Owned Enterprises: Catalysts for public value creation? https://www.pwc.com/gr/en/publications/government/state-owned-enterprises-catalysts-for-public-value-creation.html

Qian, W., & Chen, X. (2021). Corporate environmental disclosure and political connection in regulatory and leadership changes: The case of China. *The British Accounting Review, 53*(1). https://doi.org/10.1016/j.bar.2020.100935

Reed, D., Washburn, L., Rassweiler, A., Miller, R., Bell, T., & Harrer, S. (2016). Extreme warming challenges sentinel status of kelp forests as indicators of climate change. *Nature Communications, 7*(1), 1–7. https://doi.org/10.1038/ncomms13757

Tauringana, V., & Chithambo, L. (2015). The effect of DEFRA guidance on greenhouse gas disclosure. *The British Accounting Review, 47*(4), 425–444. https://doi.org/10.1016/j.bar.2014.07.002

Tingbani, I., Chithambo, L., Tauringana, V., & Papanikolaou, N. (2020). Board gender diversity, environmental committee and greenhouse gas voluntary disclosures. *Business Strategy and the Environment, 29*(6), 2194–2210. https://doi.org/10.1002/bse.2495

Tsai, W.-C., Wang, W.-Y., Ho, P.-H., & Lin, C.-Y. (2016). Bank loan supply in the financial crisis: Evidence from the role of political connection. *Emerging Markets Finance and Trade, 52*(2), 487–497. https://doi.org/10.1080/1540496X.2016.1110466

Wang, X., Hu, L., & Fan, G. (2019). *Marketization index of China's provinces: Neri report 2021.* Social Science Literature Press

World Health Organisation. (2019). Health, environment, and climate change. https://scholar.google.co.uk/scholar_url?url=https://apps.who.int/iris/bitstream/handle/10665/331959/9789240000377-eng.pdf&hl=en&sa=X&ei=W7BpYu_IDMLZmQHnraWYCA&scisig=AAGBfm10AYn67ge2V0_B3Lt76xe3zSNo2g&oi=scholarr

Xu, X., Zhao, T., Liu, N., & Kang, J. (2014). Changes of energy-related GHG emissions in China: An empirical analysis from sectoral perspective. *Applied Energy, 132*, 298–307. https://doi.org/10.1016/j.apenergy.2014.07.025

Yang, Z., Shao, S., & Yang, L. (2021). Unintended consequences of carbon regulation on the performance of SOEs in China: The role of technical efficiency. *Energy Economics, 94*. https://doi.org/10.1016/j.eneco.2020.105072

Yu, P., Hao, R., Cai, Z., Sun, Y., & Zhang, X. (2022). Does emission trading system achieve the win-win of carbon emission reduction and financial performance improvement?—Evidence from Chinese A-share listed firms in industrial sector. *Journal of Cleaner Production, 333*. https://doi.org/10.1016/j.jclepro.2021.130121

Yu, X., & Zheng, Y. (2019). The value of political ties for firms experiencing enforcement actions: Evidence from China. *The British Accounting Review, 51*(1), 24–45. https://doi.org/10.1016/j.bar.2018.08.001

CORPORATE GOVERNANCE AND GREENHOUSE GAS DISCLOSURES: EVIDENCE FROM THE UNITED STATES

Juma Bananuka (RIP), Pendo Shukrani Kasoga and Zainabu Tumwebaze

ABSTRACT

Purpose: *The purpose of this chapter is to investigate the relationship between corporate governance and greenhouse gas (GHG) disclosures using evidence from the United States.*

Design/Methodology/Approach: *The study is based on a sample of 168 firms listed on the New York Stock Exchange (NYSE) in the United States. Panel data are used covering a period from 2017 to 2020 involving 672 observations.*

Findings: *The results indicate that board size has a positive and significant effect on GHG disclosures while the effect of ownership concentration and insider ownership is negative and significant. The proportion of non-executive directors is not significant. In terms of control variables, firm size and financial slack have a positive effect on GHG disclosures.*

Originality/Value: *The study results add evidence to the already existing literature on the relationship between corporate governance and GHG disclosures using evidence from the United States.*

Keywords: Greenhouse gas disclosures; corporate governance; United States; agency theory; global warming; fixed effect modelling

Green House Gas Emissions Reporting and Management in Global Top Emitting Countries and Companies
Advances in Environmental Accounting & Management, Volume 11, 51–79
Copyright © 2023 Juma Bananuka, Pendo Shukrani Kasoga and Zainabu Tumwebaze
Published under exclusive licence by Emerald Publishing Limited
ISSN: 1479-3598/doi:10.1108/S1479-359820230000011004

INTRODUCTION

Global warming increases temperatures of the land and ocean, and negatively affects human health, migration and food security (Rosa et al., 2022). Global warming is largely attributable to greenhouse gas (GHG) emissions which result from various human activities such as burning fossil fuels, industrial activities, decomposition of organic matter, deforestation and agriculture (Fabrício et al., 2022; Rosa et al., 2022). To avert such negative effects of global warning, disclosures of GHG emissions are critical since they enable informed decision-making. Firms that disclose their GHG emissions are likely to have their reputation improved and in some instances are more likely to have tax subsidies and win grants from multinational companies. Despite the above benefits of GHG disclosures and the negative effects of global warming, wealthier countries are at the forefront of GHG (Union of Concerned Scientists, 2022). This study, therefore, focusses on the United States given that it is the leading country in the world in terms of cumulative emissions from fossil fuels and cement from 1750 to 2020. During the period (1750–2020), the United States accumulated carbon dioxide emissions of 416,738 metric megatons (Union of Concerned Scientists, 2022). This is followed by China with 235,527 metric megatons and Russia with 115,335 metric megatons (Union of Concerned Scientists, 2022). Fig. 1 indicates the top wealthy countries in the world and their carbon dioxide emissions in metric megatons.

Literature on the association between corporate governance and GHG emissions disclosures exists. For example, using evidence from the United Kingdom, Al-Qahtani and Elgharbawy (2020) found that a large proportion of directors with financial and industrial backgrounds have a negative relationship with GHG disclosures. Further, Chithambo and Tauringana (2017) found that ownership concentration and director ownership are significantly associated with GHG disclosures of listed firms in the United Kingdom. Prado-Lorenzo and Garcia-Sanchez (2010) found that board size and proportion of non-executive directors (NEDs) are negatively and significantly associated with the dissemination of GHG information as proxied by the Carbon Disclosure Leadership Index

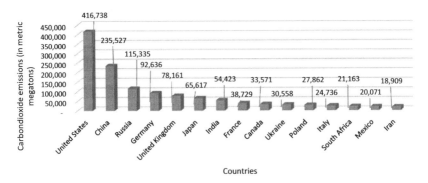

Fig. 1. The Top Wealthy Countries in the World and their Carbon dioxide Emissions in Metric Megatons from 1750 to 2020. *Source:* Union of Concerned Scientists (2022).

(CDLI). In another study, Tauringana and Chithambo (2015) found board size, ownership concentration and director ownership to significantly affect the extent of GHG information disclosure. In terms of the relationship between corporate governance and GHG disclosures using evidence from the United States, such studies are very minimal. However, some studies focus on environmental disclosures (e.g. Giannarakis et al., 2020) which document that age of the youngest director has a negative effect on environmental disclosures among the United States listed firms while independent directors are positively associated with improved environmental disclosures. There is therefore the need to investigate whether corporate governance variables such as board size, the proportion of NEDs, ownership concentration and insider ownership can have a direct impact on GHG emissions disclosures using evidence from the United States listed firms.

This research is therefore motivated by two reasons. The first reason is the need to add evidence on whether corporate governance variables such as board size, the proportion of NEDs, ownership concentration and insider ownership determine the extent of GHG disclosures using evidence from the United States. This is because how the board is structured determines the extent to which such a board executes its functions. This means that large boards are more likely to have members with diverse skills especially those related to GHG emissions disclosures. Previous studies indicate that large board members who represent various shareholder interests help to reduce information asymmetry through formulating appropriate policies and strategies to be implemented by management (Chithambo & Tauringana, 2017). The proportion of NEDs is important for improved GHG disclosures. This is because firms whose boards have more NEDs than the executive directors are independent of management and this boosts their capability to monitor and control the actions of management. Prior studies indicate that independent boards can act in the best interests of shareholders and other legitimate stakeholders of the company (Chithambo & Tauringana, 2017). Stakeholders such as the regulators, potential investors and the general public may be interested in knowing the extent of GHG emissions so that appropriate decisions are taken. In terms of ownership concentration, it may be argued that separation of ownership from control can lead to information asymmetries where managers may have more information than the owners, though such a situation could be controlled through monitoring mechanisms in place. The ownership structure is part of the governance mechanism which helps in controlling the behaviours of managers in an organisation. For example, if there is a high concentration of ownership, it is more likely that the irrational behaviours of managers are checked up since the owners have the necessary resources and the interest to monitor managerial behaviour. Insider ownership means that the directors own the company and have all the information regarding company practices. Previous studies (e.g. Chithambo & Tauringana, 2017) indicate that owner-managers can be involved in self-interest and non-value maximising costs but they may be forced by the various stakeholders to disclose information. However, if owner-managers are interested in disclosing company information, then it is easier since they have all sorts of information especially that related to GHG emissions.

The second reason is to respond to calls by previous studies to conduct a study on corporate governance and GHG disclosures in other countries (e.g. Al-Qahtani & Elgharbawy, 2020; Chithambo & Tauringana, 2017; Hollindale et al., 2019). Existing studies call for future studies largely because GHG disclosures are context-specific and this means that results from such studies may not be generalised to other national settings. For example, Hollindale et al. (2019) conducted a study on women on boards and GHG emissions disclosures using evidence from Australia but called for further studies in other national contexts because of issues of generalisability of their results. With similar reasoning, Chithambo and Tauringana (2017) called for further studies exploring corporate governance mechanisms and the extent of GHG emissions disclosures in other contexts. This means that appropriate policies and strategies can be put in place to ensure GHG emissions disclosures are improved in such contexts. For this case, companies must attract boards with members from different backgrounds but are biased towards environmental conservation. It is also important that companies in the United States are mandated to disclose their GHG emissions with more strict measures rather than fines.

To close the existing gaps, this study used panel data/secondary data to establish the effect of corporate governance variables (board size, proportion of NEDs, ownership concentration and insider ownership) on GHG information disclosures using evidence from the United States. We used 672 observations from 168 listed companies on the New York Stock Exchange (NYSE). Our results suggest that board size has a positive and significant effect on GHG disclosures. On the contrary, the proportion of NEDs has no significant effect on GHG disclosures. However, ownership concentration and insider ownership have a negative but significant effect on GHG disclosures.

This study makes two important contributions to literature. Our study results contribute to a body of growing literature on the role of corporate governance mechanisms on GHG disclosures. Specifically, this study contributes to studies such as Tauringana and Chithambo (2015) who investigated the role of board size, ownership concentration and director ownership in improving the GHG information disclosures. This study also extends previous studies (e.g. Al-Qahtani & Elgharbawy, 2020; Hollindale et al., 2019; Tauringana & Chithambo, 2015) to other contexts such as the United States. This study results also suggest that companies should aim to attract members of the board with diverse skills to improve GHG disclosures. However, firms with board share ownership need close monitoring by the government since they are more likely not to disclose any negative information about their GHG disclosures. This is because the results of this study confirm a negative relationship between insider ownership and GHG emissions disclosures. Also, block ownership is a negative force on GHG emissions disclosures in the United States since it is found to affect GHG emissions disclosures negatively. This means that the Government has the overall responsibility of ensuring that all firms disclose as much information as possible. Other than the Government, the stock market could be stricter on the GHG emissions disclosures and this means that such stock markets could hire strong auditors, especially those who are highly reputed to give an assurance on such company disclosures. Otherwise, if companies with block ownership and insider ownership are not closely monitored, global warming and its effects are bound to worsen.

The rest of the chapter is organised as follows. The next section is a literature review where the theory underpinning the study is discussed, a review of prior studies on the determinants of GHG disclosures is done and hypotheses are developed. The next section is the methodology and this is followed by the results. The discussion section then follows and lastly is the summary and conclusion.

LITERATURE REVIEW

Theoretical Foundation

Existing studies (e.g. Tauringana & Chithambo, 2015) use agency and stakeholder theories to explain the role of corporate governance mechanisms in improving GHG information disclosures. This study uses the normative branch of stakeholder theory to explain the effect of corporate governance mechanisms on GHG information disclosures. According to Freeman et al. (2010) and Dissanayake et al. (2019), the normative branch of stakeholder theory focusses on the information needs of all stakeholders without categorising them into power and less powerful. The stakeholder theory suggests that there is an implicit contract between the firm and its stakeholders (Freeman et al., 2010; Tauringana & Chithambo, 2015). In this contract, stakeholders are expected to provide a market for the entity's products and ensure a safe operating environment for the company in terms of favourable legislation. For example, the government through the regulatory authorities is expected to enact laws that enable the firm to achieve its objectives. The firm is expected to provide quality products and information regarding its operations. As such, the firm is expected to provide disclosures on its GHG emissions since these affect the natural environment and society (people) negatively. For example, increases in GHG emissions are known to contribute to global warming and climate change.

To fulfil the implicit contract between the firm and its stakeholders, there is a need for sound corporate governance mechanisms such as appropriate board size, independent directors, ownership concentration and insider directorship. Large board size is expected to have various skills and expertise in terms of GHG emissions and how they should be disclosed. Also, companies whose board of directors are largely non-executive are likely to pass decisions aimed at improving the legitimacy of the firm among its stakeholders rather than focussing on their selfish interests such as increased dividends pay, manipulated earnings to increase their allowances and other accounting-related decisions aimed at smoothening accounts. The NEDs can monitor and control the actions of executive directors and management (Tauringana & Chithambo, 2015) and this ultimately improves the GHG emissions disclosures. Firms whose ownership is concentrated on the board of directors or in one country setting are likely to be concerned with GHG, unlike those companies whose ownership is diverse. Issues of information asymmetry are unlikely to raise if there is insider ownership.

Review of Prior Studies

Prior studies establish several determinants of GHG emissions disclosures. For example, Tauringana and Chithambo (2015) found that board size, ownership concentration and NEDs have a significant effect on GHG emissions disclosures in UK firms. Chithambo and Tauringana's (2017) correlation analysis results indicate that board size and proportion of NEDs are significantly associated although the regression analysis reveals otherwise using evidence from the United Kingdom. In another study, Hollindale et al. (2021) found that companies with more women on their boards have quality GHG emissions disclosures using evidence from Australia. Tingbani et al. (2020) found that board diversity in terms of more female directors has a strong effect on GHG emissions disclosures using evidence from the United Kingdom. Chithambo et al. (2020) found that stakeholder pressures significantly affect GHG emissions disclosures. Further, Chithambo et al. (2020) found that chief executive officer (CEO) characteristics such as CEO age moderate the association between stakeholder pressures and GHG emissions disclosures among the UK listed companies.

Using evidence from multiple countries, Muttakin et al. (2022) found that countries with strong democracy have fewer disclosures of GHG emissions. This means that strong democracy gives more powers to the citizens/business people than those in authority and as such, there are fewer disclosures of GHG emissions in such countries. However, Muttakin et al. (2022) found that countries with high uncertainty avoidance and indulgence have higher GHG emissions disclosures. Muttakin et al. (2022) further found that democracy moderates the relationship between individualistic cultures and GHG information disclosures. Leng Chu et al. (2013) found that the industry sector and firm size have a significant effect on GHG disclosures. In another study, Chithambo and Tauringana (2014) found that company size, gearing, financial slack and industry type are significantly associated with GHG disclosures of UK listed firms. Using evidence from Indonesia, Faisal et al. (2018) found that profitability, leverage, company size and industry type are significant determinants of GHG disclosures. From the review of literature on the determinants of GHG emissions disclosures, there is evidence that minimal studies (if any) link corporate governance variables to GHG disclosures using evidence from the United States.

HYPOTHESIS DEVELOPMENT

Board Size and GHG Disclosures

A large-sized board has diverse knowledge, experience and skills which assist management in the processing and disclosing of information on GHG emissions appropriately (Chithambo & Tauringana, 2017). However, firms with small board sizes may have members whose knowledge, experience and skills are limited, say, to financial reporting. Such boards may only promote financial reporting and ignore the disclosure of non-financial information such as GHG emissions. In terms of listed companies, it is expected that such companies attract boards with diverse knowledge, experience and skills since they have multiple stakeholders. Such diverse stakeholders have different interests in the firm and this means that firms must disclose various pieces of information to such stakeholders. According to stakeholder theory (ethical branch), it is expected that firms treat all stakeholders equally and this means that issues of information asymmetry should be minimised as much as possible. In a bid to minimise information asymmetry, firms have to attract boards with different knowledge, experience and skills necessary to monitor the activities of management to improve disclosures.

Previous studies have documented an association between board size and GHG emissions disclosures. For example, in their study of the effect of Department for Environmental Food & Rural Affairs (DEFRA) guidance on greenhouse gas disclosure, Tauringana and Chithambo (2015) found that board size and GHG information disclosures are significantly related. In their correlational analysis, Chithambo and Tauringana (2017) found that board size and GHG disclosures are positive and significantly associated. In another study, Nuskiya et al. (2021) found that board size is a significant determinant of environmental disclosures. In their study of factors affecting environmental disclosures in emerging markets, Gerged (2021) found that board size is significantly associated with environmental disclosures. Ben Fatma and Chouaibi (2021) found that board size is significantly associated with the extent of corporate social responsibilities (CSR) disclosures. In another study, the correlation analysis results for Bananuka et al. (2019) found that board size is positive and significantly correlated with the adoption of International Financial Reporting Standards (IFRS). Therefore, this study argues that large-sized boards have members with knowledge, experience and skills in different fields which in turn positively improves GHG emissions disclosures since such boards can advise management on better ways of improving GHG emissions disclosures. The following hypothesis is thus stated:

H1. Board size has a positive impact on the extent of GHG emissions disclosures.

The Proportion of Non-Executive Directors and GHG Disclosures

Firms whose proportion of NEDs is more than that of executive directors are expected to be more independent and can best respond to calls by various stakeholders. This is because they are good at monitoring the activities of management (Tauringana & Chithambo, 2015). According to Tauringana and Chithambo (2015), the NEDs' monitoring of management activities goes beyond the financial issues to include climate change, GHG disclosures or environmental disclosures. Monitoring of management activities is crucial because management has selfish interests and may not disclose all the information regarding company activities to stakeholders. This means that, once management activities are not closely monitored by the NEDs, stakeholders may suffer from the adverse effects of information asymmetry which contradicts the tenets of the ethical branch of the stakeholder theory.

Previous studies document that the proportion of NEDs and GHG disclosures are significantly associated (e.g. Chithambo & Tauringana, 2017; Kilic & Kuzey,

2019; Liao et al., 2015; Tauringana & Chithambo, 2015). In their study of the effect of DEFRA guidance on GHG disclosure among the UK listed firms, Tauringana and Chithambo (2015) found that the proportion of independent directors and GHG information disclosures are significantly related. The correlation analysis results in their study of corporate governance and GHG disclosures reveal that the proportion of NEDs and GHG disclosures are positive and significantly associated. Using evidence from Sri Lanka, Nuskiya et al. (2021) found that board independence is significantly associated with environmental disclosures. Also, Gerged (2021) found significant positive associations between board independence and environmental disclosures. In their correlation analysis, Bananuka et al. (2019) found that board independence is positively and significantly associated with the adoption of IFRS. Subsequently, Tumwebaze et al. (2021) found board independence to be positively and significantly associated with IFRS. However, in their perception-based study of the relationship between corporate governance, internal audit quality and financial reporting quality, Kaawaase et al. (2021) found that board independence is not significantly associated with financial reporting quality. Given that previous studies suggest that independent directors promote GHG disclosures, we re-affirm this position by hypothesising that:

H2. The proportion of NEDs has a positive impact on the extent of GHG emissions disclosures.

Ownership Concentration and GHG Disclosures

The concentration of ownership structure (block ownership) means that monitoring of management activities is easier as compared to sparse ownership (Tauringana & Chithambo, 2015). This means that if the ownership structure is sparse, monitoring of management activities becomes costly and there is a likelihood of information asymmetries. The stakeholders will therefore not access information on company performance, especially GHG emissions. It is also argued that owners of companies can ally with management not to disclose information and this especially so is block ownership (Chithambo & Tauringana, 2017; Tauringana & Chithambo, 2015). However, in the circumstance that there is no alliance between company owners and management in terms of hoarding information, then disclosures of GHG emissions are possible and are fairly done.

There are also previous studies that document an association between ownership structure and GHG emissions disclosures. For example, using evidence from the UK listed firms, Tauringana and Chithambo (2015) found that ownership concentration and GHG information disclosures are significantly related. Gonzalez-Gonzalez and Zamora Ramírez (2016) found that ownership concentration is strongly associated with voluntary carbon disclosures among Spanish firms. Contrary, Gerged (2021) found that ownership concentration is negatively associated with environmental disclosures. Ben Fatma and Chouaibi (2021) found that ownership concentration has no significant association with the extent of CSR disclosures. This study argues that a block ownership structure is much better than a sparse ownership structure since the latter may limit access to adequate information disclosures to the stakeholders yet the ethical branch of stakeholder theory suggests that, various information needs should always be answered by an entity through fulfilling the implicit contract. We, therefore, hypothesise that:

H3. Ownership concentration has a positive impact on the extent of GHG emissions disclosures.

Insider Ownership and GHG Disclosures

Insider ownership means that the directors own the company or are the majority shareholders. This means that they are aware of all the activities of the company and information needs of various stakeholders. Therefore, where stakeholders demand information on GHG emissions, the directors are in a position to provide such information unless there are more incentives for not disclosing such information. Incentives for not disclosing GHG emissions by a company may include less or no fines and penalties as well as taxes. Also, companies may not accurately disclose the GHG emissions for fear of a boycott of their products by major customers. Few studies document an association between insider ownership and GHG disclosures. Tauringana and Chithambo (2015) found that director ownership is significantly associated with GHG disclosures. On the contrary, Chithambo and Tauringana (2017) found a negative significant association between director ownership and GHG disclosures. There are contradicting results on the effect of insider ownership and GHG emissions disclosures. This study argues that, once directors, CEOs and other members of management own the majority of the shares, it is easier for decisions aimed at fulfilling their responsibilities towards their stakeholders to be undertaken. So, since stakeholders are interested in information related to GHG emissions given the current debate on global warming and climate change, it is more likely that the directors will aim to disclose the GHG information to reduce the problem of information asymmetry. This leads us to hypothesise that:

H4. Insider ownership has a positive impact on the extent of GHG emissions disclosures.

METHODOLOGY

Study Design and Sample Selection

The explanatory research design was used to explain the influence of corporate governance on GHG disclosures of the firms listed on the NYSE in the United States from 2017 to 2020. The study focusses on the NYSE as it covers a wide range of industries and indexes the largest firms that are expected to take the lead in GHG voluntary disclosures. Brammer and Pavelin (2006) suggest that the use of large firms from several different industries allows a comprehensive review of disclosures and, importantly, a reasonable generalisation of the obtained results. This period was chosen because it gave a better portrayal of the cumulative emissions from fossil fuels and cement. The US stock market was chosen because it is broad enough to cover a wide range of industries and it comprises big companies that may set the pace for GHG disclosure. Brammer and Pavelin (2006) suggest that the use of large companies in a diverse range of industries permits a comprehensive review of disclosure and reasonable generalisability of results. Firms with unpublished annual reports were excluded from the sample. Also, financial-sector firms (including insurance companies, unit trusts, investment trusts, banks and real estate companies) were excluded from the sample because they are subject to different disclosure and statutory requirements. In the end, the sample of the study comprises balanced panel data from 168 firms with 672 observations.

Measurement of Variables

The variables used in the study are classified into three categories: dependent, independent and control variables. Their measurements are shown below.

Dependent Variable: GHG Disclosure

To measure GHG disclosure, an index disclosure comprising 60 items of information was used (Tauringana & Chithambo, 2014). This index is one of the most extensive in this kind of research (Prado-Lorenzo et al., 2009). Content analysis was used to quantify GHG disclosure from firms' annual reports (Mangena & Tauingana, 2007). The firm was awarded a score of 1 if an item was disclosed and a score of 0 if not (Hossain et al., 1994). The total disclosure index score was then captured for each firm sample as a ratio of the total disclosure score, divided by the maximum possible disclosure for the firm, and was finally expressed as a percentage (Tauringana & Chithambo, 2014).

Independent Variables

Four variables were used as the independent variables in the study. They were measured as follows:

Board size: The number of people making up the board of a firm (Ben Fatma & Chouaibi, 2021; Nuskiya et al., 2021; Tumwebaze et al., 2021).

Non-executive directors (NEDs): Proportion of NEDs (Chithambo & Tauringana, 2017; Kilix & Kuzey, 2019; Nuskiya et al., 2021).

Ownership concentration: Proportion of ownership by shareholders with 3% or more (Tauringana & Chithambo, 2014).

Insider ownership: Proportion of shares held by directors (Chithambo & Tauringana, 2017; Tauringana & Chithambo, 2014).

Control Variables

The study controls several firm-specific characteristics that could influence the extent of GHG disclosure. First, the study controlled for the industry. Following previous studies, it was measured as a dummy variable coded 1 if the industry is environmentally sensitive, otherwise 0 (Liao et al., 2014; Tauringana & Chithambo, 2014). Second, company size is a proxy of public visibility, measured as the natural log of total assets (Tauringana & Chithambo, 2014). According to Tauringana and Chithambo (2014), large companies tend to attract the attention of diverse stakeholders, who use intense pressure and scrutiny to force them to engage in other social and environmental activities as a way of maintaining their legitimacy within their operating environment. Previous studies have found a significant positive relationship between company size and GHG disclosure (e.g. Chithambo et al., 2020; Klç & Kuzey, 2019).

Second, gearing is controlled since it is a measure of risk borne by both equity and debt holders. In essence, creditors are worried that if a highly geared company is not properly monitored, there might be a wealth transfer from them to shareholders. If creditors are not provided with adequate information, they find their means of monitoring management behaviour (Chithambo et al., 2020; Rankin et al., 2011). It was measured as a ratio of total debt to total shareholders' equity (Prado-Lorenzo & Garcia-Sanchez, 2010).

Third, this study controls for the status of a firm's capital expenditure on property, plant and equipment. Firms with new equipment are considered to have the capacity to manage their emissions better than those with older equipment (Al-Qahtani & Elgharbawy, 2020; Tauringana & Chithambo, 2014). It was measured by dividing total capital expenditure by total sales (De Villiers & Van Staden, 2011; Tingbani et al., 2020).

Fourth, this study controls for firm profitability because empirical evidence suggests that profitability is an indicator of a firm's efficiency in resource allocation, meaning managers could be motivated to provide more information about their profitability and other areas of stakeholder interest as a way of attracting more capital than the less profitable firms (Ben Fatma & Chouaibi, 2021). It was measured by return on assets, the ratio between operating income and total assets (Ben Fatma & Chouaibi, 2021).

Fifth, the study controls for liquidity measured as current assets divided by current liabilities (Tauringana & Chithambo, 2014). According to Chithambo and Tauringana (2017), highly liquid companies are likely to disclose more information to set them apart from struggling with liquidity, and hence attract favourable business transaction terms.

Sixth, the study controls for financial slack as firms with financial slack are expected to channel resources into environmental or climate change initiatives, including disclosure, measured as cash and cash equivalents, divided by total sales (Tauringana & Chithambo, 2014). Finally, study controls for firm age are measured as the natural log of the number of years a firm has been publicly listed (Kasoga, 2020) on the NYSE.

Econometric Modelling

The study employed a fixed-effects modelling technique due to the panel time-series nature of the data, which helps to capture variation across different agents in space and changes over time (Kasoga, 2020). More importantly, this technique enables the researcher to take into account omitted or unobserved variables and to control unobserved heterogeneity among firms (Chithambo et al., 2020). The static model of panel data is as follows:

$$G_{it} = \alpha_i + \chi_{it}\beta + \mu_{it}$$

Where G_{it} is the endogenous variable (GHG disclosure index); χ_{it} are all the exogenous variables; β is a set of vector parameters and μ_{it} is a random variable.

From the basic panel fixed model, several estimations can be derived. One that resembles an ordinary least squares dummy variable model is a two-way fixed-effects model, estimated as follows:

$$G_{it} = \alpha_i + Y_t + \chi_{it}\beta + \mu_{it}$$

Where Y_t represents the (fixed) time effects.

This model gives both the group-specific dummies and time dummies. The study models are estimated as follows:

$$G_{it} = \alpha_{it} + \beta^{\text{IN}}{\cdot}\chi_{it}^{\text{IN}} + \beta^{\text{SIZE}}{\cdot}\chi_{it}^{\text{SIZE}} + \beta^{\text{GEAR}}{\cdot}\chi_{it}^{\text{GEAR}} + \beta^{\text{CAPEX}}{\cdot}\chi_{it}^{\text{CAPEX}}$$
$$+ \beta^{\text{PROF}}{\cdot}\chi_{it}^{\text{PROF}} + \beta^{\text{LIQ}}{\cdot}\chi_{it}^{\text{LIQ}} + \beta^{\text{SLACK}}{\cdot}\chi_{it}^{\text{SLACK}} + \beta^{\text{AGE}}\chi_{it}^{\text{AGE}} + \Sigma_{\alpha t}^4 + \mu_{it}$$
$$t = 1$$

Model 1

$$G_{it} = \alpha_{it} + \beta^{\text{BS}}{\cdot}\chi_{it}^{\text{BS}} + \beta^{\text{IN}}{\cdot}\chi_{it}^{\text{IN}} + \beta^{\text{SIZE}}{\cdot}\chi_{it}^{\text{SIZE}} + \beta^{\text{GEAR}}{\cdot}\chi_{it}^{\text{GEAR}} + \beta^{\text{CAPEX}}{\cdot}\chi_{it}^{\text{CAPEX}}$$
$$+ \beta^{\text{PROF}}{\cdot}\chi_{it}^{\text{PROF}} + \beta^{\text{LIQ}}{\cdot}\chi_{it}^{\text{LIQ}} + \beta^{\text{SLACK}}{\cdot}\chi_{it}^{\text{SLACK}} + \beta^{\text{AGE}}{\cdot}\chi_{it}^{\text{AGE}} + \Sigma_{\alpha t}^4 + \mu_{it}$$
$$t = 1$$

Model 2

$$G_{it} = \alpha_{it} + \beta^{\text{NED}}{\cdot}\chi_{it}^{\text{NED}} + \beta^{\text{IN}}{\cdot}\chi_{it}^{\text{IN}} + \beta^{\text{SIZE}}{\cdot}\chi_{it}^{\text{SIZE}} + \beta^{\text{GEAR}}{\cdot}\chi_{it}^{\text{GEAR}}$$
$$+ \beta^{\text{CAPEX}}{\cdot}\chi_{it}^{\text{CAPEX}} + \beta^{\text{PROF}}{\cdot}\chi_{it}^{\text{PROF}} + \beta^{\text{LIQ}}{\cdot}\chi_{it}^{\text{LIQ}} + \beta^{\text{SLACK}}{\cdot}\chi_{it}^{\text{SLACK}}$$
$$+ \beta^{\text{AGE}}{\cdot}\chi_{it}^{\text{AGE}} + \Sigma_{\alpha t}^4 + \mu_{it}$$
$$t = 1$$

Model 3

$$G_{it} = \alpha_{it} + \beta^{\text{OWC}}{\cdot}\chi_{it}^{\text{OWC}} + \beta^{\text{IN}}{\cdot}\chi_{it}^{\text{IN}} + \beta^{\text{SIZE}}{\cdot}\chi_{it}^{\text{SIZE}} + \beta^{\text{GEAR}}{\cdot}\chi_{it}^{\text{GEAR}}$$
$$+ \beta^{\text{CAPEX}}{\cdot}\chi_{it}^{\text{CAPEX}} + \beta^{\text{PROF}}{\cdot}\chi_{it}^{\text{PROF}} + \beta^{\text{LIQ}}{\cdot}\chi_{it}^{\text{LIQ}} + \beta^{\text{SLACK}}{\cdot}\chi_{it}^{\text{SLACK}}$$
$$+ \beta^{\text{AGE}}\chi_{it}^{\text{AGE}} + \Sigma_{\alpha t}^4 + \mu_{it}$$
$$t = 1$$

Model 4

$$G_{it} = \alpha_{it} + \beta^{INO} \cdot \chi_{it}^{INO} + \beta^{IN} \cdot \chi_{it}^{IN} + \beta^{SIZE} \cdot \chi_{it}^{SIZE} + \beta^{GEAR} \cdot \chi_{it}^{GEAR} + \beta^{CAPEX} \cdot \chi_{it}^{CAPEX}$$
$$+ \beta^{PROF} \cdot \chi_{it}^{PROF} + \beta^{LIQ} \cdot \chi_{it}^{LIQ} + \beta^{SLACK} \cdot \chi_{it}^{SLACK} + \beta^{AGE} \cdot \chi_{it}^{AGE} + \Sigma_{\alpha t}^{4} + \mu_{it}$$
$$t = 1$$

Model 5

$$G_{it} = \alpha_{it} + \beta^{BS} \cdot \chi_{it}^{BS} + \beta^{NED} \cdot \chi_{it}^{NED} + \beta^{OWC} \cdot \chi_{it}^{OWC} + \beta^{INO} \cdot \chi_{it}^{INO}$$
$$+ \beta^{IN} \cdot \chi_{it}^{IN} + \beta^{SIZE} \cdot \chi_{it}^{SIZE} + \beta^{GEAR} \cdot \chi_{it}^{GEAR}$$
$$+ \beta^{CAPEX} \cdot \chi_{it}^{CAPEX} + \beta^{PROF} \cdot \chi_{it}^{PROF} + \beta^{LIQ} \cdot \chi_{it}^{LIQ}$$
$$+ \beta^{SLACK} \cdot \chi_{it}^{SLACK} + \beta^{AGE} \cdot \chi_{it}^{AGE} + \Sigma_{\alpha t}^{4} + \mu_{it}$$
$$t = 1$$

Model 6

Where i is 1,......168, t is 1 (2017), 2 (2018), 3 (2019), 4 (2020) and α_{it} are intercept variables that change from year to year. They capture the difference between years, assuming the individual sample members are homogeneous. Other variables are defined as follows: BS represents board size, NED represents the proportion of NEDs, OWC represents ownership concentration, INO represents insider ownership, IN represents the industry, SIZE represents the firm size, GEAR represents gearing, CAPEX represents capital expenditure, PROF represents profitability, LIQ represents liquidity, SLACK represents financial slack and finally AGE represents firm age.

RESULTS

Descriptive Statistics: Dependent Variable

Tables 1 and 2 provide descriptive statistics for the level of GHG disclosure. The extent of disclosure about the disclosure index employed in this study is shown in Table 1. The results show that the overall mean disclosure for the four years is 39%, with a minimum of 0% and a maximum of 87%, indicating a great disparity in the amount of GHG emissions that firms disclose (Table 2). This shows that NYSE firms' GHG disclosures are still low. In general, qualitative disclosures outweigh quantitative disclosures (Table 1, Panel B). For example, in 2017, the firms disclosed about 48% of all available qualitative disclosures against only 26% of the available quantitative disclosures (Table 1, Panel B). Firms, on the other hand, gradually expanded their quantitative disclosures across the study period, reporting roughly 31% of the items in 2020, compared to 26% in 2017.

The actions/measures taken to reduce/mitigate climate change impact were the most often reported qualitative disclosures in 2017, with about 96% of the firms reporting them (Table 1, Panel A, Item 9). This could indicate a willingness on the part of the firms to divert their target audience's attention from the real to the intended consequences of climate change. The disclosure of the supplier and the

Table 1. Consolidated Disclosure Scores for All Firms.

Disclosure Item	Pane A							
	2017		2018		2019		2020	
Qualitative Disclosures	Absolute Freq.	Relative (%)	Absolute Freq.	Relative (%)	Absolute Freq.	Relative (%)	Absolute Freq.	Relative (%)
1 Institutional background	166	99	166	99	167	99	167	99
2 Periods covered by the report	166	99	166	99	167	99	167	99
3 Statement on company position on climate change and related responsibilities	157	94	158	94	159	95	160	95
4 Corporate governance on climate change	147	88	149	88	150	89	151	89
5 Climate change opportunities and company strategies	105	63	107	64	109	64	112	66
6 Climate change impact on business operations including supply chains	85	51	89	53	91	54	95	56
7 Identification of regulatory risks as a result of climate change	54	32	55	33	60	36	64	38
8 Identification of all other risks as a result of climate change	72	43	76	45	79	47	81	48
9 Actions/measures taken to reduce/mitigate climate change impact	161	96	163	97	165	98	166	99
10 Adaptation strategies to climate change effects	81	48	82	49	86	51	89	53
11 Regulated Schemes to which a firm belongs	62	37	66	39	69	41	72	43
12 Reporting guidelines used in GHG reporting	108	64	109	65	113	67	116	69
13 An assurance statement on disclosed information	62	37	64	38	66	39	69	41
14 Contact or responsible person for GHG reporting	131	78	134	80	136	81	139	83

15 Organisation boundary and consolidation approach	81	48	81	48	81	48	81	48
16 Base year	96	57	99	59	102	61	106	63
17 Explanation for a change in the base year	52	31	55	33	59	35	62	37
18 GHGs covered including those not required by the Kyoto Protocol	52	31	54	32	55	33	59	35
19 Sources and sinks used/excluded	69	41	71	42	74	44	77	46
20 Conversion factors used/methodology used to measure or calculate emissions	62	37	66	39	69	41	72	43
21 Explanation for any changes to methodology or conversion factors previously used	50	30	52	31	54	32	55	33
22 A list of facilities included in the inventory for GHG emissions	30	18	35	21	39	23	42	25
23 Information on the quality of the inventory, e.g. causes and magnitude of uncertainties in estimates	10	6	10	6	13	8	15	9
24 Information on any GHG sequestration	30	18	35	21	39	23	42	25
25 Disclosure of the supplier and the name of the purchased green tariff	10	6	10	6	10	6	12	7
26 Explanation for changes in the performance of total GHG emissions in CO_2 metric tonnes	111	66	114	68	116	69	121	72
27 Explanation of any country excluded if global total is reported	86	51	87	52	89	53	92	55
28 Explanation for changes in the performance of scope 1 emissions	47	28	52	31	54	32	57	34
29 Details of any specific exclusion of emissions from scope 1	20	12	29	17	42	25	45	27
30 Explanation for the reason for any exclusion from scope 1	35	21	39	23	42	25	47	28

Table 1. (*Continued*)

Disclosure Item	Pane A							
	2017		2018		2019		2020	
Qualitative Disclosures	Absolute Freq.	Relative (%)	Absolute Freq.	Relative (%)	Absolute Freq.	Relative (%)	Absolute Freq.	Relative (%)
31 Explanation for changes in the performance of scope 2 emissions	52	31	52	31	54	32	55	33
32 Details of any specific exclusion of emissions from scope 2	42	25	42	25	42	25	42	25
33 Explanation for the reason for any exclusion from scope 2	34	20	37	22	39	23	39	23
34 Explanation for changes in the performance of scope 3 emissions	37	22	40	24	44	26	47	28
35 Total GHG emissions in CO_2 metric tonnes	119	71	126	75	131	78	136	81
36 Comparative data of Total GHG emissions in CO_2 metric tonnes	126	75	129	77	129	77	133	79
37 Future estimates of total GHG emissions in CO_2 metric tonnes	8	5	10	6	10	6	13	8
38 GHG emission by business unit/type/country	97	58	97	58	99	59	102	61
39 GHG removals quantified in tonnes of CO_2	35	21	37	22	39	23	42	25
40 Scope 1 emissions	50	30	52	31	52	31	55	33
41 Comparative data on scope 1 emissions	45	27	49	29	49	29	52	31
42 Future estimates of scope 1 emissions	2	1	2	1	2	1	2	1
43 Scope 2 emissions	49	29	49	29	52	31	55	33
44 Comparative data on scope 2 emissions	42	25	42	25	44	26	44	26
45 Future estimates of scope 2 emissions	2	1	2	1	2	1	2	1

46 Scope 3 emissions	35	21	35	21	39	23	42	25
47 Comparative data on scope 3 emissions	35	21	35	21	35	21	35	21
48 Future estimates of scope 3 emissions	2	1	2	1	2	1	2	1
49 Emission of direct CO_2 reported separately from scopes	74	44	76	45	76	45	77	46
50 Emission not covered by Kyoto and reported separately from scopes	74	44	76	45	77	46	77	46
51 Emission attributable to own generation of electricity/heat/steam sold or transferred to another organ.	91	54	94	56	94	56	96	57
52 Emission attributable to own generation of electricity/heat/steam purchased for resale to end users	49	29	52	31	52	31	55	33
53 For purchased green tariff state the reduction in tonnes of CO_2 per year	13	8	13	8	15	9	15	9
54 Additional carbon savings associated with the tariff as a percentage	3	2	3	2	3	2	5	3
55 Quantitative data estimates the regulatory risks as a result of climate change	2	1	2	1	2	1	2	1
56 Quantitative data estimates all other risks as a result of climate change	2	1	2	1	2	1	2	1
57 GHG emission performance measurement against internal and external benchmarks including ratios	82	49	82	49	84	50	84	50
58 GHG emission targets set and achieved	108	64	108	64	109	65	111	66
59 GHG emission offsets information	37	22	39	23	39	23	42	25
60 Comparative information on targets set and achieved	104	61	106	63	108	64	108	64

Table 1. (*Continued*)

Panel B

Types of Disclosure	2017			2018			2019			2020		
	All Firms Score	Max. Poss. Score	% of Score	All Firms Score	Max. Poss. Score	% of Score	All Firms Score	Max. Poss. Score	% of Score	All Firms Score	Max. Poss. Score	% of Score
Qualitative disclosures	2,695	5,645	48	2,776	5,645	49	2,857	5,645	49	2,945	5,645	51
Quantitative disclosures	1,155	4,435	26	1,189	4,435	27	1,224	4,435	28	1,261	4,435	31
Total GHG disclosure score	3,850	10,080	38	3,965	10,080	39	4,081	10,080	40	4,206	10,080	42

Note: The maximum possible score is derived by multiplying the total number of firms and total disclosure items available per category.

Table 2. Descriptive Statistics – Aggregate (2014–2017).

Variables	N	Mean	SD	Min	Max	Skewness	Kurtosis
Disclosure	672	0.3992	0.3321	0	0.8721	0.5402	2.1604
BS	672	9.2782	2.5032	7	33	1.5435	7.5713
NED	672	0.7414	0.2212	0.3553	0.9578	−0.1518	2.8367
OWC	672	40.5421	15.7133	5.65	93.51	0.1577	2.3781
INO	672	6.5635	11.3524	0	88.2653	2.8625	10.5782
SIZE ($ million)	672	14,958.53	9,176.68	9,569.64	429,985.86	8.07	89.57
GEAR	672	1.65	11.53	0.05	255.32	13.32	211.31
CAPEX	672	0.35	0.84	0	18.73	10.14	123.18
PROF (%)	672	9.58	9.53	−65.8	119.51	2.35	25.41
LIQ	672	1.73	1.55	0.18	25.36	6.45	58.64
SLACK	672	0.82	5.56	0	106.58	10.85	126.38
AGE	672	25.52	18.23	0	83	0.78	2.36

name of the green tariff purchased was the least reported qualitative information throughout all years, with only 6% of firms sharing this information in 2017 and only 7% by 2020 (Table 1, Panel A, Item 25). In addition, the number of companies revealing their reporting framework guidelines has risen from 64% in 2017 to 69% in 2020 (Table 1, Panel A, Item 12). Over the same period, the number of firms seeking assurance services on their GHG emissions reporting increased slightly, from 37% in 2017 to 41% in 2020 (Table 1, Panel A, Item 13).

This could indicate a firm's unwillingness to devote resources to enhancing the quality of their GHG reporting, necessitating government involvement to increase disclosure quality. Managers prefer to focus on areas that suit their purposes rather than a real desire for responsibility; therefore, voluntary disclosure is regarded as less dependable (Tauringana & Chithambo, 2014). In all of the years under consideration, the most often reported quantitative item was total GHG emissions in CO_2 metric tonnes, which was reported by 81% of the firms in 2020 (Table 1, Panel A, Item 35).

During the same period, however, evidence suggests that GHG quantitative disclosure per scope was low. For example, in 2017, 30% of businesses disclosed their GHG emissions for scope 1, but by 2020, only 33% had done so (Table 1, Panel A, Item 40). Gerged (2021) made a similar observation, noting that a sample of firms had mostly declared GHG emissions in aggregate rather than by scope. Quantitative data were absent on future emissions predictions and quantifiable estimates of regulatory risks deriving from climate change, with only 1% of companies giving this information for the years 2017–2020 (Table 1, Panel A, Items 42, 45 and 48). This indicates that businesses have failed to properly integrate GHG reporting into other aspects of their operations. Due to the lack of quantitative disclosures, it is assumed that companies utilise disclosure solely to make carbon performance stories, which do not match the reality on the ground (Al-Qahtani & Elgharbawy, 2020).

Descriptive Statistics: Independent Variables

According to the descriptive statistics in Table 2 for the independent variables, the average board size was around nine directors, with a minimum of seven and a maximum of 33. Over four years, the companies had low levels of insider ownership, with a mean of 6.56%, and moderate levels of ownership concentration, with a mean of 40.54%. Firm size as assessed by total assets had a much broader range and more variation between years. Total assets, for example, varied between $9,569 million and $429,985 million, with a mean of $14,958 million and a standard deviation of $9,176 million.

The majority of the firms sampled were highly geared with a mean of 1.65. In terms of profitability, there was a lot of variation. Companies in the sample, for example, had return on assets ranging from -65.8% to 119.51%, with a standard deviation of 9.53%. It is also noticeable that the company size, gearing, profitability, financial slack, liquidity and capital expenditure variables have high levels of kurtosis. The influence of skewness and kurtosis values from normality is minimised in large samples, according to Tabachnick and Fidell (2007). As a result, the non-normal distribution of the independent variables is unlikely to affect the final result in this scenario.

Correlation of Dependent and Independent Variables

Table 3 shows the correlations between the dependent and independent variables. The results reveal that there is no problem with multicollinearity among independent variables because the variables were unrelated to one another, with a correlation of less than 0.8. A correlation of independent variables of more than 0.8, according to Field (2009), shows grounds for concern.

According to Myers (1990), multicollinearity can still occur even when none of the correlation coefficients are particularly significant. As a result, variance inflation factors were investigated further to see if multicollinearity existed. In addition, the heteroscedasticity Breusche–Pagan/Cooke–Weisberg test and the homoscedasticity White's test were performed. If heteroscedasticity is present but not managed, the standard errors and any associated tests may be incorrect, according to Breusch and Pagan (1980). The test result was highly significant in both situations, showing that heteroscedasticity was present. Heteroscedasticity can be handled in a variety of ways, according to Berry and Feldman (1985), including variable transformation and the use of robust standard errors. Options were employed in this research; some variables, particularly firm size, were converted logarithmically, and the option of robust was used.

Multivariate Results

The multivariate results are presented in Table 4. This study has four hypotheses where one hypothesis is supported and the remaining three hypotheses were not supported. Five models were run. In model 1, only control variables were included. Firm size, gearing, financial slack and industry are significantly related to GHG emissions disclosures. However, among the significant variables, the

Table 3. Correlation Among Dependent and Independent Variables.

Variable	1	2	3	4	5	6	7	8	9	10	11	12	13
1. Disclosure	1.00												
2. BS	0.28***	1.00											
3. NED	0.18***	0.12**	1.00										
4. OWC	-0.26**	-0.13**	0.03	1.00									
5. INO	-0.32**	-0.22**	-0.13**	0.23**	1.00								
6. SIZE	0.63**	0.51**	0.27**	-0.25**	-0.16**	1.00							
7. GEAR	-0.05	-0.03	-0.01	-0.05	-0.04	0.01	1.00						
8. CAPEX	0.08**	0.03	-0.05	-0.04	-0.07**	0.02		1.00					
9. PROF	-0.04	-0.02	0.05**	0.03	0.02	-0.12**	-0.01	0.13***	1.00				
10. LIQ	-0.13**	-0.13***	0.03	0.17***	0.12**	-0.03**	-0.01	-0.31***	-0.01	1.00			
11. SLACK	0.12**	0.05	0.11**	0.06**	0.01	0.04	0.01	0.03	-0.02	0.01	1.00		
12. AGE	-0.04	0.04	-0.02	-0.26**	-0.16**	0.01	0.12**	0.13***	-0.03	-0.05	-0.02	1.00	
13. IN	-0.02	0.03	0.04	0.05	0.08	0.11**	0.07**	0.19***	0.06	0.21***	0.02	-0.07***	1.00

Note: **, *** significance at 5% and 1%, respectively.

Table 4. Multivariate Results (Regression Results).

Variable	Model 1	Model 2	Model 3	Model 4	Model 5	Model 6	Robust Standard Error
Constant							
Independent variables							
BS		0.094***				0.091***	0.031
NED			−0.055			−0.061	0.082
OWC				−0.0002***		−0.001***	0.001
INO					−0.00082***	−0.0008***	0.0006
Control variables							
SIZE	0.087***	0.082***	0.086***	0.085***	0.085***	0.084***	0.021
GEAR	−0.0036**	−0.0033**	−0.0031**	−0.0034**	−0.0031**	−0.003**	0.0004
CAPEX	0.023	0.021	0.022	0.023	0.020	0.014	0.017
PROF	0.0009	0.0008	0.0008	0.0008	0.0008	0.0008	0.0005
LIQ	0.0091	0.0086	0.0085	0.0083	0.0085	0.0089	0.0025
SLACK	0.0025**	0.0023**	0.0021**	0.0022**	0.0023**	0.0023**	0.0007
AGE	−0.027	−0.024	−0.024	−0.024	−0.024	−0.024	0.002
IN	−0.06**	−0.05**	−0.05**	−0.05**	−0.05**	−0.05**	0.03
R square	0.09	0.15	0.13	0.10	0.12	0.36	
Adjusted R square	0.07	0.13	0.11	0.07	0.09	0.34	

Note: ***$p < 0.01$, **$p < 0.05$.

relationship between gearing, industry type and GHG emissions disclosures is negative. Capital expenditure, profitability, liquidity and firm age are not significantly associated with GHG emissions disclosures. Model 1 explains 7% of the variations in the GHG emissions disclosures.

In model 2, board size and the control variables are entered and results show that board size is positively and significantly related to GHG emissions disclosures. This provides support for *H1* (*Board size has a positive impact on the extent of GHG emissions disclosures*). Model 2 explains 13% of the variations in the GHG emissions disclosures. In model 3, the proportion of NEDs is entered and found negative but not significant. Therefore *H2* (*Proportion of NEDs has a positive impact on the extent of GHG emissions disclosures*) is not supported. Model 3 explains 11% of the variations in the GHG emissions disclosures. In model 4, ownership concentration is entered. Results show that ownership concentration is negatively and significantly related to GHG emissions disclosures. Therefore *H3* (*Ownership concentration has a positive impact on the extent of GHG emissions disclosures*) is not supported. Model 4 explains 7% of the variations in GHG emissions disclosures. In model 5, insider ownership is entered and found significant but negative. Thus *H4* (*Insider ownership has a positive impact on the extent of GHG emissions disclosures*) is not supported. Model 5 explains 9% of the variations in GHG emissions disclosures.

The final model is model 6 where all the variables are entered. The results indicate that corporate governance variables (board size, insider ownership and ownership concentration) and company-specific control variables (size, gearing, financial slack and industry) have a significant effect on GHG disclosure scores. All the coefficients were statistically significant ($p < 0.05$), except for board size, ownership concentration, insider ownership and firm size, which had a significance of 0.01. The NEDs and company-specific control variables (capital expenditure profitability, liquidity and firm age) have no significant relationship with GHG disclosure ($p > 0.05$). The final model explains 34% of the variation in the extent of GHG disclosure.

Robustness Check

A study like this could have several statistical flaws, including endogeneity, which occurs when a model leaves out certain important factors and thus fails to present a complete picture. One approach is to incorporate all known variables and find appropriate instruments to measure (or proxies for) other variables. The regression model in this study includes some well-known governance factors that were not included in the original model but have been extensively used in previous disclosure studies. The rationale was that governance and environmental studies research is broad, and many components of governance have been examined before, and leaving them out would have meant that our understanding was insufficient, amplifying the endogeneity problem (Tauringana & Chithambo, 2014). The audit committee, the presence of an environmental committee, gender diversity (using the proportion of female board members), directors' age and the frequency of board meetings were all non-significant, and our model's explanatory power did not exceed 34% provided in the model (Table 5). In addition, the study looked into the possibilities of including CEO duality in the model. However, because there were only two enterprises with CEO duality, this was deemed insufficient to yield relevant statistical data.

Furthermore, based on our research, we discovered that the industry variable is classified differently (e.g. Prado-Lorenzo et al., 2009, had 11 categories; Rankin et al., 2011, had four; and Freedman & Jaggi, 2005, had five). As a result, the industry variable was classed using the Industry Classification Benchmark, yielding four industry groups (having excluded). The model was examined again, this time with the reclassified industry variable, but the results were the same as before, with the explanatory variables' direction and significance remaining unchanged (Table 5). The proper model was determined using a log-likelihood ratio. Clustering the industry variable into one dummy variable resulted in a statistically significant model, according to the chi-square. The log-likelihood ratio had LR chi2 (6) of 25.41, with Prob > chi2 of 0.000 (Table 6). The model with the data in Table 4 was regarded as more appropriate based on these findings.

Table 5. Multivariate Results.

GHG Disclosure (DV)	Coefficient	Robust Standard Error
Board size	0.090***	0.032
Non-executive directors	−0.060	0.081
Ownership concentration	−0.001***	0.001
Insider ownership	−0.0007***	0.0006
Firm size	0.082***	0.024
Gearing	−0.002**	0.0004
Capital expenditure	0.013	0.018
Profitability	0.0008	0.0005
Liquidity	0.0087	0.0026
Financial slack	0.0022**	0.0008
Firm age	−0.024	0.002
Industry	−0.05**	0.03
Audit committee	−0.011	0.0613
Environmental committee	0.0031	0.0237
Board gender diversity	0.0001	0.056
Directors' age	0.0001	0.0462
Board meetings	0.0035	0.0046
R-Squared = 0.36; Adj. R-Squared = 0.34		

Note: ***$p < 0.01$, **$p < 0.05$.

Table 6. Clustering the Industry Variable Into One Dummy Variable.

GHG Disclosure (DV)	Coefficient	Robust Standard Error
Board size	0.085***	0.022
Non-executive directors	−0.050	0.063
Ownership concentration	−0.001***	0.001
Insider ownership	−0.0007***	0.0005
Firm size	0.072***	0.033
Gearing	−0.003**	0.0003
Capital expenditure	0.013	0.018
Profitability	0.0008	0.0005
Liquidity	0.0079	0.0036
Financial slack	0.0022**	0.0006
Firm age	−0.023	0.003
Industry	−0.06**	0.04
−2Log Likelihood = 25.41; Prob. χ^2 = 0.000		

Note: ***$p < 0.01$, **$p < 0.05$.

DISCUSSION OF FINDINGS

The finding that board size has a positive and significant effect on GHG disclosures means that firms with large boards have improved GHG disclosures.

This is because firms with large boards have board members with vast knowledge, experience and skills not only for financial reporting but also for other reporting paradigms such as GHG emissions disclosures. This finding is in line with the stakeholder theory, especially the ethical/normative branch which suggests that there is an implicit contract between the company and all the stakeholders. The ethical branch of stakeholder theory suggests that all stakeholders are equal. Because of the diverse information needs of various stakeholders, companies ought to have boards with members of vast knowledge, experience and skills. This study finding is also in line with previous studies such as Tauringana and Chithambo (2015) who found that board size and GHG disclosures to be positive and significantly associated. This study's results also are consistent with findings by Nuskiya et al. (2021) who found that board size is a significant determinant of environmental disclosures.

The finding that the proportion of NEDs is not significantly associated with GHG disclosures means that the NEDs have less control over management actions. This suggests that the NEDs lean on the executive directors and their decisions follow the same direction. This means NEDs are not independent of the executive directors. This partly explains the low GHG emissions disclosures among firms listed on the NYSE. The finding that the proportion of NEDs has no significant effect on GHG disclosures contradicts the stakeholder theory. This is because it is expected that when stakeholders demand information, the NEDs are partial and as such will force the executive directors to make such disclosures. This is because they are independent of the executive directors and their decisions are binding and unbiased. The NEDs are expected to pass decisions that aim to improve the legitimacy of the firm. This study's results also contradict the findings of prior studies such as Tauringana and Chithambo's (2015) study which found that the proportion of NEDs is positively and significantly associated with GHG disclosures using evidence from the United Kingdom.

In terms of the effect between ownership concentration and GHG disclosures, the result indicates a negative and significant relationship. This means that when ownership is concentrated among a few shareholders, information is confined to those shareholders and there is connivance not to disclose GHG emissions of the respective companies to various stakeholders. This finding contradicts the ethical branch of the stakeholder theory which indicates that all stakeholders are equal. In this case, results indicate that the shareholders and management have more information, unlike the other stakeholders. It is now evident that firms whose ownership is sparse can monitor management's irrational activities and represent various stakeholder needs such as the disclosure of information on GHG emissions. This study's results also contradict findings by previous studies such as Gonzalez-Gonzalez and Zamora Ramírez's (2016) study which found that ownership concentration is strongly associated with carbon disclosures among the Spanish firms.

For insider ownership, the finding that it is significant and negatively associated with GHG disclosures means that firms whose managers are also shareholders disclose less to the other stakeholders. In the circumstance where the directors own shares, information on GHG is concentrated on those directors and less information is disclosed to other stakeholders. This finding contradicts the ethical branch of stakeholder theory regarding the equality of all stakeholders. So, there is a problem of information asymmetry and this means that the stakeholders such as regulators are not able to make valid decisions. This is because information on GHG emissions is hoarded by the inside directors. This partly explains why the United States is one of those countries with more carbon dioxide emissions as indicated in Fig. 1. The finding that insider directors have a negative significant relationship is consistent with the findings by Chithambo and Tauringana (2017) who found that insider ownership has a significant negative effect on GHG disclosures in the United Kingdom. However, the study findings contradict findings by Tauringana and Chithambo (2015) who found that director ownership is significantly associated with GHG disclosures.

For control variables, only firm size and financial slack are positively and significantly associated with GHG emissions disclosures. Of course, large-sized firms are expected to have more stakeholders and these have different information needs. Large-sized firms must therefore ensure that all the stakeholders are catered for. One way to do this is to provide timely information on GHG emissions. These results are consistent with previous study findings such as Chithambo et al. (2020) who found that firm size is significantly related to GHG disclosures. In terms of financial slack, firms with financial slack are expected to channel resources into environmental or climate change initiatives, including disclosure, measured as cash and cash equivalents, divided by total sales (Tauringana & Chithambo, 2014). This result, therefore, means that financial slack improves GHG disclosures since funds are available to be invested in systems that improve GHG emissions disclosures. The negative relationship between gearing, industry type and GHG emissions means that highly geared firms may not have enough resources to commit to GHG emissions. It also means that such companies are focussed on improving the rearing level rather than the negative impacts of their activities on the environment. However, the absence of such disclosures leaves the creditors and other suppliers worried.

SUMMARY AND CONCLUSION

This study aimed to investigate the relationship between corporate governance and GHG disclosures. Using panel data from 168 firms listed on the NYSE, we found that only board size has a significant positive effect on GHG disclosures in the United States. Whereas we found the proportion of NEDs not to be significantly associated with GHG disclosures, the effect of ownership concentration and insider ownership was negative but significant with GHG disclosures.

This study makes a contribution to the existing literature on the determinants of GHG disclosures by responding to calls of previous studies to conduct such a study (e.g. Al-Qahtani & Elgharbawy, 2020; Chithambo & Tauringana, 2017; Hollindale et al., 2019). This study uses evidence from the United States and this means that what matters for the improvement of GHG in such a country is the board size. The larger the board size the better. This is because a larger board size comes with diverse skills and experience in managing big organisations with their stakeholders and this eventually improves the GHG disclosures. However, firms with board share ownership need close monitoring by the Government since all the information concerning company activities is best known by the directors and thus there is a problem of information asymmetry. Also, block ownership is a negative force on GHG emissions disclosures in the United States since it is found to affect GHG emissions disclosures negatively. This means that the Government has the overall responsibility of ensuring that all firms disclose as much information as possible. Other than the Government, the stock market could be stricter on the GHG emissions disclosures and this means that such stock markets could hire strong auditors such as the Big Four audit firms (Ernst and Young, KPMG, Deloitte and Touché and PwC) to give assurance on such company disclosures.

Like any other study, this study also has limitations which are discussed alongside areas for further research. For example, this study uses content analysis and ignores perceptions. Whereas content analysis is known to be objective, it does not establish why things happen the way they happen. This calls for perception-based studies which are capable of documenting those direct managerial motivations for GHG disclosures. This study was focussed only on the United States and this means that these results are only generalisable to the United States. Given that previous studies including this one are focussed on the developed world, such studies must be extended to the emerging world. Regardless of the above study limitations and suggestions for future research, this study's results are still useful.

REFERENCES

Al-Qahtani, M., & Elgharbawy, A. (2020). The effect of board diversity on disclosure and management of greenhouse gas information: Evidence from the United Kingdom. *Journal of Enterprise Information Management, 33*(6), 1557–1579.

Bananuka, J., Tumwebaze, Z., Musimenta, D., & Nuwagaba, P. (2019). Determinants of adoption of International Financial Reporting Standards in Ugandan micro finance institutions. *African Journal of Economic and Management Studies, 10*(3), 336–355.

Ben Fatma, H., & Chouaibi, J. (2021). Corporate governance and CSR disclosure: Evidence from European financial institutions.. *International Journal of Disclosure and Governance,* 1–16.

Berry, W. D., & Feldman, S. (1985). *Multiple regression in practice. Sage University paper series on quantitative applications in the social sciences.* Series no. 07e050. Sage.

Brammer, S., & Pavelin, S. (2006). Voluntary environmental disclosures by large UK companies. *Journal of Business Finance & Accounting, 33*(7), 1168–1188.

Breusch, T. S., & Pagan, A. R. (1980). The Lagrange multiplier test and its applications to model specification in econometrics. *The Review of Economic Studies, 47*(1), 239–253.

Chithambo, L., & Tauringana, V. (2014). Company specific determinants of greenhouse gases disclosures. *Journal of Applied Accounting Research, 15*(3), 323–338.

Chithambo, L., & Tauringana, V. (2017). Corporate governance and greenhouse gas disclosure: A mixed-methods approach. *Corporate Governance, 17*(4), 678–699.

Chithambo, L., Tingbani, I., Agyapong, G. A., Gyapong, E., & Damoah, I. S. (2020). Corporate voluntary greenhouse gas reporting: Stakeholder pressure and the mediating role of the chief executive officer. *Business Strategy and the Environment, 29*(4), 1666–1683.

De Villiers, C., & Van Staden, C. J. (2011). Where firms choose to disclose voluntary environmental information. *Journal of Accounting and Public Policy*, *30*(1), 504–525.

Dissanayake, D., Tilt, C., & Qian, W. (2019). Factors influencing sustainability reporting by Sri Lankan companies. *Pacific Accounting Review*, *31*(1), 84–109.

Fabrício, S. A., Ferreira, D. D. M., & Rover, S. (2022). Female representation on boards of directors and environmental disclosure: Evidence of the Brazilian GHG protocol program. *Gender in Management*, *37*(5), 619–637.

Faisal, F., Andiningtyas, E. D., Achmad, T., Haryanto, H., & Meiranto, W. (2018). The content and determinants of greenhouse gas emission disclosure: Evidence from Indonesian companies. *Corporate Social Responsibility and Environmental Management*, *25*(6), 1397–1406.

Field, A. (2009). *Discovering statistics using SPSS* (3rd ed.). Sage Publishers.

Freedman, M., & Jaggi, B. (2005). Global warming, commitment to the Kyoto Protocol, and accounting disclosures by the largest global public firms from polluting industries. *The International Journal of Accounting*, *40*(3), 215–232.

Freeman, R. E., Harrison, J. S., Wicks, A. C., Parmar, B. L., & De Colle, S. (2010). *Stakeholder theory: The state of the art*. Cambridge University Press.

Gerged, A. M. (2021). Factors affecting corporate environmental disclosure in emerging markets: The role of corporate governance structures. *Business Strategy and the Environment*, *30*(1), 609–629.

Giannarakis, G., Andronikidis, A., & Sariannidis, N. (2020). Determinants of environmental disclosure: Investigating new and conventional corporate governance characteristics. *Annals of Operations Research*, *294*, 87–105.

Gonzalez-Gonzalez, J. M., & Zamora Ramírez, C. (2016). Voluntary carbon disclosure by Spanish companies: An empirical analysis. *International Journal of Climate Change Strategies and Management*, *8*(1), 57–79.

Hollindale, J., Kent, P., Routledge, J., & Chapple, L. (2019). Women on boards and greenhouse gas emission disclosures. *Accounting and Finance*, *59*(1), 277–308.

Hossain, M., Tan, L. M., & Adams, M. (1994). Voluntary disclosure in an emerging capital market: Some empirical evidence from companies listed on the K.L. stock exchange. *International Journal of Accounting*, *29*(1), 334–351.

Kaawaase, T. K., Nairuba, C., Akankunda, B., & Bananuka, J. (2021). Corporate governance, internal audit quality and financial reporting quality of financial institutions. *Asian Journal of Accounting Research*, *6*(3), 348–366.

Kasoga, P. S. (2020). Does investing in intellectual capital improve financial performance? Panel evidence from firms listed in Tanzania DSE. *Cogent Economics and Finance*, *8*(1), 1–26.

Kılıç, M., & Kuzey, C. (2019). The effect of corporate governance on carbon emission disclosures: Evidence from Turkey. *International Journal of Climate Change Strategies and Management*, *11*(1), 35–53.

Leng Chu, C., Chatterjee, B., & Brown, A. (2013). The current status of greenhouse gas reporting by Chinese companies: A test of legitimacy theory. *Managerial Auditing Journal*, *28*(2), 114–139.

Liao, L., Luo, L., & Tang, Q. (2014). Gender diversity, board independence, environmental committee and greenhouse gas disclosure. *The British Accounting Review*, *1*(1), 1–16.

Liao, L., Luo, L., & Tang, Q. (2015). Gender diversity, board independence, environmental committee and greenhouse gas disclosure. *The British Accounting Review*, *47*(4), 409–424.

Mangena, M., & Tauingana, V. (2007). Corporate compliance with non-mandatory statements of best practice: The case of the ASB statement on interim reports. *European Accounting Review*, *16*(2), 1–29.

Muttakin, M. B., Rana, T., & Mihret, D. G. (2022). Democracy, national culture and greenhouse gas emissions: An international study. *Business Strategy and the Environment*. https://doi.org/10.1002/bse.3059

Myers, R. H. (1990). *Classical and modern regression with applications*. PWS-Kent Publishing Company.

Nuskiya, M. N. F., Ekanayake, A., Beddewela, E., & Meftah Gerged, A. (2021). Determinants of corporate environmental disclosures in Sri Lanka: The role of corporate governance. *Journal of Accounting in Emerging Economies*, *11*(3), 367–394.

Prado-Lorenzo, J. M., & Garcia-Sanchez, I. M. (2010). The role of the board of directors in disseminating relevant information on greenhouse gases. *Journal of Business Ethics, 97*(3), 391–424.

Prado-Lorenzo, J. M., Rodríguez-Domínguez, L., Gallego-Álvarez, I., & García-Sánchez, I. M. (2009). Factors influencing the disclosure of greenhouse gas emissions in companies worldwide. *Management Decision, 47*(7), 1133–1157.

Rankin, M., Windsor, C., & Wahyum, D. (2011). An investigation of voluntary corporate greenhouse gas emissions reporting in a market governance system Australian evidence. *Accounting, Auditing & Accountability Journal, 24*(8), 1037–1070.

Rosa, F. S., Bartolacelli, A., & Lunkes, R. J. (2022). Post-regulation effects on driving factors (no) environmental disclosures about greenhouse gas emissions in Italian companies. *Journal of Financial Reporting & Accounting, 20*(3/4), 712–733.

Tabachnick, B. G., & Fidell, L. S. (2007). *Using multivariate statistics* (5th ed.). Pearson Education.

Tauringana, V., & Chithambo, L. (2014). The effect of DEFRA guidance on greenhouse gas disclosure. *The British Accounting Review, 47*(1), 425–444.

Tauringana, V., & Chithambo, L. (2015). The effect of DEFRA guidance on greenhouse gas disclosure. *The British Accounting Review, 47*(4), 425–444.

Tingbani, I., Chithambo, L., Tauringana, V., & Papanikolaou, N. (2020). Board gender diversity, environmental committee and greenhouse gas voluntary disclosures. *Business Strategy and the Environment, 29*(6), 2194–2210.

Tumwebaze, Z., Bananuka, J., Alinda, K., & Dorcus, K. (2021). Intellectual capital: Mediator of board of directors' effectiveness and adoption of International Financial Reporting Standards. *Journal of Financial Reporting & Accounting, 19*(2), 272–298.

Union of Concerned Scientists. (2022). Each country's share of CO2 emissions: The wealthy nations of the world are responsible for most carbon emissions. https://www.ucsusa.org/resources/each-countrys-share-co2-emissions. Accessed on April 14, 2022.

BOARD INTERLOCKS AND CARBON EMISSIONS PERFORMANCE: EMPIRICAL EVIDENCE FROM INDIA

Albert Ochien'g Abang'a and Chipo Simbi

ABSTRACT

Purpose: *Utilising the resource dependency theory, this study investigates the impact of board interlocks (CEOs' interlocks, women board interlocks, independent board interlocks and total board interlocks) on carbon emissions performance in India.*

Design/Methodology/Approach: *This research applies varieties of regression methods comprising robust least squares, generalised method of moments and Heckman's regression on a final sample of 63 of India's top 200 Bombay Stock Exchange (BSE) listed companies that voluntarily participate in the Carbon Disclosure Project's (CDP) Climate Change Program and disclose their climate change data for years 2013–2020.*

Findings: *We provide strong evidence for a strong negative association between CEOs' interlocks and women board interlocks on carbon emissions performance. Independent and total board interlocks are not found to significantly affect carbon emissions performance.*

Research Limitations: *Our sample is restricted to the proportion of the top 200 BSE firms that voluntarily submit their carbon emissions data to CDP. Also, the study's focus is India, limiting the generalisation of our findings to other emerging economies.*

Practical Implication: *The study's findings provide valuable insight for regulators and corporate board of directors on the important role of CEOs and women board who interlock with other firms in steering the carbon emissions reduction. Specifically, the corporate board of directors should encourage*

Green House Gas Emissions Reporting and Management in Global Top Emitting
Countries and Companies
Advances in Environmental Accounting & Management, Volume 11, 81–106
Copyright © 2023 Albert Ochien'g Abang'a and Chipo Simbi
Published under exclusive licence by Emerald Publishing Limited
ISSN: 1479-3598/doi:10.1108/S1479-359820230000011005

CEOs to build more networks through outside board memberships. The regulators should revisit the Companies Act, 2013 and the Securities Exchange Board of India (SEBI) regulation to increase the number of multiple directorships of CEOs and women board of directors.

Originality/Value: *This study responds to the dearth of literature on the efficacy of board interlocks on carbon emissions performance in emerging economies.*

Keywords: Board interlocks; Bombay Stock Exchange; carbon emissions performance; India; resource dependency theory; CDP (Carbon Disclosure Project)

INTRODUCTION

Greenhouse gas (GHG) emissions and climate change have become a global concern that endangers the earth's ecosystem. Since the formation of The United Nations Framework Convention on Climate Change (UNFCCC) in 1992, the focus has been on how to reduce GHG in the atmosphere to address the deterioration of natural resources and their impact on the environment. It is observed that carbon dioxide (CO_2) makes up the largest share of the GHG contributing to global warming and climate change (CDP India Annual Report, 2018; Nasih et al., 2019). The increased carbon emissions are attributed mainly to human activities, such as manufacturing, especially in the chemical, forestry, mining and oil/gas extraction (Lu et al., 2021b; Nasih et al., 2019), which have caused extreme weather events across the world.

India is one of the countries that has felt the adverse effect of climate change through floods, cyclone Amphan and COVID-19 (CDP India Annual Report, 2020). India ranks fifth in the Global Climate Risk Index 2020 (CDP India Annual Report, 2020) and fourth global emitter of CO_2 according to emission data for 2019 (Ritchie & Roser, 2020). GHG emissions reporting and reduction policy in India is under the purview of the Ministry of Environment, Forest and Climate Change (MoEF), together with the central and state pollution control board. Similar to other emerging economies, disclosure of GHG in India is not mandatory under the Kyoto Protocol, and the managers have the option to disclose or not disclose their emission data publicly (Desai et al., 2021). According to CDP India Annual Report (2020), India disclosed 704 million tons of scope 1 and scope 2 carbon emissions compared to 557 million tons in 2019, showing an increase of 26%. This is an improvement compared to the 86% increase reported from 2018 to 2019, which is in tandem with the country's targets of reducing the emissions intensity by 33%–35% by 2030 below 2005 levels. However, there is a generally upward trajectory of carbon emissions from 2012 to 2020. This rise is probably due to the increase in the number of companies volunteering to provide their carbon emissions data (Fig. 1).

The responsibility of overseeing climate-related issues is usually placed on companies' leadership who are at the top of the corporate ladder, such as chief

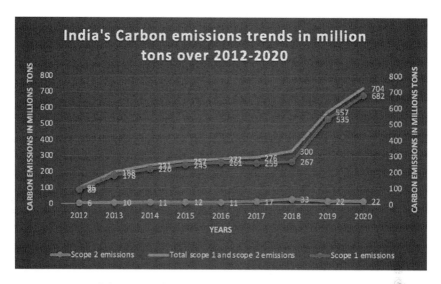

Fig. 1.   India's CO$_2$ Emissions (Metric Tons per Capita). *Source:* India's
CDP Annual Reports 2012–2020.

executive officers (CEOs) and the board of directors (CDP India Annual Report, 2020; Glass et al., 2016; Tauringana & Chithambo, 2015). However, to oversee their mandate on environmental sustainability, the board of directors and CEOs should network to gather and share knowledge on how best to respond to climate challenges. One way of networking and sharing knowledge is through board interlocks (Lu et al., 2021a; O'Hagan, 2017). A board interlock occurs when one director sits on the boards of two or more different firms (Lu et al., 2021a, 2021b; O'Hagan, 2017).

Despite the growing awareness of board interlocks for gathering and sharing knowledge on climate change mitigations (Cucari et al., 2018; Lu et al., 2021a, 2021b; Ortiz-de-Mandojana & Aragon-Correa, 2015), the role of board inter-locks in reducing carbon emissions has not been investigated widely, with the exception of Lu et al. (2021a, 2021b). Prior literature has emphasised on the relationship between board interlocks and financial performance (Hundal, 2017; Tjondro et al., 2021; Zona et al., 2018) or board interlocks and corporate social responsibility (CSR) reporting (Al-Dah, 2019; De Villiers et al., 2011; Ortiz-de-Mandojana & Aragon-Correa, 2015). But as pointed out by Shahin and Zairi (2007) and Bui et al. (2020), the success of the company is not only envisioned from its economic success but also through its environmental accountability. In addition, whereas CSR reporting incorporates environmental information (Cordeiro et al., 2020), such information is based on environmental disclosure practices. Some scholars argue that environmental disclosure is not the same as environmental performance (Clarkson et al., 2008; Haque & Ntim, 2020; Luo & Tang, 2021) since the former reflects what is being done in a firm relating to environmental risk management, strategy, target setting and other ways aimed at reducing emissions while the latter is about the outcome of the implemented strategy (the rate of absolute reduction of carbon emissions). Furthermore, the only available study focussing on board interlocks and carbon emissions performance is in the United States, where the Kyoto Protocol enforces carbon emissions limits (Lu et al., 2021a). Finally, extant literature that studies board interlocks either looks at the impact of total board interlocks (Lu et al., 2021a, 2021b; Sun et al., 2020) or independent board interlocks (Al-Dah, 2019), CEOs interlocks (Ratri et al., 2021) or women board interlocks (Glass et al., 2016) in separate studies. Hernández-Lara and Gonzales-Bustos (2019) argue that the role of interlocking directorate changes depending on the type of director, which suggests that a corporate board of directors comprises different categories of directors with different roles and who represent various stakeholders. Also, different governance frameworks have different guidelines on the proportion of each category of directors such as those relating to independent directors, board gender representations and the limits of board interlocks of some categories of boards which are likely to influence their responsibilities on environmental performance differently. Therefore, in addition to investigating the synergy brought about by the total board interlocks, there is a need also to examine various categories of board interlocks to ascertain how each performs in their networks.

Thus, based on the resource dependency theory, we investigate the impact of board interlocks (CEOs interlocks, independent board interlocks, women board interlocks and total board interlocks) on carbon emissions performance in India, an emerging economy.

Our research contributes to the literature in four main areas. First, unlike the majority of previous studies that focus on the relationship between board interlocks and financial performance (Hundal, 2017; Tjondro et al., 2021; Zona et al., 2018), we investigate the impact of board interlocks on carbon emissions performance. Excessive carbon emissions into the atmosphere have resulted in adverse climate change, which is the biggest crisis facing the planet. Therefore, there is an urgent need to look for ways to address its adversarial impact. This argument is also supported by Bui et al. (2020), which encourages firms to be accountable not only for financial performance but also for environmental performance. Secondly, our study focusses on environmental performance (Carbon emissions) as opposed to environmental disclosure. Clarkson et al. (2008), Haque and Ntim (2020), and Luo and Tang (2021) opine that environmental disclosure is different from environmental performance since the former reflects what is being done in a firm relating to carbon risk management, strategy, target setting and other ways aimed at reducing emissions while the latter is about the outcome of the implemented strategy. Thirdly, India, being an emerging country and fourth-largest emitter of carbon emissions, warrants a study that has predominantly been concentrated in developed economies like the United States (Lu et al., 2021a, 2021b; Matsumura et al., 2014; Ortiz-de-Mandojana & Aragon-Correa, 2015) and industrialised European Union countries (Haque & Ntim, 2020; Luo & Tang, 2021). India's regulatory environment does not prescribe the limits of carbon emissions and does not punish heavy carbon emitters, nor does it reward little carbon emissions (Desai et al., 2021) as contained in the Kyoto Protocol. Finally, on the basis that the role of interlocking directorate change depending on the type of board of directors (Hernández-Lara & Gonzales-Bustos, 2019), we offer a comprehensive set of measures of board interlocks encompassing CEOs, women board, board independent and total board interlocks in a single study as opposed to previous studies (Al-Dah, 2019; Glass et al., 2016; Lu et al., 2021a, 2021b; Ratri et al., 2021; Sun et al., 2020) that only focus on one type of board interlock in different studies.

The findings of this study indicate that CEOs and women board interlocks have an inverse relationship with carbon emissions performance, whereas the impact of an independent board and total board interlocks are inconclusive.

The remainder of this chapter is structured as follows: Multiple directorships Environment in India, Theoretical Framework and Hypotheses Development, Methodology, Empirical Results, Discussion, Summary and Conclusion.

MULTIPLE DIRECTORSHIPS ENVIRONMENT IN INDIA

Multiple directorships became a phenomenon in India soon after its independence in 1947. There were shortages of experienced and qualified individuals who could participate in corporate leadership. This necessitated firms to approach relatively experienced and successful boards to join their corporate boards. Thereafter, multiple directorships became a common practice in India, and as time passed by, it became apparent that some directors held directorships in more than 50 companies (Hundal, 2017; Sarkar & Sarkar, 2009), and the need for regulation was therefore necessary. The first attempt at such regulation was contained in Section 275 of the Companies Act of India (MCA, 1956), which specified the maximum number of directorships to 15. Currently, the regulation of multiple directorships in India is contained in the Securities and Exchange Board of India (SEBI), having been established in 1992, as well as the Companies Act, 2013. The Companies Act, 2013, section 165 specifies that a board of directors are not supposed to have directorship in more than 10 public limited companies or act as independent directors in more than seven listed companies or three listed companies if they serve as a whole-time director in any listed company as per the regulation 25 of SEBI Listing Obligations and Disclosure Requirements (LODR). This means that CEOs who in most cases are whole-time directors of the listed companies are not permitted to serve as independent directors in more than three listed company.

THEORETICAL FRAMEWORK AND HYPOTHESES

Resource Dependency Theory

We base this study's assumptions on the resource dependency theory to gain insight into the impact of board interlocks and carbon emissions performance. The theory posits that corporations depend on their external environment for survival (Pfeffer & Salancik, 1978). Board interlocks can be a critical path to invaluable resources and information for organisation success. The theory alludes that links to the external environment are crucial because firms are unable to internally generate all the required inputs for production. Thus, resource dependency is the best justification for board interlocks in today's global knowledge economy (O'Hagan, 2017).

The dangers posed by carbon emissions require extra capabilities and expertise beyond what is available within a single organisation. Accordingly, Pfeffer and Salancik (1978) suggest that firms can formulate various plans to acquire capabilities that are outside their reach. For instance, employing the resource dependency theory, a CEO who holds multiple directorships may be equipped with the experience and knowledge required for environmental performance gained from exposure to different external environments. In addition, women board members who are regarded as more sensitive than men when it comes to environmental performance (Cordeiro et al., 2020) can use their network to inculcate environmental conservation. Moreover, independent boards with multiple directorships are better positioned to put pressure on CEOs to guarantee environmental performance. Earlier studies such as Lu et al. (2021a, 2021b) have used the resource dependency theory to demonstrate that a greater number of board interlocks achieve better environmental performance. Other studies have also documented the role that board interlocks can play in helping the firm achieve environmental performance (Al-Dah, 2019; De Villiers et al., 2011). We discuss in the next section how board interlocks can influence carbon emissions performance.

Hypotheses Development

Chief Executive Officer Interlocks

A CEO is regarded as the primary driver of the organisation's strategy (Glass et al., 2016). Organisation strategy incorporates environmental conservation and preservation effort. Based on resource dependency theory, a CEO who serves on other boards is able to get experience and knowledge (Pfeffer & Salancik, 1978), which is essential for environmental performance. However, based on the busyness hypothesis, holding multiple directorships by CEOs reduces their effectiveness in managing firms' affairs (Ferris et al., 2003). This observation is in tandem with Saleh et al.'s (2020) findings that CEOs' multiple directorships are associated with company losses.

According to the Indian Companies Act, 2013, and regulation 25 of SEBI LODR, executives such as CEOs cannot hold outside directorships as independent directors on any listed company. This requirement could suggest that CEOs can hold other directorships in other companies as long as the outside directorships are not independent in nature. The National Association of Corporate Director's guideline recommends that senior corporate executives and CEOs hold no more than three outside directorships. Besides, the Council for Institutional Investors suggests that individuals with full-time jobs should not serve on more than two other boards.

On the basis of the busyness hypothesis that holding multiple directorships by CEOs reduces their effectiveness in managing firms' affairs, we propose the following hypothesis:

H1. A higher number of CEO interlocks are associated with higher carbon emissions.

Women Board Interlocks

Under-representation of women membership in corporate boards has elicited the interest of both academic scholars and policymakers (Joecks et al., 2013). The proposition of resource dependency theory justifies the need for more women in corporate board membership. SEBI mandated all listed companies in India to have at least one woman director on their boards by 1 October 2014. Similarly, the Kotak Committee on corporate governance and SEBI recommended that there should be at least one independent woman director in the top 500 listed entities by market capitalisation by 2019. Given that Indian public Ltd companies are male-dominated, the role of women in corporate board membership is likely to face challenges, especially when it comes to interlocking because under-representation means that only a handful of women boards would be available for other directorships. This argument is echoed by Zenou et al. (2012) when they averred that the chances of appointing a woman to another board are higher when she already has a similar appointment elsewhere.

There is a dearth of empirical evidence on the impact of women interlocks and carbon emissions. That notwithstanding, the arguments advanced are similar to those underpinning women board and women board interlocks and CSR and GHG disclosure studies. Drawing from available literature, there are two main contrasting arguments. On the one hand, women are regarded as more sensitive than men regarding environmental performance (Cordeiro et al., 2020). They are also portrayed as better at developing business contacts networks than men (Zenou et al., 2012). It is also argued that women on the board increase the likelihood of board understanding ethical and social demands regarding GHG emission disclosure (Hollindale et al., 2019). According to Liao et al. (2015) and Tingbani et al. (2020), in studies undertaken in the United Kingdom, a board with more women tends to disclose more GHG information. Macchioni et al. (2022), in a study involving European countries, establish that women's membership in the corporate board is associated with reduced carbon emission. Similarly, Glass et al. (2016) observe better environmental strength when women board interlock.

On the other hand, board membership with women has been faulted on some grounds with respect to environmental performance. Nielsen and Huse (2010) assert that women boards are risk-averse and are more conservative in decision-making. Nonetheless, Hernández-Lara and Gonzales-Bustos (2019) observe that such weakness can be diminished when women board interlock. When they do, they get empowered and gain more experience and knowledge than other women directors who do not hold multiple directorships. Therefore, we state our second hypothesis as follows:

H2. A higher number of women board interlocks are associated with lower carbon emissions.

Independent Board Interlocks

Board independence refers to the power balance on the board (Liao et al., 2015). To ensure a proper balance of power, it is argued that independent boards should be of a higher percentage of the total number of board members. The Indian Listing Regulation 17 (1) (b) of 2015 requires that the board of directors of listed companies should comprise at least 50% non-executive independent directors.[1] While there is no specific limit on the number of outside directorships that can be held by independent directors, the general rule for all directors of listed companies in India is that the board of directors is not supposed to have directorship in more than 10 public limited companies or act as independent directors in more than seven listed companies. However, the maximum threshold recommended by the Act does not prohibit directorships in unlisted and foreign entities. Lei and Deng (2014) argue that in emerging markets where qualified independent directors are not enough, those with greater reputation, knowledge or experience might obtain more directorships, confirming Lamb and Roundy's (2016) line of reasoning that interlocked independent directors are appointed to the board due to their large social network and wide access to resources.

Lei and Deng (2014) found a significant positive relationship between interlocked independent directors and the firm value in Hong Kong. Similarly, Sarkar and Sarkar (2009) found that interlocked independent directors correlate positively with firm value. In contrast, the independent board with many outside directorships has also been shown not to perform its role effectively (Jackling & Johl, 2009; Mallin & Michelon, 2011). Various reasons why this is likely to be the case are documented. First is the issue of monitoring, where it is argued that as the busyness of the outside independent directors increases, so is the decrease in the monitoring of the management (Jackling & Johl, 2009). Second is the conflict of interest that is likely to prop up, especially if they are serving on the boards of competitor firms. From resource dependency theory, a higher number of outside boards coupled with multiple memberships should be in a position to put pressure on CEOs to guarantee environmental performance. Thus, the proposed hypothesis is:

H3. A higher number of independent board interlocks are associated with lower carbon emissions.

Total Board Interlocks

It has become a common practice for the board of directors to sit on the board of other firms to build networks and links (Finkelstein & Mooney, 2003), which may benefit the firm in realising its performance objective consistent with the proposition of resource dependency theory. Accordingly, Hundal (2017) corroborates this assertion by pointing out that appointing a board of directors who also serve on other corporate boards adds to its resources in the form of education, experience, expertise and skills, and external ties with other firms. On the downside, though, is the argument that interlocking directorates reduce the independence and commitments of the directors from their core responsibilities, such as the inability to attend or plan adequately for meetings (Chiranga & Chiwira, 2014; Finkelstein & Mooney, 2003; Saleh et al., 2020). In other studies, Jiraporn et al. (2009) found conflicting results. On the one hand, they find support for the busyness hypothesis in that, at lower levels of multiple board seats, directors holding more outside directorships tend to serve on fewer board committees. On the other hand, at higher levels of multiple board seats, the reputation hypothesis is supported because findings suggested that more outside directorships are associated with serving a higher number of committees. Lu et al. (2021a, 2021b) found that a firm with a higher number of total board interlocks achieves better environmental performance.

The central question that unravels scholars is how many directorships a person can undertake and still perform to the expected level (Kiel & Nicholson, 2006). There is a claim that policies that try to limit the number of directorships ignore the rich tradition of empirical literature supporting directors' resource dependence role. Looking at the Indian context, the Companies Act, 2013, section 165 specifies that the board of directors is not supposed to have directorship in more than 10 public limited companies. The merit of this requirement is debatable because the legislation does not include private firms, unlimited companies and non-profit organisations except subsidiaries or holding companies of a publicly traded firm. This means that the directors get leeway to exceed the required limit of directorships. Currently, there are varied board directorships within public limited companies and other associations not covered under regulations. However, as explained earlier, the overall directorships in most cases exceed the required limit when private firms, unlimited companies and non-profit organisations are considered. Therefore, it is an open debate as to whether such an opaque requirement is of merit as a concern for the performance of an enterprise.

The following hypothesis is proposed in light of the abundant supporting empirical evidence:

H4. A higher number of total board interlocks are associated with lower carbon emissions.

METHODOLOGY

Data and Sample Selection

Our study uses the top 200 Bombay Stock Exchange (BSE) listed companies that voluntarily participate in the Carbon Disclosure Project[2] (CDP) Climate Change Program and disclose their climate change data. However, given that the participation is voluntary, not all the top 200 BSE companies submit their annual emissions data. The top 200 BSE are the largest firms by capitalisation and are exposed to significant pressures from society and stakeholders on carbon emissions. We use the CDP Project, which provides the largest and most comprehensive database of voluntary reporting of carbon-related performance and activities (Barka & Dardour, 2015) and is also reliable (Wang et al., 2014). Data are collected from 2013 to 2020 because the Indian Company Act became operational in 2013, and the end of the period is 2020. This was the latest report available on CDP annual reporting relating to India at the time of this study. Secondly, data for 2020 are considered ideal since CDP reported after 2 March 2020[3] had a sharp drop of emissions (CDP India Annual Report, 2020) as a result of lockdown and slow business operations due to COVID-19. Data on carbon emissions performance are extracted from CDP databases while data on board directorships and firm-level control variables are obtained from annual reports, corporate governance reports and integrated reports from the individual company websites. Our final sample after excluding firms with missing data is 289 firm-year observations (see Table 1). Sample distribution by industry is outlined in Table 2.

Measurement of Variables

The present study analyses the impact of board interlocks on the carbon emissions performance of Indian companies. Variable definitions of dependent, independent and control variables and supporting literature are given in Table 3.

Model Specification

To test our hypotheses (*H1–H4*), with an unbalanced panel of 289 observations (23, 29, 32, 35, 38, 38, 43 and 51 observations in 2013, 2014, 2015, 2016, 2017, 2018, 2019 and 2020, respectively) from 63 firms, we first examine linear regression assumptions of multicollinearity, autocorrelation, normality, homoscedasticity and linearity consistent with prior literature (Abang'a et al., 2021; Ntim et al., 2012). The results suggest that the tested regression assumptions of linearity (Appendix 1), normality (Appendix 2) and multicollinearity (Table 4, Panel A) were met except for homoscedasticity (Appendix 3) and autocorrelation (Appendix 4). We, therefore, used robust linear squares regression with Huber–White robust standard errors to control for serial autocorrelation and heteroscedasticity (Macchioni et al., 2022; Matsumura et al., 2014). The empirical model estimated using EVIEWS, version 12, is specified below.

Table 1. Sample Selection Procedure.

	Observations
Top 200 BSE firms that provided CDP data between 2013 and 2020	326
Less	
Observations with no scope 1 emissions	(1)
Observations with no scope 2 emissions	(2)
Observations missing board directorships and control variables	(34)
Final sample	289

Table 2. Sample Distribution by Industry Based on CDP India Annual Report (2020) Classification.

Industry	2013	2014	2015	2016	2017	2018	2019	2020	Total
Bars, hotels and restaurants	0	0	1	1	1	1	1	1	6
Biotech and pharma Cement	1	1	1	1	2	1	2	2	11
Cement and concrete	4	4	4	5	5	4	4	5	35
Chemicals	2	2	4	5	4	3	4	4	28
Energy utility networks	1	1	1	1	1	3	1	2	11
Financial services	3	4	5	5	5	5	6	6	39
Agricultural commodities	1	1	1	1	0	1	2	2	9
Intermodal transport and logistics	0	0	0	0	0	0	1	1	2
IT and software development	3	5	5	5	5	6	6	5	40
Land and property ownership and development	0	0	0	0	1	1	1	2	5
Leisure and home manufacturing	0	0	0	0	0	0	1	0	1
Light manufacturing	0	0	0	0	0	0	0	1	1
Media, telecommunication and data centre services	1	0	0	1	2	2	2	1	9
Metal smelting, refining and forming	3	5	3	4	3	3	3	4	28
Metallic mineral mining	0	0	1	0	0	0	0	1	2
Oil and gas processing	1	1	0	1	1	1	2	2	9
Renewable power generation	0	0	0	0	0	0	0	1	1
Specialised professional services	1	2	2	1	2	2	2	3	15
Textiles and fabric goods	0	0	0	0	1	1	1	1	4
Thermal power generation	1	1	1	1	2	2	2	4	14
Tobacco	1	1	1	1	1	0	0	1	6
Transportation equipment	0	1	2	2	2	2	2	2	13
Total	23	29	32	35	38	38	43	51	289

$$Y = \beta_0 + \beta_1 CEIL + \beta_2 WEIL + \beta_3 IBIL + \beta_4 TBIL + \beta_5 LEV + \beta_6 IND \\ + \beta_7 FMSIZE + \beta_8 ROA + \beta_9 BSIZE + \varepsilon_i \tag{1}$$

Control Variables

Following previous studies on board interlocks (Lu et al., 2021a, 2021b), GHG emissions (Macchioni et al., 2022; Tingbani et al., 2020) and environmental performance (Braam et al., 2016; Ortiz-de-Mandojana & Aragon-Correa, 2015), several control variables are included that could affect the relationships proposed. Leverage is considered a control variable because the ability of companies to engage in carbon emissions reduction strategies is influenced by the level of indebtedness such that if they are highly indebted, funds become unavailable for carbon emissions strategies (Sun et al., 2020). We, therefore, expect a positive coefficient between leverage and carbon emissions. In addition, we include an

Table 3. Operationalisation of the Variables.

Variables	Short Name	Measurement	Supporting Literature
Dependent variable			
Carbon emissions performance	CEP	Natural logarithm of the total scope 1 and scope 2 CO_2 emissions[a]	Matsumura et al. (2014), Wang et al. (2014), Braam et al. (2016), Haque and Ntim (2020), Macchioni et al. (2022)
Independent variables			
CEO interlocks	CEIL	Number of outside directorships held by a CEO	Booth and Deli (1996), Saleh et al. (2020)
Women interlocks	WEIL	The proportion of female directors who interlock the total board members of the company	O'Hagan (2017), Hernández-Lara and Gonzales-Bustos (2019), Tjondro et al. (2021)
Independent board of 'directors' interlocks	IBIL	The proportion between the number of independent directors who interlock the total board members of the company.	Saleh et al. (2020), Tjondro et al. (2021)
Total directorships interlocks	TBIL	The sum of all directorships held by directors who served at the end of the trading period.	Kiel and Nicholson (2006), Ming and Lee (2014)
Control variable			
Leverage	LEV	Represents the outside liabilities as proportion of total assets of the firm	Wang et al. (2014), Desai et al. (2021), Macchioni et al. (2022)
Industry	IND	Dummy variable indicating 1 if the company belongs to carbon-intensive sector such as energy, chemicals, metals, utilities, machineries, mining, cement and transportation, otherwise 0	Wang et al. (2014), Tingbani et al. (2020)
Firm size	FMSIZE	Total assets expressed as natural log	Liao et al. (2015), Tingbani et al. (2020), Macchioni et al. (2022)
Return on assets	ROA	EBIT divided by total assets of firm i in year t.	Desai et al. (2021)
Board size	BSIZE	The number of members on the board of an individual firm	Tauringana and Chithambo (2015), Lu et al. (2021a)

[a]Scope 1 refers to direct emissions related to the combustion of fossil fuels or the processes of chemicals and materials from sources that are owned or controlled by the company. Scope 2 refers to indirect emissions from the generation of the purchased electricity consumed by the company.

industry dummy because different companies in different industries have different carbon emissions intensity (Wang et al., 2014). We expect a positive coefficient on this variable. Moreover, we consider firm size a control variable because larger firms with lots of resources also have higher carbon emissions (Matsumura et al., 2014). We, therefore, expect a positive coefficient on the variable. Furthermore, return on assets has been considered among the control variables because profitable firms can accommodate high environmental compliance costs (De Villiers et al., 2011). We, therefore, expect a negative coefficient on the variable. Finally,

Table 4. Descriptive Statistics – Aggregate (2013–2020).

Variables	Obs.	Mean	Median	Maximum	Minimum	Std. Dev.
CEP (ln)	289	13.4345	12.9771	20.7507	7.5480	2.6865
CEIL	289	2.6332	1.0000	14.0000	0.0000	2.9716
WEIL	289	0.1103	0.1000	0.4167	0.0000	0.0897
IBIL	289	0.4365	0.4615	0.8889	0.0000	0.1649
TBIL	289	40.7924	40.0000	91.0000	0.0000	19.1757
LEV	289	0.5766	0.5539	5.4022	0.0360	0.3854
IND	289	0.6920	1.0000	1.0000	0.0000	0.4625
FMSIZE(ln)	289	10.8197	10.8817	15.2500	7.4104	1.4160
ROA	289	0.0950	0.0570	1.8017	−0.2708	0.1423
BSIZE	289	10.9792	11.0000	21.0000	5.0000	2.6193
PARIS	289	0.8270	1.0000	1.0000	0.0000	0.3789

Note: This table provides the sample characteristics of 289 firm-year across 63 top 200 BSE listed firms over the period 2013–2020.

we include board size as control variable because larger boards are likely to have experts on environmental performance (De Villiers et al., 2011). We, therefore, expect a negative coefficient on the variable.

EMPIRICAL RESULTS

Descriptive Statistics

Table 4 presents the mean, median, maximum, minimum and standard deviation for all the independent and dependent variables. Carbon emission values range from 7.5480 to 20.7507, with a mean value of 13.4345 and a standard deviation of 2.6865. Table 5 shows that the mean of CEOs with outside directorships is 3. In addition, the proportion of women board of directors with outside directorships is about 11%. Regarding the proportion of independent directors with outside directorships, Table 5 shows a mean value of 44%, and the minimum and maximum values range between 0 and 89%. Total board interlock has a mean value of 40.7924 and ranges between 0 (minimum) and 91 (maximum).

Among the control variables, the firm's leverage varies between 0.0360 and 5.4022, with a mean of 0.5766 and a standard deviation of 0.3854. The mean being below 1 reflects that the firms in our dataset are not highly levered. The size of the firm, measured by the natural logarithm of its total assets, varies between 7.4104 and 15.2500, with a mean of 10.8197 and a standard deviation of 1.4160. Return on assets has a mean and standard deviation of 0.0950 and 0.1423, respectively. Finally, Table 6 also shows that the average board size is approximately 11. Hundal (2017) also found that the average board size of non-financial firms listed in BSE, India, was approximately 11, the same as our finding.

Table 5. Spearman Correlation Coefficients Matrix.

Variable	1	2	3	4	5	6	7	8	9	10	11
1. CEP	1										
2. CEIL	−0.0493	1									
	0.4040										
3. WEIL	−0.2368***	0.0620	1								
	0.0000	0.2935									
4. IBIL	−0.1927***	0.2619***	0.4080***	1							
	0.0010	0.0000	0.0000								
5. TBIL	0.0839	0.3652***	0.0845	0.3849***	1						
	0.1548	0.0000	0.1519	0.0000							
6. LEV	−0.1042*	0.1711***	0.0399	0.0585	0.0057	1					
	0.0769	0.0035	0.4991	0.3220	0.9226						
7. IND	0.5685***	0.2732***	−0.0298	0.0071	0.2672***	−0.2189***	1				
	0.0000	0.0000	0.6145	0.9043	0.0000	0.0002					
8. FMSIZE	0.1155**	−0.0666	−0.2301***	−0.1398**	−0.1792***	0.4591***	−0.3128***	1			
	0.0499	0.2592	0.0001	0.0174	0.0022	0.0000	0.0000				
9. ROA	0.0341	−0.1615***	−0.1011*	−0.0795	0.0505	−0.7161***	0.0906	−0.3695***	1		
	0.5637	0.0059	0.0861	0.1775	0.3921	0.0000	0.1245	0.0000			
10. BSIZE	0.2138***	−0.1065*	−0.3795***	−0.2294***	0.2874***	−0.0826	0.1346**	0.1382**	0.1631***	1	
	0.0003	0.0707	0.0000	0.0001	0.0000	0.1616	0.0221	0.0187	0.0054		
11. PARIS	−0.0587	0.0460	0.2383***	0.0728	−0.0844	0.0118	0.0317	0.0135	−0.0955	−0.1138*	1
	0.3199	0.4361	0.0000	0.2175	0.1524	0.8411	0.5909	0.8194	0.1052	0.0533	

Notes: * Significant at the 10% level (2-tailed), ** significant at the 5% level (2-tailed), *** significant at the 1% level (2-tailed).

Table 6. Panel A: Robust Linear Squares.

Variable	Coefficient	Std. Error	z-stats	p Value	VIF
Constant	6.0837	1.2877	4.7244	0.0000	N/A
Independent					
CEIL	−0.2605	0.0475	−5.4807	0.0000***	1.3540
WEIL	−4.6765	1.5311	−3.0544	0.0023***	1.2802
IBIL	−0.3586	0.9018	−0.3976	0.6909	1.5004
TBIL	0.0083	0.0081	1.0258	0.3050	1.6418
Control					
LEV	−1.4360	0.3328	−4.3135	0.0000****	1.1167
IND	3.9874	0.2971	13.4206	0.0000****	1.2812
FMSIZE	0.6465	0.1047	6.1720	0.0000****	1.4927
ROA	−0.1915	0.9115	−0.2101	0.8336	1.1421
BSIZE	−0.0513	0.0580	−0.8847	0.3763	1.5677
R-squared	44%				
Adjusted *R*-squared	43%				
Significance	0.0000***				
Observations	289				

Note: *** significant at the 1% level (2-tailed).

Table 6. Panel B: Generalised Methods of Moments.

Variable	Coefficient	Std. Error	t-Stats	p Value	VIF
Constant	4.5795	3.4908	1.3119	0.1909	N/A
Independent variables					
CEIL	−0.3852	0.0947	−4.0680	0.0001***	1.3540
WEIL	−5.9628	2.8194	−2.1149	0.0356**	1.2802
IBIL	2.0170	1.7685	1.1405	0.2553	1.5004
TBIL	−0.0028	0.0126	−0.2245	0.8226	1.6418
Control variables					
LEV	0.9214	2.9668	0.3106	0.7564	1.1167
IND	5.0743	0.5293	9.5875	0.0000****	1.2812
FMSIZE	0.5670	0.1543	3.6738	0.0003****	1.4927
ROA	4.6976	9.3796	0.5008	0.6170	1.1421
BSIZE	−0.0705	0.1111	−0.8847	0.3763	1.5677
Wald (Joint)	121.811***				
J-statistics	37.755				
AR (1) statistics (p value)	4.260 (0.0000)				
AR (2) statistics (p value)	0.365 (0.8562)				
R-squared	46%				
Adjusted *R*-squared	43%				
Significance	0.0000***				
Observations	289				

Notes: ** significant at the 5% level (2-tailed), *** significant at the 1% level (2-tailed).

Table 6. Panel C: Heckman's Selection Regression.

Variable	Coefficient	Std. Error	*t*-Stats	*p* Value	VIF
Constant	5.4539	1.5443	3.5317	0.0005	N/A
Independent					
CEIL	−0.2320	0.0485	−4.7810	0.0000***	1.3540
WEIL	−2.9100	1.3300	−2.1879	0.0295**	1.2802
IBIL	−0.8961	0.8288	1.0812	0.2806	1.5004
TBIL	0.0065	0.0081	0.8083	0.4197	1.6418
Control					
LEV	0.4102	0.4009	1.0233	0.3071	1.1167
IND	4.5862	0.3656	11.1005	0.0000****	1.2812
FMSIZE	0.6083	0.1295	4.6966	0.0000****	1.4927
ROA	0.2376	1.5338	0.1549	0.8770	1.1421
BSIZE	−0.1292	0.0689	−1.8743	0.0620	1.5677
Observations	289				

Notes: ** significant at the 5% level (2-tailed), *** significant at the 1% level (2-tailed).

Correlation Matrix and Multicollinearity

One of the pre-conditions for regression analysis is the assessment of the correlation coefficient, which indicates the strength of the linear relationships among the variables under study. Table 5 summarises the Spearman's rank-order correlation of the variables under study. Women and independent board interlocks have a strong and negative relationship with carbon emissions performance at a 1% level. Additionally, firm size is positively correlated to carbon emissions performance at the 5% level. Further, the industry has reported a strong and positive relationship with carbon emissions performance at 1%. In contrast, leverage has reported a weak inverse relation with carbon emissions performance at the 10% level. Finally, board size demonstrates a positive and significant association with carbon emission at the 1% level.

The correlation matrix in Table 5 indicates low or moderate correlations among the variables. Multicollinearity is a problem if the absolute value of the simple correlation coefficient exceeds 0.8 (Manes-Rossi et al., 2020). Our results show a correlation coefficient below 0.8 since the highest is −0.71 between the return on assets and leverage. Multicollinearity is thus not a problem. In addition, we examined the variance inflation factors (VIFs). Since the highest VIF value is 1.6418 (Table 6, panel A), and the threshold considered a problem is 2, we conclude that there is no multicollinearity problem.

Main Results

Table 6, panel A shows robust linear squares regression results of board interlocks and other specific control variables on carbon emissions performance (CEP). The R^2 adjusted is 44%. It is revealed that CEOs and women board interlocks have statistically significant negative association with CEP ($\beta = -4.6765$, $\rho = 0.0023$; $\beta = -0.2605$, $\rho = 0.0000$). The results suggest that *H1* is rejected while *H2* is confirmed. The results also indicate that independent board and total board interlocks have insignificant association with CEP ($\beta = -0.3586$, $\rho = 0.6909$; $\beta = 0.0083$, $\rho = 0.3050$). This implies that *H3* and *H4* are rejected. Among the control variables, leverage shows inverse relationships ($\beta = -1.4360$, $\rho = 0.00000$), whereas industry and firm size show positive association with CEP ($\beta = 3.9874$, $\rho = 0.0000$; $\beta = 0.6465$, $\rho = 0.0000$). On the contrast, return on assets and board size are insignificantly related to CEP ($\beta = -0.1915$, $\rho = 0.8336$; $\beta = -0.0513$, $\rho = 0.3763$).

To ensure that our results are not driven by a possible endogeneity, and consistent with earlier studies such as Haque and Ntim (2020) and Desai et al. (2021), we re-estimate the same set of variables using generalised method of moments (GMM), with first lags of all independent variables used as instruments. To confirm the efficacy of GMM, three diagnostic tests are performed: Wald test, second-order autocorrelation test and Sargan test (J-statistics) for the validity of the instruments. The R^2 adjusted is 46%. The results in Table 6, panel B, consistently show that the impact of CEOs and women board interlocks is negative and statistically significant ($\beta = -0.3852$, $\rho = 0.0001$; $\beta = -5.9628$, $\rho = 0.0356$) whereas independent board and total board interlocks have insignificant association with CEP ($\beta = 2.017$, $\rho = 0.2553$; $\beta = -0.0028$, $\rho = 0.8226$). Among the control variables, industry and firm size maintain their positive association with CEP ($\beta = 5.0744$ $\rho = 0.0000$; $\beta = 0.5670$, $\rho = 0.0003$), whereas leverage changes the sign and significance of the relationship ($\beta = 0.9214$, $\rho = 0.764$) while return on assets and board size remain insignificantly related ($\beta = 4.6976$, $\rho = 0.6170$; $\beta = -0.0706$, $\rho = 0.5263$). Thus, generally, the results reinforce the main findings presented in Table 6, panel A.

Finally, a concern may be raised that our sample is not random due to the voluntary nature of carbon emissions reporting. To address this concern, we estimate the Heckman's model. Heckman's regression model allows one to control for self-selection bias and represents inferences for the whole sample instead of disclosing firms only (Heckman, 1979). This procedure is also consistent with similar studies in the past (Desai et al., 2021; Lu et al., 2021a, 2021b; Luo & Tang, 2021). We employ the Full Information Maximum Likelihood (FIML) approach. That is, we estimate the board interlocks model Eq. (1), jointly with Eq. (2), depicting the Paris Climate Agreement as an indicator that is coded as one if the company provides carbon emissions data after the year 2015 when India ratified the Paris Climate Agreement, and zero values for disclosures made before the year 2015. The selection model is as follows:

$$Y = \beta_0 + \beta_1\text{LEV} + \beta_2\text{IND} + \beta_3\text{FMSIZE} + \beta_4\text{ROA} + \beta_5\text{BSIZE} + \varepsilon_i \quad (2)$$

Where,

Y = Dummy variable that is equal to 1 if the carbon emission disclosure is made in 2015–2020 and 0 for disclosure made between 2013 and 2014, LEV = Leverage, FMSIZE = Firm size, ROA = Return on assets, BSIZE = Board size, ε_t = Residual error.

Consistently, the results presented in Table 6, panel C, convey similar results as those reported earlier in the main findings. CEOs and women interlocks are found to have significant negative relationship with CEP ($\beta = -0.2320$, $\rho = 0.0000$; $\beta = -2.9100$, $\rho = 0.0295$). Similarly, independent board and total board interlocks show insignificant association with CEP ($\beta = -0.8961$, $\rho = 0.2806$; $\beta = 0.0065$, $\rho = 0.4197$). With regard to control variables, industry and firm size are positively and significantly related to CEP ($\beta = 4.0586$, $\rho = 0.0000$; $\beta = 0.6083$, $\rho = 0.0000$), while leverage is positively but insignificantly related to CEP ($\beta = 0.4102$, $\rho = 0.3071$). On the contrast, return on assets is positively but insignificantly related to CEP ($\beta = -0.2376$, $\rho = 0.8770$) yet board size is negatively and significantly related to CEP ($\beta = -0.1292$, $\rho = 0.0620$).

Sensitivity Tests

Consistent with Elsayih et al. (2021), we further examine the sensitivity of our main findings to an alternative measure of CEP by decomposing the dependent variable into scope 1 and scope 2 carbon emissions to establish if the impact of CEOs and women board interlocks is different on each of these compared to overall CEP. To do this, we employ the three regression methods discussed earlier to test the variables under focus. Table 7 presents the findings of board interlocks and the control variables using both scope 1 and scope 2 carbon emissions as dependent variables. The results do not differ materially from those already reported in the main findings. CEOs and women board interlocks largely maintained their original model status except for the impact of women board interlocks on scope 1 emissions under GMM and Heckman's regression analyses, where the significance level changed, but the direction of the relationship remains unchanged. Another slight difference in findings is the impact of an independent board and total board interlocks. Previous results revealed insignificant relationships under the different regression models, which now show a mixture of findings under different regression models and different measures of CEP. A similar trend is observed among the control variables, where industry and firm size results largely remain consistent with the main findings, and some notable differences were observed for leverage, return on assets and board size.

DISCUSSION

Our study analysed the impact of board interlocks on carbon emissions performance. The regression results confirmed that CEOs and women board interlocks are important for carbon emissions performance. The results were drawn from a sample of 63 firms (289 observations) from the top 200 BSE listed companies that voluntarily participated in CDP from 2013 to 2020.

Our results demonstrate that CEOs' interlocks (CEIL) are significantly and negatively related to carbon emissions performance. The findings are consistent with the resource dependency theory proposition (Pfeffer & Salancik, 1978). A

Table 7. Alternative Measure of Carbon Emissions Performance.

Variable	ROBULS		GMM		HECKMAN'S	
	Scope 1	Scope 2	Scope 1	Scope 2	Scope 1	Scope 2
Constant	4.6719****	6.3329****	3.1826	5.2704	4.5861**	5.1130****
	(2.6604)	(7.2996)	(1.0301)	(2.7757)	(2.3681)	(4.3462)
Independent						
CEIL	−0.3767****	−0.1624****	−0.5159****	−0.3372****	−0.2903****	−1.9274****
	(−5.8112)	(−5.0709)	(−3.8793)	(−4.1256)	(−4.6843)	(−4.6347)
WEIL	−5.1483**	−3.6668****	−5.9559	−5.8364**	−0.2580	−3.0033**
	(−2.4658)	(−3.5548)	(−1.6120)	(−2.5703)	(−0.1607)	(−2.2777)
IBIL	−0.9890	1.0620*	1.2073	4.0733	−2.2703* (−	1.5774*
	(−0.8042)	(1.7479)	(0.4716)	(2.5890)	1.9849)	(1.9478)
TBIL	0.0221*	0.0172	0.0165	0.0142**	0.0148	0.0151**
	(1.9953)	(3.1423)	(0.9112)	(1.2717)	(1.4934)	(2.0425)
Control						
LEV	−2.3396****	−1.3807****	1.7735	−1.6618	0.2859	−0.0066
	(−5.1544)	(−6.1573)	(0.7249)	(−0.5372)	(0.5609)	(−0.0240)
IND	6.3168****	1.4160****	7.4324****	2.1732****	5.9679****	1.6783****
	(15.5902)	(7.0735)	(12.3120)	(5.8577)	(12.7994)	(6.0280)
FMSIZE	0.5727****	0.5204****	0.3649	0.6029****	0.4102*	0.4853****
	(4.0097)	(7.3753)	(1.0934)	(2.9395)	(2.5176)	(5.1490)
ROA	−0.4067	0.6170	6.8599	1.0785	1.3208	3.4996****
	(−0.3272)	(1.0048)	(0.5172)	(0.1323)	(0.6739)	(2.7616)
BSIZE	−0.0517	−0.0734*	−0.0910	−0.1337	0.0504	−0.0588
	(−0.6537)	(−1.8779)	(−0.6180)	(−1.4781)	(0.5812)	(−0.9477)
Control for industry effect	Yes	Yes	Yes	Yes	Yes	Yes
R-squared	49%	25%	–	–	50%	7%
Adjusted *R*-squared	47%	23%	–	–	48%	3%
Significance	0.0000	0.0000	–	–	0.0000	0.0000
Observations	289	289	289	289	289	289

Notes: This table reports ROBULS, GMM and Heckman's regression results for independent and control variables on scopes 1 and 2 emissions. *, ** and *** indicate significance at the 10%, 5% and 1% levels, respectively (2-tailed). *z*/*t*-statistics are in parentheses. Detailed variable definitions and supporting literature are provided in Table 3.

CEO who serves on other boards can get the experience and knowledge required to manage the firm's affairs. The result disapproves of the busyness hypothesis that CEOs who serve on other boards are detrimental to the success of firms' activities and associated with losses in the companies (Ferris et al., 2003; Saleh et al., 2020). This means that firms achieve carbon emission reduction as the number of CEOs with outside directorships increases.

In respect to women board interlocks (WEIL), our results of a strong and negative relationship with carbon emissions performance provide supportive

evidence of resource dependency theory and for the enforcement of the requirement of appointment of at least one woman on board as per the recommendation
of SEBI that mandated all listed companies in India to have at least one woman
director on their boards by 1 October 2014. Similarly, the finding supports the
Kotak Committee on corporate governance and SEBI recommendation that
there should be at least one independent woman director in the top 500 listed
entities by market capitalisation by 2019. The increased membership of women
board of directors enhances the chances of women board interlocks. Zenou et al.
(2012) argued that the chances of appointing a woman to a board are higher
when she already has a similar appointment elsewhere. The result confirms
arguments made by prior scholars on the role of women on board, such as the
claim that women are more sensitive than men when it comes to environmental
performance (Cordeiro et al., 2020), they are good at developing business contacts networks between them than men (Zenou et al., 2012) and the argument
that women on board increase the likelihood of board to understand ethical and
social demand regarding GHG emissions disclosure (Hollindale et al., 2019).

Results of independent board interlocks (IBIL) show an insignificant negative
association with carbon emissions performance. The insignificant effect of independent board interlock confirms the assertion made by Jackling and Johl (2009)
and Mallin and Michelon (2011) that as the busyness of the outside independent
directors increases as a result of multiple directorships, so is the decrease in the
monitoring of the management. The insignificant effect may also be explained by
the conflict of interest of independent directors who serve on the boards of
competitor firms. Thus, the argument of resource dependency theory on the
impact of independent board interlocks on carbon emissions performance is not
confirmed.

Similarly, the impact of total board interlocks (TBIL) on carbon emissions
performance is positive and insignificant. The finding is consistent with the
argument that interlocking directorates reduce the independence and commitments of the directors from their core responsibilities, such as the inability to
attend or plan adequately for meetings to discuss environmental issues (Chiranga
& Chiwira, 2014; Finkelstein & Mooney, 2003; Saleh et al., 2020). The finding
contradicts Lu et al. (2021a, 2021b), who found a favourable impact between
total board interlocks and environmental performance. Therefore, the resource
dependency theory proposition on the impact of total board interlocks on carbon
emissions is not supported.

Among the control variables, leverage has a significant and negative impact on
carbon emissions performance from the main result, which is inconsistent with
our prediction. In the additional analyses, leverage turns out to be positive but
insignificant under different regression methods. When alternative carbon performance measures were introduced, a similar result was observed under robust
linear squares regression for scope 1 and scope 2. However, the insignificant
positive and negative association is observed under GMM and Heckman's
regression methods. Overall, the result suggests that investors are willing to
supply funds as long as it is used in carbon reduction initiatives. The industry has
a positive and significant impact on carbon emissions performance which is

consistent across different regression methods and alternative carbon emission performance. The result is also consistent with our prediction (Wang et al., 2014). This means that companies from carbon-intensive industries are heavy emitters of carbon emissions. The main analysis observed a positive and significant impact between firm size and carbon emissions performance. The result is largely exhibited across all the regression methods as well as on alternative carbon emissions performance measures. The result confirms that large firms have higher carbon emissions due to their activities (Matsumura et al., 2014). The result is consistent with our prediction. In contrast, results show that the influence of return on assets and board size on carbon emissions is insignificant and remains insignificant across all the additional analyses.

SUMMARY AND CONCLUSIONS

This study investigates through the lenses of resource dependency theory whether board interlocks (CEO interlocks, women board interlocks, independent board interlocks and total board interlocks) have an impact on carbon emission performance among the top 200 BSE listed companies in India that voluntarily submit their carbon emissions data to CDP for the 2013–2020 period.

The unbalanced panel of 289 observations was modelled using EVIEWS, version 12, and applied varieties of regression methods comprising robust least squares, generalised method of moments and Heckman's regression.

Regression results showed that CEOs and women board interlocks contribute to lowering carbon emissions. This is because CEOs who serve on other boards can get the experience and knowledge required to respond to environmental challenges such as carbon emissions. Moreover, women are regarded as more sensitive than men when it comes to environmental performance. They are also portrayed as better at developing business contacts between them than men (Zenou et al., 2012). The study provided robust results regarding endogeneity and self-selection bias and an alternative measure of carbon emissions performance. The results were largely similar, albeit with few differences in control variables.

The findings reported in our study should be interpreted with caution in light of the following limitations. First, our sample is restricted to a proportion of the top 200 BSE firms that voluntarily submit their carbon emissions data to CDP. There is a likelihood of different results if different firms that do not fall within our sample are used. Future research may extend the sample to include other firms other than firms within the top 200 BSE. Finally, we focus our study on India, which means that our findings cannot be generalised to other emerging economies due to different regulatory regimes. Future studies may investigate other emerging economies like Russia, China and South Africa to compare and contrast the results.

The above limitations notwithstanding, our study enriches the literature on board interlocks and carbon emissions performance in several ways. First, unlike the majority of previous studies that focus on the relationship between board interlocks and financial performance (Hundal, 2017; Tjondro et al., 2021; Zona et al., 2018), this study investigated the impact of board interlocks on carbon emissions performance which is the biggest crisis facing the planet currently. Secondly, our study is focussed on environmental performance (carbon emissions) as opposed to environmental disclosure. Environmental disclosure is different from environmental performance since the former reflects what is being done in a firm relating to carbon risk management, strategy, target setting and other ways aimed at reducing emissions while the latter is about the outcome of the implemented strategy (Clarkson et al., 2008; Haque & Ntim, 2020; Luo & Tang, 2021). Thirdly, the study was based in India, which is an emerging economy and the fourth largest emitter of carbon emissions unlike previous studies that had predominantly been concentrated in developed economies (Lu et al., 2021a, 2021b). Based on the Kyoto Protocol, India, an emerging economy, is not obligated to report its carbon emissions data (Desai et al., 2021). Finally, we offer a comprehensive set of measures of board interlocks encompassing CEOs, women board, board independence and total board interlocks in a single study as opposed to previous studies (Al-Dah, 2019; Glass et al., 2016; Lu et al., 2021a, 2021b; Ratri et al., 2021; Sun et al., 2020) that only focus on one type of board interlock in different studies.

The negative association between CEOs and women board interlocks and carbon emissions performance has a policy and theoretical implications. The results add to an ongoing debate about the degree of regulation imposed by the Companies Act, 2013, and SEBI on the number of directorships held by an executive (CEOs). The empirical evidence suggests that CEOs should be allowed flexibility to outside directorships, which grants greater knowledge sharing towards environmental sustainability involving carbon emission reduction. Also, the negative impact between women board interlocks and carbon emissions performance implies that more women directorships enhance carbon emissions reduction. The study's results call for more actions for regulatory authorities to enforce previous recommendations on women board memberships and increase the number of women board members. This is in line with the argument made by Zenou et al. (2012) that the chances of appointing a woman to a board are higher when she already has a similar appointment elsewhere. Theoretically, the results support the resource dependency theory that through CEOs and women board interlocks, knowledge acquired can help address carbon emissions reduction.

NOTES

1. According to Clause 49, Independent directors are not paid employees and do not have family connection to the company.
2. According to CDP Climate Change Report (2012), CDP is an independent non-profit organisation that captures information on climate change and GHG from various firms across the globe.
3. The financial year in India runs from April 1 to March 31 of the following year. Thus, the financial year 2020 covers the period from 1 April 2019 to 31 March 2020.

REFERENCES

Abang'a, A. O., Tauringana, V., Wang'ombe, D., & Achiro, L. O. (2021). Corporate governance and performance of state-owned enterprises in Kenya. *Corporate Governance: The International Journal of Business in Society*, 22(4), 798–820.

Al-Dah, B. (2019). Director interlocks and the strategic pacing of CSR activities. *Management Decision*, 57(10), 2782–2798.

Barka, H. B., & Dardour, A. (2015). Investigating the relationship between director's profile, board interlocks and corporate social responsibility. *Management Decision*, 34(1), 1–5.

Booth, J. R., & Deli, D. N. (1996). Factors affecting the number of outside directorships held by CEOs. *Journal of Financial Economics*, 40(1), 81–104.

Braam, G. J., De Weerd, L. U., Hauck, M., & Huijbregts, M. A. (2016). Determinants of corporate environmental reporting: The importance of environmental performance and assurance. *Journal of Cleaner Production*, 129, 724–734.

Bui, B., Houqe, M. N., & Zaman, M. (2020). Climate governance effects on carbon disclosure and performance. *The British Accounting Review*, 52(2), 100880.

CDP Climate Change Report. (2012). *CDP climate change report*. CDP India.

CDP India Annual Report. (2020, March). *Building back greener*. CDP India.

Chiranga, N., & Chiwira, O. (2014). Impact of multiple directorships on performance for companies listed on the Johannesburg Stock Exchange (JSE). *Economics*, 2(6), 378–387.

Clarkson, P. M., Li, Y., Richardson, G. D., & Vasvari, F. (2008). Revisiting the relation between environmental performance and environmental disclosure: An empirical analysis. *Accounting, Organizations and Society*, 33(4–5), 303–327.

Cordeiro, J. J., Profumo, G., & Tutore, I. (2020). Board gender diversity and corporate environmental performance: The moderating role of family and dual-class majority ownership structures. *Business Strategy and the Environment*, 29(3), 1127–1144.

Cucari, N., Esposito de Falco, S., & Orlando, B. (2018). Diversity of board of directors and environmental social governance: Evidence from Italian listed companies. *Corporate Social Responsibility and Environmental Management*, 25(3), 250–266.

De Villiers, C., Naiker, V., & Van Staden, C. (2011). The effect of board characteristics on firm environmental performance. *Journal of Management*, 37(6), 1636–1663.

Desai, R., Raval, A., Baser, N., & Desai, J. (2021). Impact of carbon emission on financial performance: Empirical evidence from India. *South Asian Journal of Business Studies*, 11(4), 450–470.

Elsayih, J., Datt, R., & Tang, Q. (2021). Corporate governance and carbon emissions performance: Empirical evidence from Australia. *Australasian Journal of Environmental Management*, 28(4), 433–459.

Ferris, S. P., Jagannathan, M., & Pritchard, A. C. (2003). Too busy to mind the business? Monitoring by directors with multiple board appointments. *The Journal of Finance*, 58(3), 1087–1111.

Finkelstein, S., & Mooney, A. C. (2003). Not the usual suspects: How to use board process to make boards better. *The Academy of Management Executive*, 17(2), 101–113.

Glass, C., Cook, A., & Ingersoll, A. R. (2016). Do women leaders promote sustainability? Analyzing the effect of corporate governance composition on environmental performance. *Business Strategy and the Environment*, 25(7), 495–511.

Haque, F., & Ntim, C. G. (2020). Executive compensation, sustainable compensation policy, carbon performance and market value. *British Journal of Management*, 31(3), 1–22.

Heckman, J. J. (1979). Sample selection bias as a specification error. *Econometrica*, 47(1), 153–161.

Hernández-Lara, A. B., & Gonzales-Bustos, J. P. (2019). The impact of interlocking directorates on innovation: The effects of business and social ties. *Management Decision*, 57(10), 2799–2815.

Hollindale, J., Kent, P., Routledge, J., & Chapple, L. (2019). Women on boards and greenhouse gas emission disclosures. *Accounting and Finance*, 59(1), 277–308.

Hundal, S. (2017). Multiple directorships of corporate boards and firm performance in India. *Corporate Ownership and Control*, 14(4), 150–164.

Jackling, B., & Johl, S. (2009). Board structure and firm performance: Evidence from India's top companies. *Corporate Governance: An International Review*, 17(4), 492–509.

Jiraporn, P., Singh, M., & Lee, C. I. (2009). Ineffective corporate governance: Director busyness and board committee memberships. *Journal of Banking & Finance, 33*(5), 819–828.

Joecks, J., Pull, K., & Vetter, K. (2013). Gender diversity in the boardroom and firm performance: What exactly constitutes a "critical mass?" *Journal of Business Ethics, 118*(1), 61–72.

Kiel, G. C., & Nicholson, G. (2006). Multiple directorships and corporate performance in Australian listed companies. *Corporate Governance: An International Review, 14*(6), 530–546.

Lamb, N. H., & Roundy, P. (2016). The "ties that bind" board interlocks research: A systematic review. *Management Research Review, 39*(11), 1516–1542.

Lei, A. C. H., & Deng, J. (2014). Do multiple directorships increase firm value? Evidence from independent directors in Hong Kong. *Journal of International Financial Management & Accounting, 25*(2), 121–181.

Liao, L., Luo, L., & Tang, Q. (2015). Gender diversity, board independence, environmental committee and greenhouse gas disclosure. *The British Accounting Review, 47*(4), 409–424.

Lu, J., Mahmoudian, F., Yu, D., Nazari, J. A., & Herremans, I. M. (2021). Board interlocks, absorptive capacity, and environmental performance. *Business Strategy and the Environment, 30*(8), 3425–3443.

Lu, J., Yu, D., Mahmoudian, F., Nazari, J. A., & Herremans, I. M. (2021). Board interlocks and greenhouse gas emissions. *Business Strategy and the Environment, 30*(1), 92–108.

Luo, L., & Tang, Q. (2021). Corporate governance and carbon performance: Role of carbon strategy and awareness of climate risk. *Accounting and Finance, 61*(2), 2891–2934.

Macchioni, R., Prisco, M., Santonastaso, R., & Zagaria, C. (2022). Carbon emission and board gender diversity: The moderating role of CEO duality. *International Journal of Business and Management Studies, 3*(1).

Mallin, C. A., & Michelon, G. (2011). Board reputation attributes and corporate social performance: An empirical investigation of the US best corporate citizens. *Accounting and Business Research, 41*(2), 119–144.

Manes-Rossi, F., Nicolò, G., Tudor, A. T., & Zanellato, G. (2020). Drivers of integrated reporting by state-owned enterprises in Europe: A longitudinal analysis. *Meditari Accountancy Research, 29*(3), 586–616.

Matsumura, E. M., Prakash, R., & Vera-Muñoz, S. C. (2014). Firm-value effects of carbon emissions and carbon disclosures. *The Accounting Review, 89*(2), 695–724.

Ming, T. C., & Lee, C. L. (2014). Board structure and firm performance: Some evidence from Malaysian government linked companies. *Corporate Ownership and Control, 12*(1), 345–351.

Ministry of Corporate Affairs of India (MCA). (1956). *Companies Act.*

Nasih, M., Harymawan, I., Paramitasari, Y. I., & Handayani, A. (2019). Carbon emissions, firm size, and corporate governance structure: Evidence from the mining and agricultural industries in Indonesia. *Sustainability, 11*(9), 2483.

Nielsen, S., & Huse, M. (2010). Women directors' contribution to board decision-making and strategic involvement: The role of equality perception. *European Management Review, 7*(1), 16–29.

Ntim, C. G., Quadrangle, W., & Building, G. S. (2012). Director shareownership and corporate performance in South Africa. *African Journal of Accounting, Auditing and Finance, 1*(4), 359–373.

O'Hagan, S. B. (2017). An exploration of gender, interlocking directorates, and corporate performance. *International Journal of Gender and Entrepreneurship, 9*(3), 269–282.

Ortiz-de-Mandojana, N., & Aragon-Correa, J. A. (2015). Boards and sustainability: The contingent influence of director interlocks on corporate environmental performance. *Business Strategy and the Environment, 24*(6), 499–517.

Pfeffer, J., & Salancik, G. R. (1978). *The external control of organizations: A resource dependence perspective.* Harper & Row.

Ratri, M. C., Harymawan, I., & Kamarudin, K. A. (2021). Busyness, tenure, meeting frequency of the ceos, and corporate social responsibility disclosure. *Sustainability, 13*(10), 1–22.

Ritchie, H., & Roser, M. (2020). CO_2 and greenhouse gas emissions. Our World in Data. https://ourworldindata.org/co2-and-other-greenhouse-gas-emissions

Saleh, M. W., Shurafa, R., Shukeri, S. N., Nour, A. I., & Maigosh, Z. S. (2020). The effect of board multiple directorships and CEO characteristics on firm performance: Evidence from Palestine. *Journal of Accounting in Emerging Economies, 10*(4), 637–654.

Sarkar, J., & Sarkar, S. (2009). Multiple board appointments and firm performance in emerging economies: Evidence from India. *Pacific-Basin Finance Journal, 17*(2), 271–293.

Shahin, A., & Zairi, M. (2007). Corporate governance as a critical element for driving excellence in corporate social responsibility. *International Journal of Quality & Reliability Management, 24*(7), 753–770.

Sun, W., Li, X., Geng, Y., Yang, J., & Zhang, Y. (2020). Board interlocks and the diffusion of CSR reporting practices: The role of market development. *Corporate Social Responsibility and Environmental Management, 27*(3), 1333–1343.

Tauringana, V., & Chithambo, L. (2015). The effect of DEFRA guidance on greenhouse gas disclosure. *The British Accounting Review, 47*(4), 425–444.

Tingbani, I., Chithambo, L., Tauringana, V., & Papanikolaou, N. (2020). Board gender diversity, environmental committee and greenhouse gas voluntary disclosures. *Business Strategy and the Environment, 29*(6), 2194–2210.

Tjondro, E., Chang, N., Lianata, I., Yuliani, V., & Prayitno, N. (2021). Does board interlock control high-tech firm performance? Evidence from ASEAN's growth triangle countries. *AKRUAL: Jurnal Akuntansi, 12*(2), 117.

Wang, L., Li, S., & Gao, S. (2014). Do greenhouse gas emissions affect financial performance? – An empirical examination of Australian public firms. *Business Strategy and the Environment, 23*(8), 505–519.

Zenou, E., Allemand, I., & Brullebaut, B. (2012). At the origins of female directors' networks: A study of the French case. *Research in Finance, 28*(8), 177–192.

Zona, F., Gomez-Mejia, L. R., & Withers, M. C. (2018). Board interlocks and firm performance: Toward a combined agency–Resource dependence perspective. *Journal of Management, 44*(2), 589–618.

APPENDICES

(1) *Ramsey's RESET test for linearity*

	Value	df	Probability
t-statistic	1.4800	278	0.1397
F-statistic	2.1933	(1, 2738)	0.1397
Likelihood ratio	2.2711	1	0.1318

(2) *Jarque–Bera test for normality*

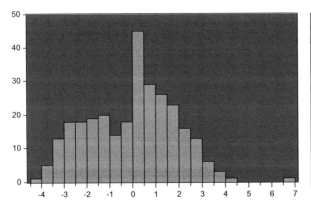

Series: Residuals
Sample 1 289
Observations 289

Mean	-5.19e-16
Median	0.274805
Maximum	6.744259
Minimum	-4.192389
Std. Dev.	1.903151
Skewness	-0.029512
Kurtosis	2.595002
Jarque-Bera	2.017064
Probability	0.364754

(3) *Heteroscedasticity Test: Breusch–Pagan–Godfrey*

F-Statistic	5.5093	Prob. $F(9,271)$	0.0000
Obs*R-squared	43.6106	Prob. Chi-Square(9)	0.0000
Scaled explained SS	32.4143	Prob. Chi-Square(9)	0.0002

(4) *Breusch–Godfrey Serial Correlation LM Test*

F-Statistics	163.3033	Prob. F (2.297)	0.0000
Obs*R-squared	156.3755	Prob. Chi-Square (2)	0.0000

THE IMPACT OF THE PARIS CLIMATE CHANGE AGREEMENT AND OTHER FACTORS ON CLIMATE CHANGE DISCLOSURE IN SOUTH AFRICA*

Caitlin Mongie, Gizelle Willows and Shelly Herbert

ABSTRACT

Purpose: *This study investigates the impact of the Paris Agreement (and other factors) on carbon information disclosures to the Carbon Disclosure Project (CDP).*

Design/Methodology/Approach: *A sample of South African listed companies was selected and data analysed from 2013 to 2017. A random effect panel data model using SPSS was used to determine whether the Paris Agreement had an effect on carbon information disclosure.*

Findings: *The results indicate that (1) the Paris Agreement, as an example of an intergovernmental coordination initiative, is significant in creating awareness and increasing the carbon disclosures to the CDP. Furthermore, (2) in terms of the other factors examined, providing incentives for managing climate change and assessing climate risks further into the future improves disclosure quality, while no relationship was found between the CDP score and the approval by key management personnel.*

---

*This chapter has been developed from the theses: Claire Mongie, C. (2019). Voluntary climate change disclosure in South Africa. University of Cape Town.

Green House Gas Emissions Reporting and Management in Global Top Emitting Countries and Companies
Advances in Environmental Accounting & Management, Volume 11, 107–125
Copyright © 2023 Caitlin Mongie, Gizelle Willows and Shelly Herbert
Published under exclusive licence by Emerald Publishing Limited
ISSN: 1479-3598/doi:10.1108/S1479-359820230000011006

Originality: *This research examines CDP disclosures for an emerging market before and after the signing of the Paris Agreement.*

Practical Implications: *This research shows the importance of supportive government policy. Furthermore, a commitment to climate change disclosure is manageable and achievable and needs to be implemented at the management level.*

Keywords: Climate change; incentives; institutional theory; Paris Agreement; sociopolitical theory; voluntary disclosure

INTRODUCTION

Climate change is referred to as the 'greatest challenge of our time' (DEA, 2016, p. 4) and is cited as a contributing factor to events such as the COVID-19 pandemic (Lorentzen et al., 2020). In response, companies are engaging in various climate change mitigation efforts and are reporting on these efforts to their stakeholders (Siew, 2015). Companies use voluntary climate change disclosure as one mechanism to acknowledge the gravity of the climate issue (Ihlen, 2009) and to appease stakeholders who want to see a response to climate change. As well as general climate change disclosures, many companies voluntarily disclose emissions and carbon information. Disclosure made to the CDP (formerly the Carbon Disclosure Project) is an example of such voluntary disclosure. The CDP measures a company's progress towards environmental stewardship (CDP, 2016a). In addition to the benefits for the climate of these efforts, the companies benefit by increasing their legitimacy. Various studies have also found many financial benefits for companies (Hopkins et al., 2009; Maroun, 2018).

The extent of companies reporting on climate change efforts has increased significantly over the preceding decades (KPMG, 2020). The extent of reporting is influenced by numerous factors, including age and size of the company, industry classification and senior management's attitudes (Nazari et al., 2015). In addition to these company-specific factors, societal pressure and the external environment also play a role (Luo et al., 2012). The changing climate has required intergovernmental coordination of environmental management and mitigation strategies under the Kyoto Protocol and, more recently, in the Paris Agreement, both international sub-treaties under the United Nations Framework Convention on Climate Change (UNFCCC) (Gupta & Mason, 2016).

The Paris Agreement provides ongoing focus and structure for global leaders at gatherings such as the annual UNFCCC climate change conferences, with COP26 being the most recent conference (Hobert & Toth, 2021). The Paris Agreement is the first treaty negotiated in 25 years that envisages all countries participating in climate action (Wolfgang et al., 2016) and has been adopted by 195 countries (UN, 2018). Therefore, the Paris Agreement is considered a turning point for climate action (DEA, 2016), particularly since, under the Kyoto Protocol, only 35 countries were prepared to limit their greenhouse gas (GHG) emissions (Spash, 2016). However, prior studies have not examined the impact of the Paris Agreement on the climate change disclosures provided by companies.

Other factors that may influence the level of CDP disclosures are how far into the future climate risks are considered, the incentives provided to management for managing risks and who approves the CDP disclosures among the key management personnel. There is likely to be better environmental stewardship the further into the future a company's management considers climate change (Christensen & Wessel, 2012). Monetary and non-monetary incentives are generally found to be effective in promoting a change of behaviour among management and may provide a key to encouraging management to prioritise climate change (Renwick et al., 2013; Saeed et al., 2019). Finally, the involvement of top management in climate change initiatives has been found to be positively related to the success of these initiatives (Esser & Delport, 2018).

The primary research question for this study is: *What was the impact of the Paris Agreement on CDP climate change scores?* The secondary research question is: *Which other factors (assessment of future risk, management incentives and approval by key management personnel) influence a higher CDP climate change score?* Prior research has concentrated on Forbes Global 500 and US S&P 500 companies (Luo et al., 2012; Oktay et al., 2021; Stanny & Ely, 2008). However, the CDP considers South Africa's domestic companies to be 'unquestionably performing on a par with their global peers' and 'in many cases outperforming them' (NBI, 2016, p. 2). If it can be determined which factors influence a higher CDP score for South African companies, these factors might indicate why South African companies are outperforming their global peers. A sample of 57 top 100 Johannesburg Stock Exchange (JSE) listed companies was selected, and an analysis was done over 5 years from 2013 to 2017. A random effect panel data model is used to conduct the quantitative analysis of the impact of the variables. This study has three findings. Firstly, in answering the primary research question, the Paris Agreement had a positive impact of carbon disclosures. In examining the secondary research question, CDP disclosures were increased the further into the future a company's management considers climate change; where companies provide incentives for managing climate change issues, these companies are more likely to have a higher CDP score; and no relationship was found between the approval by key management personnel of the CDP disclosures and the final score.

This research contributes to the literature by making recommendations for managers and policymakers. The effectiveness of intergovernmental coordination is seen through the positive impact of the Paris Agreement on climate disclosure scores, and the impact of manager commitment towards climate change disclosure is shown in the quality of output by companies. Additionally, a more thorough understanding of disclosure theories is established from these results, as explained by institutional and sociopolitical theories. Managers should be made aware that the further into the future they consider climate change risk management, the better. This consideration will improve the company's CDP score, enhance stakeholders' perceptions of the company and align disclosure to the Paris Agreement's objectives. Companies should also incentivise staff to manage climate change and reduce GHG emissions. These results provide policymakers globally with necessary information on the environmental management and climate change debate. The changing climate requires intergovernmental coordination in the first instance. Furthermore, the private sector can no longer play a passive role. The results show that a commitment to climate change disclosure is manageable and achievable. The measures are consistent with voluntary disclosure frameworks and need to be implemented at the management level.

The remainder of this chapter is organised as follows. The theoretical framework and prior studies are discussed. The hypotheses for this study are then developed, followed by an outline of the methodology used. The results are then presented and discussed, followed by the summary and conclusion.

LITERATURE REVIEW

Theoretical Framework

Voluntary disclosure occurs when information is provided by a company even though there is no legal requirement to do so. It represents management's choice to provide information that it deems to be decision-useful. In South Africa, carbon disclosure, an aspect of sustainability reporting, is entirely voluntary.

Despite the voluntary nature of carbon disclosure, all JSE-listed companies must comply with the King Code (IoDSA, 2016; JSE, 2017). Of relevance for this research is that King IV recognises climate change as a driver of change and states that 'continuing business as usual' in light of climate change is simply 'no longer possible' (IoDSA, 2016, p. 3). Furthermore, the recommended practice suggests that all JSE-listed companies should have oversight and monitor their impact on the environment in order to be, and to be seen as, responsible corporate citizens. Companies must also produce integrated reports, focusing on value creation across the six capitals over the short, medium and long term (IoDSA, 2016).

The recommendations from the King Code further increase the societal pressure for businesses to respond to climate change, in addition to government policies, pressure from consumers and other stakeholders. The response from business needs to harness financial, technological and organisational resources (Okereke et al., 2012).

In addition to the societal pressures, climate change could directly change a company's external environment. This transformation will impact its ability to acquire, retain and grow the capitals required to create value and, therefore, result in a cost to the company (Lemma et al., 2019). This negative outcome indicates that organisations should effectively and proactively manage their environmental impact and natural resource stewardship.

The South African Department of Environmental Affairs (DEA) (2017) states that they will evaluate the private sector's transition to a lower-carbon economy based on their participation and activities disclosed in their responses to the CDP. The CDP is a global not-for-profit company that sends out three separate questionnaires on climate change, forests and water security to cities and companies worldwide (CDP, 2017). More than 570 cities, 100 states and 6,300 companies worldwide participate by disclosing their environmental data every year to the CDP (Appleby, 2018; CDP, 2017). The CDP uses a scoring methodology to incentivise participating companies to measure and manage their impact on climate change, water and forests (CDP, 2016a).

Voluntary disclosure practices can be explained using sociopolitical and institutional theories (Garcia et al., 2020). The application of each of these theories is discussed below.

Sociopolitical theories of voluntary disclosure explain that the disclosure produced by organisations is due to political or social pressure from multiple stakeholders (Hahn et al., 2015). Disclosure produced in response to such coercion tends to vary based on the social or political focus of the time, particularly when the disclosure is not required by regulation. Sociopolitical theories can be further subdivided into stakeholder theory and legitimacy theory.

Stakeholder theory refers to an organisation implementing different strategies in the interests of different stakeholder groups (Roberts, 1992). The social pressure for climate change information explains the need for carbon disclosure (Hahn et al., 2015). The urgency of a company's response depends on the power of the stakeholders (Hahn et al., 2015) and thus varies from one company to another.

Legitimacy theory refers to how the actions of an organisation are considered appropriate because of societal norms and values (Suchman, 1995). Legitimacy theory also motivates for carbon disclosure in reaction to external social or political pressure and improves the public's perception of a company's sustainability performance (Hahn et al., 2015; Suchman, 1995). Environmental disclosure essentially maintains a social contract between the company and society (Hahn et al., 2015). The higher the level of stakeholder engagement, the higher the incentive for companies to safeguard their legitimacy. Larger and more profitable companies are pressured to legitimise their actions since they are usually more visible and have greater media exposure (Hahn et al., 2015). In Spain, Andrades Peña and Jorge (2019) found that the most significant predictor of disclosure of non-financial information was institution size.

However, because of the voluntary element of CDP reporting and the pressure to maintain legitimacy (Theoharakis et al., 2021), 'greenwashing' can be prevalent as managers tend to opportunistically not report on the "bad" sustainability information (Hahn & Lülfs, 2014; Manning, 2017). This practice also negatively impacts consumers' perceptions of the company and their willingness to interact with them (Szabo & Webster, 2021).

Institutional theory has some overlap with sociopolitical theories. The theory states that an organisation is driven by the requirements of different institutions and not only the organisation's aim to maximise profits, which implies that external institutions create pressure that causes organisations to adjust their behaviours and social performance (Jepperson, 1991). Companies act as agents by selecting which institutional influences match their priorities (Ismaeel & Zakaria, 2019). By performing in a socially acceptable manner, corporations increase their legitimacy and survival prospects.

With voluntary disclosure, research has examined the role of institutional actors, such as the CDP, who use disclosure as a method of monitoring companies' climate change mitigation actions and performance (Gupta & Mason, 2016). Companies who voluntarily disclose information about their activities meet the demands imposed by institutional stakeholders for information and are essentially responding to public pressure. Disclosures around GHG emissions and carbon are used as part of a legitimacy exercise wherein the quality of reporting is perhaps more important for understanding how companies respond to stakeholder expectations (Pitrakkos & Maroun, 2020). As the purpose of voluntary environmental disclosure is to manage the public's impression of a company's activities (Cormier et al., 2005), investors and stakeholders will utilise this information to gain a more thorough understanding of the company's carbon performance and its responses to climate change (Jaggi et al., 2017). Furthermore, voluntary emissions and carbon disclosure should reduce information asymmetry (Barboza et al., 2021) and enable investors to make investment decisions after evaluating a company's risk exposure to climate change (Jaggi et al., 2017). The response to institutional pressure is consistent with either what other companies in the same industry have disclosed or what companies have disclosed because of routine and regulation (Cormier et al., 2005).

Prior Studies and Hypotheses Development

Paris Agreement

The Kyoto Protocol was effected on 16 February 2005 (UNFCCC, 1998) and promised substantial emission reductions for the developed world. However, it was criticised as economically inefficient, politically impractical and inadequate to address global warming (Rosen, 2015). Thus, a new climate treaty, the Paris Agreement, was agreed to on 12 December 2015 (Falkner, 2016; Wolfgang et al., 2016). This treaty acknowledged that domestic politics around climate change vary from nation to nation and allows countries to set their own climate change mitigation strategies (Falkner, 2016).

The Paris Agreement is the first treaty negotiated in 25 years that envisages all countries partaking in climate action (Wolfgang et al., 2016) and has been adopted by 195 countries as of 18 December 2018 (Gupta & Mason, 2016; UK Telegraph, 2018; UN, 2018). Therefore, the Paris Agreement is considered a turning point for climate action (DEA, 2016), particularly since, under the Kyoto Protocol, only 35 countries were prepared to limit their GHG emissions (Spash, 2016). A further difference between the Paris Agreement and the Kyoto Protocol is that under the Paris Agreement, developing countries must commit to reducing their emissions (Stowe, 2015). In terms of institutional theory, the external pressure created by the Paris Agreement is expected to increase the level of engagement with climate action (Jepperson, 1991).

Given that the Paris Agreement was expected to bring about real climate action (Stowe, 2015), the following hypothesis is presented:

H1: The Paris Agreement has a significant positive impact on carbon dioxide information disclosure.

Management Incentives

Numerous studies have examined the relationship between management incentives and climate change performance, and incentives and compensation are often assumed to be one of the most effective mechanisms to drive positive climate change behaviour (Jackson et al., 2011). In terms of institutional theory, institutional investors can create pressure for organisations to implement incentives that will cause management behaviour to align with their objectives (Chung et al., 2002). Haque (2017) studied 256 non-financial UK companies and found a positive relationship between initiatives aimed at carbon reduction, and the compensation policy of the board, relating to environmental, social and governance factors. In a study of North American and European compensation packages for Chief Executive Officers, Jouber (2019) also found a positive relationship between the compensation and the implementation of sustainability initiatives.

Although monetary incentives are generally considered the most effective measure to change behaviour (Saeed et al., 2019), combining monetary and non-monetary rewards, such as recognition, may produce better results (Renwick et al., 2013). Studying employee responses to various forms of monetary and non-monetary incentives for positive climate change behaviour, Saeed et al. (2019) also found a positive relationship for all levels of employees. They conclude that a combination of monetary and non-monetary rewards is most effective in incentivising employees.

Following on from the studies above, the following hypotheses are offered:

H2: Management monetary rewards incentives have a significant positive impact on carbon dioxide information disclosure.

H3: Management monetary rewards and recognition have a significant impact on carbon dioxide information disclosure.

Assessment of Future Risk

The assessment of future risk is an essential function of the management of an organisation (Institute of Directors Southern Africa, 2016), and organisations are increasingly considering future risks (Di Vaio et al., 2020). The further into the future risks are considered holistically, meeting the needs of all stakeholders, the better the advantages for all parties affected (Khare et al., 2011). Companies can create a competitive advantage by considering sustainability risks (Berns et al., 2009). How far into the future climate change risk is considered indicates how the current business is likely to overcome disruptions such as climate change (Christensen & Wessel, 2012).

Several studies have examined the assessment of carbon risks and their effect on carbon management. In a study of 500 companies across 38 countries, Hossain and Farooque (2019) found that the presence of a risk management committee was positively correlated with a higher CDP score. Examining 45 Australian companies, Tang and Luo (2014) found that carbon risk and opportunity assessments were one of the drivers of sound carbon management systems.

However, there appears to be a lack of studies considering the assessment of carbon risks into the future and for different assessment time frames. The Paris Agreement is a forward-looking agreement based on expectations for future risks (United Nations Framework Convention on Climate Change, 2016), which would meet the needs of a broader group of stakeholders, in line with stakeholder theory (Roberts, 1992). Therefore, it is appropriate to propose the following hypothesis:

H4: Management consideration of future carbon risks has a positive impact on carbon dioxide information disclosure.

Key Management Personnel

When a company's top management is involved in sustainability issues, the company has a greater level of sustainability disclosures (Herbert & Graham, 2020a). The top management is most likely to be concerned about the legitimacy of the organisation, and is best placed to act to maintain the legitimacy (Herbert & Graham, 2021). Furthermore, the establishment of a social and ethics committee, or having designated directors responsible for sustainability issues, including carbon and GHG emissions, is increasingly common (Esser & Delport, 2018) and are encouraged to be involved in the drafting of disclosures (Integrated Reporting Committee of South Africa, 2014).

Peters and Romi (2014) found a positive correlation between the existence of an environmental committee and a Chief Sustainability Officer in a company and the level of GHG disclosure presented. Their study used companies submitting to the CDP between 2002 and 2006. As cited by Haque (2017), Lam and Li (2008) also found a positive relationship between the carbon disclosures and the presence of a committee dedicated to environmental concerns. Finally, Baraibar-Diez and Odriozola (2019) also found a significant relationship between the existence of a corporate social responsibility committee and disclosures in their study of European companies between 2005 and 2015.

Examining the quality of integrated report disclosures of large listed South African companies, Malola and Maroun (2019) found no relationship between the existence of a dedicated, independent committee and the quality of disclosures. Although this study examined integrated reporting, integrated reports should integrate environmental disclosures within the report (Herbert & Graham, 2020b; International Integrated Reporting Council, 2021). Ullah and Nasim (2021) also found no relationship in their study of 202 companies from BRICS countries from 2009 to 2018.

Based on the above discussion, the following hypothesis is proposed:

H5: Key management personnel approval has a significant positive impact on carbon dioxide information disclosure.

RESEARCH METHODOLOGY

To answer the primary and secondary research questions, the CDP score for the top 100 JSE-listed companies will be assessed against selected companies' characteristics and their responses to questions asked within the CDP questionnaire.

The list of top 100 companies, ranked by market capitalisation, was obtained on 31 March 2017. Selected company-specific variables were sourced from the INET BFA portal for each company. Additionally, the CDP climate change programme score and individual company responses to the climate change questionnaire were obtained directly from the CDP.

The CDP Questionnaire

The rationale for using data from the CDP is fourfold: Firstly, 6,300 companies elect to participate in the CDP's climate change programme every year, indicating that the CDP is a source of company-specific voluntary environmental disclosure information (CDP, 2017). Secondly, because the disclosure made to the CDP is via a questionnaire, there is a lack of discretion in the companies' answers, which allows for simplified data collection and comparison. Thirdly, extensive comparative data are available since companies have disclosed information to the CDP since 2001. Finally, the CDP's scoring allows companies to compare themselves yearly and similarly allows comparisons between companies (Appleby, 2018). This practice of comparison corresponds with institutional theories in that what other companies in the same industry have disclosed often encourages voluntary disclosure (Cormier et al., 2005).

This study will analyse CDP questionnaires between 2013 and 2017 ('the period'), spanning before and after the signing of the Paris Agreement, to address *H1*. In total, a responding company must answer 77 questions in the CDP climate change questionnaire. The researchers assessed each of these questions for comparability and completeness across the period and to determine which questions address the hypotheses offered in this study. This process resulted in three questions to be included in this analysis, which addressed incentives provided to management, how far into the future climate risks are considered, and the approval of the CDP responses, addressing *H2–H5*.

Given the 5 year period (2013–2017), a 100% response rate would equal 500 company responses. However, only 305 responses were available. Furthermore, of the 305 responses to the CDP, 63 responses were excluded because of incomplete information. Therefore, the final sample over the period consists of 242 responses. The 242 responses can be disaggregated into the different years, with 50 responses in 2017, 53 in 2016, 55 in 2015, 38 in 2014 and 46 in 2013. The 242 responses are representative of 57 unique companies. Therefore, this study will only assess the results for these 57 companies.

One can speculate that those companies not responding were likely those with poorer CDP scores and thus did not submit or participate. This limitation is similar to prior research on CDP disclosures (Stanny, 2018) and does not negate the value of the study. The study aims to assess the factors determining the CDP score, and this objective can still be achieved by limiting the analysis to these 57 unique companies. This study does not aim to assess who is and who is not participating in the CDP questionnaire. Instead, this study aims to determine if individual company responses within the CDP questionnaire influence a higher CDP climate change score.

Information on the Paris Agreement, the three selected climate change questionnaire responses to be included in the testing, and each selected company-specific variable are presented in Table 1. The variable name is shown in the first column, with further descriptive information on how that variable was determined, why it is appropriate to include in the testing and the related theoretical frameworks in the remaining columns.

Research Approach

Panel data refer to repeated measurements of the same individual at different points in time (Cameron & Trivedi, 2009), which in this case is the sampled companies over the period. In a fixed-effect model, the random individual-specific effects (a_i) are permitted to be correlated with the independent variables, while in the random effects model it is assumed that a_i are purely random and uncorrelated with the independent variables (Cameron & Trivedi, 2009). A Hausman's test establishes whether a fixed effect or random-effects model is more appropriate. With a p-value of 0.0757, the null hypothesis is rejected. It is, thus, appropriate to use the random effect panel data model for the data. Spearman's rank correlation coefficients confirmed no collinearity of independent variables. The random effect panel data model formula is presented below (Eq. 1). Refer to Table 1 for the definition of the variables.

$$
\begin{aligned}
\text{CDP Score} = {} & \beta_1 \text{Size} + \beta_2 \text{FSP} + \beta_3 \text{Leverage} + \beta_4 \text{ROA} + \beta_5 \text{Incentives} \\
& + \beta_6 \text{Key management} + \beta_7 \text{Paris Agreement} \\
& + \beta_8 \text{Industry} + \beta_{9-11} \text{Future risks} + u_{it} + \varepsilon_{it}
\end{aligned} \tag{1}
$$

To determine the best fit for the model, the data were inspected for outliers and run three times: (1) using the data in their original format ($n = 242$), (2) using winsorised data ($n = 240$) and (3) using the original data but excluding outliers ($n = 229$). The best model fit upon examination of the residuals plotted against the model fit was for the winsorised data. Therefore, all results presented in the remainder of this study are presented for the winsorised data.

RESULTS AND DISCUSSION

Descriptive Statistics

The dependent variable, the CDP score, will be discussed first. The CDP scores, which were ranked within a range between A (better environmental stewardship) and E (poorer environmental stewardship), were re-coded as $A = 5$, $B = 4$, $C = 3$, $D = 2$ and $E = 1$. The mean score of the 242 responses is 3.67 (i.e. between B and C), with a standard deviation of 0.94 and a mode of 4 (i.e. B). This result indicates that most companies that elected to provide the voluntary disclosure show good environmental management (CDP, 2016b).

Summary statistics for each of the variables in Table 1 are given in Table 2 and Table 3. Firstly, Table 2 details the number of observations, the mean value, the

Table 1. Variables.

Variable Name	Variable Description	Explanation for Inclusion and Theoretical Framework[a]
Paris Agreement	Paris Agreement is a *binary variable* that indicates the period before (2013–2015) and after (2016–2017) the agreement was affected.	A driving factor for institutional theories disclosure is what companies have disclosed because of routine and regulation (Cormier et al., 2005). The Paris Agreement is an example of a regulation that might drive disclosure to the CDP.
Incentives	This variable is derived from the following question in the CDP questionnaire. 'Do you provide incentives for the management of climate change issues, including the attainment of targets?' If incentives were provided, companies had to select the type of incentive given. This variable is coded as a *categorical variable*: (1) no incentive is provided ($n = 52$), (2) management's incentive is monetary ($n = 128$) and (3) management's incentive is based on both a monetary reward and recognition ($n = 62$).	If institutional investors call for the integration of environmental metrics in managerial incentivisation schemes, then revised reward structures are likely to be introduced by companies (Deegan & Islam, 2012).
Future risks	CDP questionnaire derivation: 'Please select the option that best describes your risk management procedures with regard to climate change risks and opportunities – how far into the future is climate risk considered?' Response options are coded as a *categorical variable* accordingly: 1–3 years = 1 ($n = 37$); 3–6 years = 2 ($n = 55$); >6 years = 3 ($n = 101$); Unknown or not provided = 4 ($n = 49$).	Managers use their future climate change risk management activities rather than their historical carbon emissions levels to manage stakeholders' perceptions (Najah & Cotter, 2012). Thus, companies implement different strategies to manage their stakeholders in terms of stakeholder theory (Roberts, 1992).
Key management	CDP questionnaire derivative: 'Please provide the following information for the person who has signed off (approved) your CDP climate change response'. Companies have to select the job title of the person who was responsible. Where either the Environment or Sustainability Manager or the Group Head of Safety and Sustainable Development was selected, a value of 1 is assigned. All other job titles are coded as 0. This variable is, therefore, a *binary variable*.	The level of responsibility delegated to key management to manage emissions disclosures and climate change issues enhances shareholder value (Najah & Cotter, 2012).
Size	A *continuous variable* calculated as market capitalisation over the shareholders' equity.	Larger companies are pressured to legitimise their actions since they are usually more visible and have greater media scrutiny (Hahn et al., 2015).
Foreign sales percentage (FSP)	A *continuous variable* calculated as total foreign sales, divided by total turnover.	Companies are driven by the requirements of different stakeholders,

Table 1. *(Continued)*

Variable Name	Variable Description	Explanation for Inclusion and Theoretical Framework[a]
		including customers, and not only the company's aim to maximise profits (Jepperson, 1991).
Leverage	A *continuous variable* calculated as total debt divided by total assets.	Providing more information voluntarily about the environment improves management's reputation because it is more transparent and signalling that management takes responsibility for the environment increases legitimacy (Hahn et al., 2015). This is more prevalent for companies belonging to carbon-intensive industries.
Return on assets (ROA)	A proxy for a firm's profitability. This *continuous variable* is calculated as the earnings before interest and tax, divided by total assets.	Profitability is a predicator of carbon disclosure due to the increased public scrutiny (Hahn et al., 2015)
Industry	A *binary variable* coded as 1 for industries considered carbon-intensive industries (industrials and basic materials) and 0 for the other industries.	Affiliation with a carbon-intensive industry is a predicator of carbon disclosure (Hahn et al., 2015).

[a]For some of the variables included in this table there is an overlap with the three theories. However, the authors have included the most relevant theory.

standard deviation and the minimum and maximum values for each continuous variable.

The four continuous variables (i.e. FSP, Size, ROA and Leverage) are financial ratios. The average proportion of total revenue earned from foreign sales is 37%. A maximum of 100% was obtained by six companies that generate revenue solely outside South Africa. For the leverage variable, the maximum value of 0.95 shows that the company has a risky level of debt because it is more dependent on creditors than the other sampled companies. The average ROA, which indicates how profitable the company is, is 9%. The highest ROA percentage of 64% for an iron ore company in 2013 reflects the stronger market conditions in crude steel over that period. The lowest ROA percentage is negative 26% for a company that made losses in 2013.

Table 2. Summary Statistics for the Continuous Variables ($N = 242$).

Continuous Variable	Mean	Standard Deviation	Minimum	Maximum
Size	10.25	31.74	0.06	302.16
Foreign sales percentage (FSP)	37%	0.35%	0%	100%
Leverage	0.54	0.21	0.00	0.95
Return on assets (ROA)	9%	0.10%	−26%	64%

The number of observations and frequency for each binary variable are presented separately. Table 3 details these observations and frequency below.

Table 3 shows that over half (57%) of the sampled responses come from 2013 to 2015 (i.e. pre-signing of the Paris Agreement), and 60% of the sampled companies are not operating in carbon-intensive industries. Furthermore, 34% of key management indicates that the majority (66%) of the sampled companies were not requiring either the Environment or Sustainability Manager or the Group Head of Safety and Sustainable Development to approve the CDP questionnaire.

Finally, consideration of the categorical variables is necessary. The results are included in Table 1 above. 79% of responses indicated that incentives are provided to manage climate change issues in some form. Thus, the majority of responding companies are providing incentives. The most significant proportion of companies indicated that they consider climate change risk more than 6 years into the future.

Table 4 shows that the statistically significant variables related to the CDP score are the Paris Agreement, Incentives and Future Risk. The first two variables support institutional theories of voluntary disclosure, while the third aligns with stakeholder theory. *H5* is rejected as there was no significant relationship found between the CDP score and the approval of the disclosures by key management personnel.

Supporting *H1*, companies who completed the CDP questionnaire after the Paris Agreement are expected to have a CDP score, on average, 0.51 times higher than companies who completed the CDP questionnaire before the Paris Agreement. Wolfgang et al. (2016) suggest that the years following the Paris Agreement would indicate whether the global community is willing to seriously tackle the challenges of climate change. Based on these results, South African companies are considering the seriousness of the climate change issue after the signing of the Paris Agreement. The influence of the Paris Agreement supports institutional theory, whereby the issuing of regulations influences behaviour.

The results are in line with the predictions of *H2* and *H3*. The statistical significance of Incentives makes sense as prior research (Greiner & Sun, 2021; Ihlen, 2009) indicates that incentives can effectively reward responsible corporations. Companies providing either or both monetary incentive and recognition are expected to have, on average, a CDP score of 0.79 or 0.80 more when compared to companies that do not provide incentives, holding all other variables in the model constant. Given no notable difference in the statistical significance of

Table 3. Summary Statistics for the Binary Variables ($N = 242$).

Binary Variables	Frequency
Paris Agreement	103 (43%)
Industry	97 (40%)
Key management	82 (34%)

Table 4. Predictors of CDP Score.

	Coefficients	Z
Paris Agreement	0.51***	5.61
	(0.09)	
Incentive: Monetary	0.79***	5.25
	(0.15)	
Incentive: Monetary and recognition	0.80***	5.04
	(0.16)	
Future risk: 3–6 years	0.52***	3.08
	(0.17)	
Future risk: >6 years	0.50***	3.06
	(0.16)	
Future risk: not provided	0.38**	2.51
	(0.15)	
Key management	0.07	0.57
	(0.12)	
Size	0.01	0.79
	(0.02)	
FSP	0.30	1.55
	(0.19)	
Leverage	0.07	0.23
	(0.32)	
ROA	−1.15	−1.84
	(0.62)	
Industry	0.24	1.50
	(0.16)	
Constant	2.31	8.19
R^2	0.30	
N	240	

***$p < 0.01$, **$p < 0.05$, *$p < 0.1$.

the two types of incentives, the results suggest that it is not the type of incentive given that assists in driving better environmental stewardship but rather the practice of providing incentives in the first instance. Being able to identify and understand managers' incentives is considered by Luo et al. (2012) to be a driving force in creating a low-carbon economy. Practically, various types of incentives can be provided to align managers' behaviour with institutional investors' goals, which have important implications for managerial behaviour (Deegan & Islam, 2012). Hartmann et al. (2013) indicated that monetary incentives make management more eager to promote environmental risk-reducing activities. Non-monetary incentives, such as recognition, are the most cost-effective, and workers exert more effort when the meaning of work is higher (Kosfeld et al., 2014). Therefore, companies should consider the structure of incentives for managing climate change issues, as providing incentives is important. In terms of institutional theories, institutional investors should call for incentives to motivate for climate change management because companies might then be more likely to receive a better CDP score.

The future risk variable assessed how long into the future management was considering climate change in its disclosure to the CDP. Companies with a 3–6 years future risk assessment or more than 6 years future risk assessment are, on average, expected to have a CDP score of 0.52 and 0.50 more when compared to companies with a 1–3 years future risk assessment. This result suggests better environmental stewardship for companies with a longer-term view of their risk assessment and supports *H4*. In line with stakeholder theory, companies must adopt a longer-term view for issues of sustainability, such as climate change, that are material to their business and their stakeholders. This result aligns with Karwowski and Raulinajtys-Grzybek (2021), finding a correlation between risk identification and mitigating actions.

SUMMARY AND CONCLUSION

This study aimed to determine the impact of the Paris Agreement on CDP disclosures and which factors influence a higher CDP climate change score, indicating, among other things, better management of GHG emissions. The period chosen was able to assess whether the signing of the Paris Agreement impacted the quality of voluntary disclosure regarding the climate change debate. The results indicate that CDP scores have improved post the signing of the Paris Agreement. This finding suggests that policymakers and intergovernmental coordination are succeeding in creating awareness of climate change, and companies are participating. In terms of institutional theories, if regulations stipulated in the Paris Agreement are implemented, this process might be a driving force for corporate climate change disclosure (Cormier et al., 2005). This result is encouraging, as the mitigation strategies of the UNFCC appear to be effective, and the commitment of the South African DEA has provided additional societal pressure for companies to respond to climate change and reduce emissions.

Providing incentives for managing climate change has also led to improvements in the CDP score, resulting in improved climate change disclosure. In terms of institutional theories, where institutional investors call for incentives to motivate climate change management, companies are more likely to introduce these incentive schemes and make the appropriate disclosures (Deegan & Islam, 2012). This finding provides a measurable action that companies can implement to show their commitment against climate change.

Furthermore, the longer the company assesses climate change risks and opportunities into the future, the better its CDP score is. This study's findings indicate that managers should be made aware that the further into the future they consider climate change risk management, the better. This practice will improve the company's CDP score and simultaneously manage stakeholders' perceptions. Additionally, by considering climate change risks over a longer time frame, the company can proactively put measures in place to mitigate the risks in advance.

The study is not without limitations, however. The scope relates to the outcome of the CDP score which measures how well a company discloses information about climate change only. This study is not claiming to assess what drives good responses to climate change, only to assess climate change disclosures made to the CDP on climate change. This limitation does not hinder the relevance of this research because disclosure of climate change is indicative of companies acknowledging the importance of the climate change issue (Doran et al., 2009) and companies detailing their risk exposure to climate change which has been lacking in practice (Doran et al., 2009).

These results provide policymakers globally with necessary information on the debate on GHG emissions and climate change. The findings from this research represent the environmental management practices of South African companies. The CDP considers South Africa's domestic companies to be 'unquestionably performing on a par with their global peers' and 'in many cases outperforming them' (NBI, 2016, p. 2). A unique factor in South Africa is the mandatory nature of integrated reporting for listed companies (JSE, 2017). The focus of integrated reporting on considering all six capitals and adopting a long-term view of value creation may explain the relatively better performance of South African companies in their CDP scores. Furthermore, the presence of the South African DEA evaluating the private sector's transition to a lower-carbon economy based on companies' participation and activities disclosed in their responses to the CDP might also suggest the necessity of intergovernmental and policymaker coordination and oversight. These findings provide insight for other nations in their environmental management. In addition to country-specific actions, the changing climate requires intergovernmental coordination, with initiatives such as the Paris Agreement. It will be interesting to note the success of future agreements and events such as the annual UNFCCC climate change conferences, in bringing about further cooperation between government leaders, given the findings of this study that the Paris Agreement did bring about significant change. Furthermore, the private sector can no longer play a passive role. The results show that a commitment to climate change disclosure is manageable and achievable. The measures are consistent with voluntary disclosure frameworks and need to be implemented at the management level.

REFERENCES

Andrades Peña, J., & Jorge, M. L. (2019). Examining the amount of mandatory non-financial information disclosed by Spanish state-owned enterprises and its potential influential variables. *Meditari Accountancy Research*, 27(4), 534–555.

Appleby, K. (2018). Why should cities, states and regions disclose through CDP? *CDP Portal*.

Baraibar-Diez, E., & Odriozola, M. D. (2019). CSR committees and their effect on ESG performance in UK, France, Germany, and Spain. *Sustainability*, 11(18). https://doi.org/10.3390/su11185077

Barboza, G., Pede, V., & Madero, S. (2021). Shared social responsibility. Dual role of consumers as stakeholders in firm strategy. *Social Responsibility Journal*, 17(1), 48–68.

Berns, M., Townend, A., Khayat, Z., Balagopal, B., Reeves, M., Hopkins, M. S., & Kruschwitz, N. (2009). Sustainability and competitive advantage. *MIT Sloan Management Review*, 51(1), 19–20.

Cameron, A. C., & Trivedi, P. K. (2009). *Microeconometrics using stata*. Stata Press Books, Stata Press Publication.

CDP. (2016a). *Scoring introduction 2017*.

CDP. (2016b). *CDP 2016 climate change scoring methodology*.

CDP. (2017). *CDP South Africa climate change 2017: Executive Summary.*

Christensen, C. M., & Wessel, M. (2012, June). Surviving disruption – Spotlight on how to manage disruption. *Harvard Business Review.* https://hbr.org/2012/12/surviving-disruption

Chung, R., Firth, M., & Kim, J. B. (2002). Institutional monitoring and opportunistic earnings management. *Journal of Corporate Finance, 8*(1), 29–48.

Cormier, D., Magnan, M., & Van Velthoven, B. (2005). Environmental disclosure quality in large German companies: Economic incentives, public pressures or institutional conditions? *European Accounting Review, 14*(1), 3–39.

DEA. (2016). *South Africa's 1st annual climate change report: A synopsis of South Africa's 2015 annual report on monitoring climate change responses.*

Deegan, C., & Islam, M. A. (2012). Corporate commitment to sustainability – Is it all hot air? An Australian review of the linkage between executive pay and sustainable performance. *Australian Accounting Review, 22*(4), 384–397.

Doran, K. L., Quinn, E. L., & Roberts, M. G. (2009). *Reclaiming transparency in a changing climate: Trends in climate risk disclosure by the S & P 500 from 1995 to the present.* Center for Energy & Environmental Security.

Esser, I., & Delport, P. (2018). The South African King IV Report on corporate governance: Is the crown shiny enough? *Company Lawyer, 39*(11), 378–384.

Falkner, R. (2016). The Paris Agreement and the new logic of international climate politics. *International Affairs, 92*(5), 1107–1125.

Garcia, E. A. da R., de Carvalho, G. M., Boaventura, J. M. G., & de Souza Filho, J. M. (2020). Determinants of corporate social performance disclosure: A literature review. *Social Responsibility Journal, 17*(4), 445–468.

Greiner, M., & Sun, J. (2021). How corporate social responsibility can incentivize top managers: A commitment to sustainability as an agency intervention. *Corporate Social Responsibility and Environmental Management, 28*(4), 1360–1375.

Gupta, A., & Mason, M. (2016, January). Disclosing or obscuring? The politics of transparency in global climate governance. *Current Opinion in Environmental Sustainability, 18*, 82–90.

Hahn, R., & Lülfs, R. (2014). Legitimizing negative aspects in GRI-oriented sustainability reporting: A qualitative analysis of corporate disclosure strategies. *Journal of Business Ethics, 123*, 401–420.

Hahn, R., Reimsbach, D., & Schiemann, F. (2015). Organizations, climate change, and transparency: Reviewing the literature on carbon disclosure. *Organization and Environment, 28*(1), 80–102.

Haque, F. (2017). The effects of board characteristics and sustainable compensation policy on carbon performance of UK firms. *British Accounting Review, 49*(3), 347–364.

Hartmann, F., Perego, P., & Young, A. (2013). Carbon accounting: Challenges for research in management control and performance measurement. *Abacus, 49*(4), 539–563. https://doi.org/10.1111/abac.12018

Herbert, S., & Graham, M. (2020a). Sustainability disclosures within the management commentary in the integrated reports of South African listed companies. In *Meditari/SAAA Conference* (pp. 1–33).

Herbert, S., & Graham, M. (2020b). Application of principles from the International <IR> Framework for including sustainability disclosures within South African integrated reports reports. *South African Journal of Accounting Research, 35*(1), 42–68.

Herbert, S., & Graham, M. (2021). Applying legitimacy theory to understand sustainability reporting behaviour within South African integrated reports. *South African Journal of Accounting Research, 36*(2), 147–169.

Hobert, R., & Toth, E. (2021). COP 26 explained: What to know about the UN climate change conference. *United Nations Foundation.*

Hopkins, M. S., Townend, A., Khayat, Z., Balagopal, B., Reeves, M., & Berns, M. (2009). The business of sustainability: What it means to managers now. *MIT Sloan Management Review, 51*(1), 20–26.

Hossain, M., & Farooque, O. (2019). The emission trading system, risk management committee and voluntary corporate response to climate change – A CDP study. *International Journal of Accounting and Information Management, 27*(2), 262–283.

Ihlen, Ø. (2009). Business and climate change: The climate response of the world's 30 largest corporations. *Environmental Communication: A Journal of Nature and Culture, 3*(2), 244–262.

Institute of Directors Southern Africa. (2016). *Report on corporate governance for South Africa 2016, King IV Report on corporate governance for South Africa.*

Integrated Reporting Committee of South Africa. (2014). *Preparing an integrated report: A Starter's guide.* http://integratedreportingsa.org/ircsa/wp-content/uploads/2017/05/IRCSA_StartersGuide.pdf. Accessed on November 9, 2018.

International Integrated Reporting Council. (2021). International <IR> Framework. https://integratedreporting.org/wp-content/uploads/2021/01/InternationalIntegratedReportingFramework.pdf

IoDSA. (2016). *The King IV Report.* The Institute of Directors in Southern Africa.

Ismaeel, M., & Zakaria, Z. (2019). *Perception of preparers of sustainability reports in the Middle East: Contrasting between local and global.* Meditari Accountancy Research.

Jackson, S. E., Renwick, D. W. S., Jabbour, C. J. C., & Muller-Camen, M. (2011). State-of-the-art and future directions for green human resource management: Introduction to the special issue. *German Journal of Human Resource Management: Zeitschrift Für Personalforschung, 25*(2), 99–116.

Jaggi, B., Allini, A., Macchioni, R., & Zampella, A. (2017). Do investors find carbon information useful? Evidence from Italian firms. *Review of Quantitative Finance and Accounting, 50*(4), 1–26.

Jepperson, R. L. (1991). Institutions, institutional effects and institutionalism. In W. Powell & P. Dimaggio (Eds.), *The new institutionalism on organisational analysis* (pp. 143–163). University of Chicago Press.

Jouber, H. (2019). How does CEO pay slice influence corporate social responsibility? U.S.–Canadian versus Spanish–French listed firms. *Corporate Social Responsibility and Environmental Management, 26*(2), 502–517.

JSE. (2017). *JSE limited listings requirements.* Lexis Nexis.

Khare, A., Beckman, T., & Crouse, N. (2011). Cities addressing climate change: Introducing a tripartite model for sustainable partnership. *Sustainable Cities and Society, 1*(4), 227–235.

Karwowski, M., & Raulinajtys-Grzybek, M. (2021). The application of corporate social responsibility (CSR) actions for mitigation of environmental, social, corporate governance (ESG) and reputational risk in integrated reports. *Corporate Social Responsibility and Environmental Management, 28*(4), 1270–1284.

Kosfeld, M., Neckermann, S., & Yang, X. (2014). *Knowing that you matter, matters! The interplay of meaning, monetary incentives, and worker recognition* (pp. 1–29). Tinbergen Institute Discussion Paper.

KPMG. (2020). *The time has come! The KPMG survey of sustainability reporting 2020.* https://doi.org/10.6004/jnccn.2019.0020

Lemma, T. T., Feedman, M., Mlilo, M., & Park, J. D. (2019). Corporate carbon risk, voluntary disclosure, and cost of capital: South African evidence. *Business Strategy and the Environment, 28*(1), 111–126.

Lorentzen, H. F., Benfield, T., Stisen, S., & Rahbek, C. (2020). COVID-19 is possibly a consequence of the anthropogenic biodiversity crisis and climate changes. *Danish Medical Journal, 67*(5), 1–6.

Luo, L., Lan, Y. C., & Tang, Q. (2012). Corporate incentives to disclose carbon information: Evidence from the CDP global 500 report. *Journal of International Financial Management and Accounting, 23*(2), 93–120.

Malola, A., & Maroun, W. (2019). The measurement and potential drivers of integrated report quality: Evidence from a pioneer in integrated reporting. *South African Journal of Accounting Research, 33*(2), 114–144.

Manning, B. (2017). Corporate governance mechanisms, sustainability performance and sustainability disclosure quality.

Maroun, W. (2018). Consequences of reporting. In C. de Villiers & W. Maroun (Eds.), *Sustainability accounting and integrated reporting* (1st ed., pp. 90–100). Routledge.

Najah, M. M., & Cotter, J. (2012). Are climate change disclosures an indicator of superior climate change risk management? In *Australian Centre for Sustainable Business and Development* (pp. 1–47).

Nazari, J. A., Herremans, I. M., & Warsame, H. A. (2015). Sustainability reporting: External motivators and internal facilitators. *Corporate Governance: The International Journal of Business in Society, 15*(3), 375–390.

NBI. (2016). *CDP South Africa climate change 2016: Executive summary.*

Okereke, C., Wittneben, B., & Bowen, F. (2012). Climate change: Challenging business, transforming politics. *Business & Society, 51*(1), 7–30.

Oktay, S., Bozkurt, S., & Yazıcı, K. (2021). The relationship between carbon disclosure project scores and global 500 companies: A perspective from national culture. *SAGE Open, 11*(2). https://doi.org/10.1177/21582440211014521

Peters, G. F., & Romi, A. M. (2014). Does the voluntary adoption of corporate governance mechanisms improve environmental risk disclosures? Evidence from greenhouse gas emission accounting. *Journal of Business Ethics, 125*(4), 637–666.

Pitrakkos, P., & Maroun, W. (2020). Evaluating the quality of carbon disclosures. *Sustainability Accounting, Management and Policy Journal, 11*(3), 553–589.

Renwick, D. W. S., Redman, T., & Maguire, S. (2013). Green human resource management: A review and research agenda. *International Journal of Management Reviews, 15*(1), 1–14.

Roberts, R. W. (1992). Determinants of corporate social responsibility disclosure: An application of stakeholder theory. *Accounting, Organizations and Society, 17*(6), 595–612.

Rosen, A. M. (2015). The wrong solution at the right time: The failure of the Kyoto protocol on climate change. *Politics and Policy, 43*(1), 30–58.

Saeed, B. B., Afsar, B., Hafeez, S., Khan, I., Tahir, M., & Afridi, M. A. (2019). Promoting employee's proenvironmental behavior through green human resource management practices. *Corporate Social Responsibility and Environmental Management, 26*(2), 424–438.

Siew, R. Y. J. (2015). A review of corporate sustainability reporting tools (SRTs). *Journal of Environmental Management.* https://doi.org/10.1016/j.jenvman.2015.09.010

Spash, C. L. (2016). The political economy of the Paris Agreement on human induced climate change: A brief guide. *Real-World Economics Review, 1*(75), 67–75.

Stanny, E. (2018). Reliability and comparability of GHG disclosures to the CDP by US electric utilities. *Social and Environmental Accountability Journal, 38*(2), 111–130.

Stanny, E., & Ely, K. (2008, October). Corporate environmental disclosures about the effects of climate change. *Corporate Social Responsibility and Environmental Management, 15*, 338–348.

Stowe, R. (2015). Differentiation, financial support, and the Paris climate talks. *The Energy Collective.*

Suchman, M. C. (1995). Managing legitimacy: Strategic and institutional approaches. *The Academy of Management Review, 20*(3), 571–610.

Szabo, S., & Webster, J. (2021). Perceived greenwashing: The effects of green marketing on environmental and product perceptions. *Journal of Business Ethics, 171*(4), 719–739.

Tang, Q., & Luo, L. (2014). Carbon management systems and carbon mitigation. *Australian Accounting Review, 24*(1), 84–98.

Theoharakis, V., Voliotis, S., & Pollack, J. M. (2021). Going down the slippery slope of legitimacy lies in early-stage ventures: The role of moral disengagement. *Journal of Business Ethics, 172*(4), 673–690.

UK Telegraph. (2018). What is the Paris agreement on climate change? Everything you need to know. *UK Telegraph.*

Ullah, S., & Nasim, A. (2021, April). Do firm-level sustainability targets drive environmental innovation? Insights from BRICS economies. *Journal of Environmental Management, 294*, 112754.

UN. (2018). S7(d) Paris Agreement.

UNFCCC. (1998). *Kyoto protocol to the United Nations Framework Convention on Climate Change.*

United Nations Framework Convention on Climate Change. (2016). The Paris Agreement.

Di Vaio, A., Syriopoulos, T., Alvino, F., & Palladino, R. (2020). 'Integrated thinking and reporting' towards sustainable business models: A concise bibliometric analysis. *Meditari Accountancy Research.* https://doi.org/10.1108/MEDAR-12-2019-0641

Wolfgang, B., Arens, C., Hermwille, L., Kreibich, N., Ott, H. E., & Wang-helmreich, H. (2016). *Phoenix from the ashes—An analysis of the Paris Agreement to the United Nations Framework Convention on Climate Change* (pp. 1–53). Wuppertal Institute for Climate, Environment and Energy.

SOCIAL DETERMINANTS OF GREENHOUSE GAS EMISSIONS IN THE TOP 100 DEVELOPED AND DEVELOPING EMITTING COUNTRIES

Venancio Tauringana, Laura Achiro and Babajide Oyewo

ABSTRACT

This chapter investigates the social determinants (urbanisation, population, literacy and corruption) of greenhouse gas (GHG) emissions in the top 100 developed and developing emitting countries. The data were collected from central repositories for the different variables explored for the period 2012–2020 in a cross-country analysis. Fixed effects ordinary least squares (OLS) regression was used to analyse the data. The results for all top 100 countries and developing countries show that urbanisation and corruption are significantly positive and negative determinants of GHG emissions, respectively. In addition, literacy is a significant positive determinant of GHG emissions in developing countries but not in the top 100 and developed countries. Population is not significant in the top 100 developed and developing countries. The results for the control variables suggest that primary energy consumption is a positive significant determinant of GHG emissions in the top 100 developed and developing countries. However, gross domestic product (GDP) is not a significant determinant of GHG emissions. The findings have important policy implications.

Keywords: Social; determinants; greenhouse gas emissions; developed; developing; countries

Green House Gas Emissions Reporting and Management in Global Top Emitting Countries and Companies
Advances in Environmental Accounting & Management, Volume 11, 127–158
Copyright © 2023 Venancio Tauringana, Laura Achiro and Babajide Oyewo
Published under exclusive licence by Emerald Publishing Limited
ISSN: 1479-3598/doi:10.1108/S1479-359820230000011007

INTRODUCTION

Human-induced actions such as industrial processes, deforestation, land clearing for agriculture, degradation of soils and fossil fuel burning for electricity, transportation, heat and industry are all related to greenhouse gas (GHG) emissions (Coskuner et al., 2020; Moses et al., 2019). GHG is a leading causal factor for climate-related risks globally and contributes to climate change by trapping heat, leading to extreme weather such as droughts and cyclones. Food shortages, wildfires and respiratory diseases also result from extreme events (IPCC, 2014). These climatic implications of GHG emissions have raised public interest in its causes, and this increased interest has consequently triggered attempts to understand the factors that induce GHG emissions worldwide (Coskuner et al., 2020). As a result, several studies on the determinants of GHG emissions (e.g. Friedl & Getzner, 2003; Lau et al., 2014; Puertas & Marti, 2021) have been motivated by the need to identify measures capable of lowering GHG emissions as consensus on the determinants of GHG emissions could have important implications for sustainable development.

This chapter addresses the following gaps in research relating to the determinants of GHG emissions literature. First, most studies have focussed on environmental determinants and economic determinants, with less focus on social determinants of GHG (e.g. Akadiri, Bekun, & Sarkodie, 2019; Akadiri, Bekun, Taheri, et al., 2019; Akadiri, Lasisi, et al., 2019; Al-Mulali, Weng-Wai, et al., 2015; Alola et al., 2019; Baek, 2015; Balogh & Jámbor, 2017). For example, Al-Mulali, Weng-Wai, et al. (2015) investigated the determinants of GHG emissions by analysing empirical evidence from 93 developed and developing countries, focussing on economic determinants (proxied by GDP growth rate) and environmental determinants (in terms of ecological footprint). Akadiri, Bekun, & Sarkodie (2019) investigation of GHG emission in South Africa focussed on real GDP and kg oil equivalent per capita energy consumed as economic and environmental determinants of GHG emissions, respectively. Saboori et al. (2012) examined the long-run and causal relationship between economic growth and carbon dioxide (CO_2) emissions in Malaysia. The findings suggest the existence of a long-run relationship between per capita CO_2 emissions and real per capita gross domestic product (GDP). Overall, most of the studies have examined environmental and economic determinants of GHG emission, but few studies have covered the social determinants (e.g. Akadiri, Alola, et al., 2019; Allard et al., 2018; Cosmas et al., 2019). There is, therefore, a dearth of studies on how social factors determine GHG emissions.

Second, there is little appreciation that the determinants of GHG emissions may differ due to the country's development status. This suggestion is based on the observation that among the studies that have investigated the determinants of GHG emissions using data from both developed and developing countries, only a few have separately analysed the determinants of GHG emissions. For example, only a few studies separately analysed the determinants of GHG emissions according to income status, such as low-income, lower middle-income, upper-middle income and high-income countries (e.g. Al-Mulali, Weng-Wai, et al., 2015; Allard et al., 2018; Alola et al., 2019). However, several studies made no attempt to distinguish determinants of GHG emissions in developed and developing countries. Akadiri, Bekun, Taheri, et al. (2019), for example, investigated determinants of GHG emission from 16 developed and developing countries and only reported the pooled results. Similarly, Balogh and Jámbor (2017) did not distinguish between the determinants of GHG emissions in developed and developing countries. Given that the environmental Kuznets curve (EKC) suggests that environmental degradation initially rises with economic growth and then, at a certain point of economic growth, starts to decline (Allard et al., 2018; Hussein, 2005), the relationship between determinants of GHG emissions may not be the same for developing and developed countries.

Third, to develop sustainably, it has been suggested that the three dimensions of economic, environmental and social sustainability should be accorded equal priority (Moses et al., 2022; Saboori et al., 2012). As suggested above, current research has mostly concentrated on the relationship between the economic dimension (economic growth) and environmental degradation Al-Mulali, Weng-Wai, et al., 2015; Cosmas et al., 2019; Saboori & Sulaiman, 2013). However, very few studies have comprehensively investigated economic, environmental and social factors that determine GHG emissions (e.g. Akadiri, Alola, et al., 2019; Al-Mulali, Saboori, et al., 2015; Alola, 2019a; Amin et al., 2020). The discourse on determinants of GHG emission is, therefore, incomplete without an exposition on the social determinants of GHG emission. This stems from the argument that the formulation of policies to address the challenges of GHG emission should be robust enough to tackle the economic, environmental and social challenges. Policy formulation and implementations that focus on only economic and environmental challenges without addressing the social solutions may be counter-productive considering the interrelationship between the economic, environmental and social dimensions of sustainable development (Coskuner et al., 2020).

Fourth, most studies on the determinants of GHG emission have not covered the top emitting countries but have focused on either a country (e.g. Cosmas et al., 2019; Gill et al., 2018; Ivanovski & Churchill, 2020) or region/group of countries (e.g. Dogan & Seker, 2016; Gozgor, 2017; Lapinskienė et al., 2017). Very few studies have analysed empirical evidence from a minimum of 100 top emitting countries (e.g. Balogh & Jámbor, 2017), as most studies have examined fewer than 100 top emitting countries in their studies (e.g. Le Quéré et al., 2019; Tan et al., 2014). Meanwhile, it is important to investigate GHG emission in the top 100 emitting countries because of two key considerations – one, they account for about 95% of GHG emissions all over the world (Azam & Khan, 2016; Puertas & Marti, 2021), and two, such investigation can enhance generalisability of results on determinants of GHG emission.

To address these research gaps, the current study focusses on the investigation of the social determinants of GHG emission in the top 100 emitting countries in the world using international evidence that spans across a 9-year period (2012–2020) controlling for economic and environmental determinants (GDP and primary energy use). We use univariate analysis to determine the correlation between variables, and multivariate analysis to determine the relationships and the statistical significance between the total CO_2 (GHG) emissions and the determinants for emissions in the selected countries. The study utilises panel data; therefore, the multivariate analysis is conducted using the ordinary least squares regression model. Results show that urbanisation and corruption are significant positive and negative determinants of GHG emissions, respectively, for all top 100 countries and developing countries. Literacy is a significant positive determinant of GHG emissions in developing countries but not in the top 100 and developed countries. Population is not significant in the top 100 developed and developing countries. The results for the control variables suggest that primary energy consumption is a positive significant determinant of GHG emissions in the top 100 developed and developing countries. However, GDP is not a significant determinant of GHG emissions.

The study contributes to knowledge by providing an exposition on the social determinants of GHG emissions. This is against the backdrop that most studies have focussed on environmental determinants and economic determinants, with less focus on social determinants of GHG. Second, separately analysing the determinants of GHG emissions in developed and developing countries contributes to increasing our understanding of whether the way social factors affect GHG emissions differ in these countries. Third, the findings from this study could inform policy formulation on addressing the challenges of GHG emission from the social sustainability standpoint. This is because policies should be robust enough to tackle the economic, environmental and social challenges of GHG emissions. Finally, the analyses of data from top 100 GHG-emitting developed and developing countries in the world contributes to the existing literature by enhancing generalisability of the results, considering that the top 100 emitting countries account for about 95% of GHG emission worldwide.

The rest of the chapter proceeds as follows: Literature Review and Hypotheses Development, Methodology, Discussion of Findings, and Conclusion.

LITERATURE REVIEW AND HYPOTHESES DEVELOPMENT

Literature Review

Previous research on the determinants of GHG emissions is characterised by its focus on economic and environmental factors, with limited studies investigating social factors. This is surprising given that humans are mostly to blame for GHG emissions. For example, a study by Akadiri, Bekun, Taheri, et al. (2019) examined the causal and long-run relationship between carbon emissions, energy consumptions and economic growth in Iraq. The findings suggest a unidirectional causality relationship from fossil fuel to carbon emissions and from GDP to per capita to fossil fuel. Al-Mulali, Saboori, et al. (2015) also investigated how economic factors affect an increase in pollution in the context of Vietnam. The findings, among others, indicate that imports increase pollution, suggesting that

Vietnam's imported products are energy intensive. In another study focussing on environmental and economic variables as determinants of GHG emissions, Alola et al. (2019) examined the dynamic long-run nexus of CO_2 emissions with renewable energy, food production and the inflation rate in 16 coastline Mediterranean countries. The study reported a negative and significant relationship between CO_2 emissions and renewable energy consumption. The study also found a significant positive relationship between food production and CO_2 emissions. The relationship between CO_2 emissions and inflation was found to be significant and negative in the long run. Yildirim and Yildirim (2021) also examined how environmental (energy usage) and economic variables (real GDP, trade, financial development and construction sector activities) are related to CO_2 emissions in Turkey. The results suggest that an increase in construction sector activities, GDP and trade openness have a significant positive impact on CO_2 emissions, but financial development has no significant influence.

Liobikienė et al. (2016) examined how the implementation of Europe 2020 energy and climate policy contributed to changes in GHG emissions in the Baltic States and reported a 55% reduction in GHG emissions between 1990 and 2012. An Indian-based study by Tiwari et al. (2013) tested the dynamic relationship between coal consumption, economic growth, trade openness and CO_2 emissions and concluded that both coal consumption and trade openness contribute to CO_2 emissions. Shahbaz et al. (2013), in Romanian, examined the relationship between one economic variable (economic growth), one environmental variable (energy consumption) and CO_2 emissions. The results confirmed the long-run relationship between economic growth, energy consumption and energy pollutants, confirming the EKC in the short and long runs. In a study based in Austria, Friedl and Getzner (2003) found a cubic (i.e. N-shaped) relationship between gross domestic product and CO_2 emissions. However, in Singapore, Tan et al. (2014) found a significant rise in CO_2 emissions as GDP rises over the years, confirming a short-run trade-off between environmental degradation and economic growth. In one of the most comprehensive studies in terms of the number of countries covered, Balogh and Jámbor (2017) also investigated the relationship between environmental and economic factors with CO_2 emissions based on data from 168 countries over 24 years. The results confirmed the standard EKC hypothesis.

The limited number of studies that have included social factors include Akadiri, Alola, et al. (2019) who investigated the role of one social determinant (globalisation) in addition to electricity consumption and economic growth in CO_2 emissions in Turkey between 1970 and 2014. The study found that globalisation has a negative but non-significant relationship with carbon emissions. However, both electricity consumption and economic growth were found to cause carbon emissions. Ivanovski and Churchill (2020) who included urbanisation (a social determinant) in their study based on Australia (state and territory) concluded that urbanisation alongside income per capita, trade and industry are key determinants in GHG emission accumulation. However, they suggested that these determinants are dependent on the specific type of GHG. A Turkish study by Pata (2018) revealed that economic growth, financial development and urbanisation increased environmental degradation. However, total renewable energy consumption, hydropower consumption and alternative energy consumption had no effect on CO_2 emissions. In an investigation of economic and social determinants of carbon emissions in the Organization of Petroleum Exporting Countries (OPEC), Coskuner et al. (2020) report that urbanisation is responsible for a significant proportion of carbon emissions in the OPEC countries. Per-capita GDP, fossil fuel energy consumption and international trade were also found to be significant drivers of GHG emissions.

Another feature of existing research on the determinants of GHG emissions is its inclusion of data from either developed or developing countries. For example, among developed countries-based studies are Bekun et al. (2019) who found that CO_2 emissions are associated with economic growth, natural resources rent, renewable and non-renewable energy consumption. Le Quéré et al. (2019) in a study based on 18 developed countries reported that the displacement of fossil fuel by renewable energy and decrease in energy use explain decreasing CO_2 emissions. In a study of the OECD countries, Dogan and Seker (2016) found that financial development and trade openness decrease carbon emissions, but energy consumption increases carbon emissions. In three studies based on the United States, Alola (2019a) reports that migration and carbon emissions are positively related, but trade policy was only significant in the short run. Alola (2019b) reports that trade policy, monetary policy and migration index exert positive and significant impacts on carbon emissions in the long run. In the third study, Dogan and Turkekul (2016) showed that in the long run, energy consumption and urbanisation increase environmental degradation while financial development has no effect on it and trade leads to environmental improvements. Regarding developing countries-based studies, Zmami and Ben-Salha (2020) examined the relationship between CO_2, per capita GDP, energy consumption, urbanisation, international trade and foreign direct investments in Gulf Cooperation Council countries between 1980 and 2017 and found evidence consistent with the EKC hypothesis. The results by Wang et al. (2011) in China indicate that energy consumption and economic growth are the long-run causes of CO_2 emissions.

Of the studies that have included data from both developed and developing countries, a limited number of such studies have separately analysed the determinants of GHG emissions. For example, Onafowora and Owoye (2014) tested the EKC hypothesis using data from Brazil, China, Egypt, Japan, Mexico, Nigeria, South Korea and South Africa. The results show that the inverted U-shaped EKC hypothesis holds for Japan and South Korea. However, in the other six countries, the long-run relationship between economic growth and CO_2 emissions follows an N-shaped trajectory. Azam and Khan (2016) investigated the EKC hypothesis for four countries from low income, lower middle income, upper middle income and high-income countries, namely, Tanzania, Guatemala, China and the United States. Specifically, they examined the relationship between CO_2 emissions, income, income square, energy consumption, urbanisation growth rate and trade openness for the period 1975–2014. The results show support for EKC for low and lower middle-income countries. However, the study failed to find support for the validity of an EKC for upper middle income and high-income countries, implying that the determinants of CO_2 emissions may differ according to the country's income level or development.

Existing research can also be criticised in that it is not holistic because most research papers include factors drawn from only two of the three pillars of sustainable development (environmental and economic dimensions) and exclude the social (e.g. Gozgor, 2017; Lau et al., 2014). Examples of a limited number of studies that included determinants from all three pillars of sustainability include Amin et al. (2020) who examined urbanisation (a social determinant) alongside environmental variables (renewable energy consumption) and economic variable (economic growth) on transport CO_2 emissions for European countries. The findings suggest that urbanisation has a statistically insignificant positive impact on pollution, while increases in renewable energy consumption mitigate CO_2 emissions from transportation. Cosmas et al. (2019), in Nigeria, found population was not related to carbon emissions. However, GDP per capita caused a rise in carbon emissions. In addition, changes in energy consumption, GDP per capita and manufacturing were shown to be related to CO_2 emissions. Ozturk and Al-Mulali (2015), in Cambodia, found that GDP, urbanisation, energy consumption and trade openness increase CO_2 emissions while controlling corruption and governance can reduce emissions. Allard et al. (2018) investigated how renewable energy consumption, technological development, trade and institutional quality determine GHG emissions. Their findings suggest that institutional quality has a negative effect on carbon emissions for lower-middle income countries, thus concluding that improvement in institutional quality is most important for these countries (Table 1).

Determinants of GHG emissions research also tend to be single-country-based with exceptions such as Cho et al. (2014), Lapinskienė et al. (2017), Balogh and Jámbor (2017), Al-Mulali, Weng-Wai, et al. (2015), and Allard et al. (2018). For example, Akadiri, Alola, et al. (2019) based on Turkey found that in the long run, electricity consumption, economic growth and carbon emissions are linked. However, the study did not find evidence of a relationship between globalisation and carbon emissions. A Malaysian study by Gill et al. (2018) found an insignificant relationship between GHG emissions and GDP, and that renewable energy production has a negative effect on CO_2 emissions. Also, in Malaysia, Saboori and Sulaiman (2013) showed no support for U-shaped relationship (EKC) when aggregated energy consumption data were used, but there was support when data were disaggregated. A further study based on Malaysia by Lau et al. (2014) indicated that an inverted U-shaped relationship exists between economic growth and CO_2 after controlling for foreign direct investment and trade openness. In another single country-based study, Iwata et al. (2010) investigated the relationship between energy consumption and carbon emissions in France. Their estimation results provide evidence supporting the EKC hypothesis, and the estimated models are shown to be stable over the sample period. In a study of the relationship between carbon emissions and energy consumption, income and foreign trade based on China, Jalil and Mahmud (2009) reported that carbon emissions are mainly determined by income and energy consumption.

Table 1. Summary of Sustainability Pillars in GHG Studies.

No	Author	Period	Country/Countries	No of Countries	Developed/Developing/Income Class	Methodology	Sustainability Pillars Variables		
							Economic	Environmental	Social
1	Akadiri, Alola, et al. (2019)	1970–2014	Turkey	1	Developing	ARDL	GDP, tourism		Globalisation
2	Akadiri, Bekun, & Sarkodie (2019)	1973–2014	South Africa	1	Developing	Autoregressive Distributive Lag model and Toda–Yamamoto procedure for testing Granger causality	GDP as measure of real income	kg oil equivalent per capita energy consumed	
3	Akadiri, Bekun, Taheri, et al. (2019)	1972–2013	Iraq	1	Developing	Cointegration test and Toda–Yamamoto for a Granger causality test	GDP	Carbon emissions, energy consumption	
4	Akadiri, Lasisi, et al. (2019)	1995–2014	Various	16	Developed/Developing	Hausman test, random effects regression model, fixed effects estimation	GDP as measure of real income, international tourism	Carbon dioxide (CO_2) emissions	
5	Akadiri, Bekun, Taheri, et al. (2019)	1990–2016	France, Germany, UK	3	Developed	FMOLS, DOLS	Renewable energy consumption, GDP	Ecological footprint	
6	Akadiri, Lasisi, et al. (2019)	1970–2014	Turkey	1	Developing	ARDL	Economic growth	Electricity consumption	Globalisation
7	Allard et al. (2018)	1994–2012	Various	74	Developed/Developing	Panel quantile regression analysis	GDP, technological development, trade	Renewable energy consumption	Institutional quality
8	Al-Mulali, Saboori, et al. (2015)	1981–2011	Vietnam	1	Developing	ARDL	Imports, exports, capital, GDP	Fossil fuel energy consumption, renewable energy consumption	Labour force
9	Al-Mulali, Weng-Wai, et al. (2015)	1980–2008	Multiple countries	93	Developed/Developing	Fixed effects and the generalised method of moments	GDP growth	Ecological footprint	
10	Alola (2019a)	1990–2018	USA	1	Developed	ARDL	Trade, GDP	Renewable energy consumption,	Health impact, Migration

	Author	Period	Country	No.	Development	Method			
11	Alola (2019b)	1990–2018	USA	1	Developed	ARDL	Trade, monetary policy	Renewable energy consumption	Migration
12	Alola et al. (2019)	1995–2014	Coastline Mediterranean countries	16	Developed/ Developing	ARDL	Food production, inflation rate	Renewable energy consumption	Urbanisation
13	Amin et al. (2020)	1980–2014	European countries		Developed	Second-generation panel long-run estimates, non-causality test	Economic growth	Renewable energy consumption	Urbanisation
14	Azam and Khan (2016)	1975–2014	Tanzania, China, Guatemala, USA	4	Developed/ Developing	Johansen co-integration test, Pearson correlation	Trade openness, income, income square	Energy consumption	
15	Baek (2015)	1960–2010	Arctic countries		Developed	ARDL	GDP	Energy consumption	
16	Balogh and Jámbor (2017)		Various	168	Developed/ Developing	GMM	International tourism, trade openness, financial development, Per capita real GDP growth, FDI	Nuclear energy, renewable energy production, energy from coal, agricultural production	
17	Bekun et al. (2019)	1996–2014	EU	16	Developed	Panel Pooled Mean Group-Autoregressive Auto regressive distributive lag model (PMG-ARDL)	GDP	Renewable energy consumption, non-renewable energy consumption, natural resource rent	
18	Calbick and Gunton (2014)		OECD countries		Developed	Assessment	Energy prices, economic output per capita, Real GDP per capita, the square of GDP per capita, technological development, industrial structure	Environmental governance, climate, population pressure (measured as both growth and density), pollution abatement and control expenditures, environmental pricing	

Table 1. (*Continued*)

No	Author	Period	Country/ Countries	No of Countries	Developed/ Developing/ Income Class	Methodology	Economic	Environmental	Social
								Energy use	
19	Cho et al. (2014)	1971–2000	OECD countries	22	Developed	Panel unit root and panel cointegration tests, OLS			
20	Coskuner et al. (2020)	1995–2016	Organisation of Petroleum Exporting Countries (OPECs)	13	Developing	Kao, Pedroni and Johansen panel cointegration tests, OLS	Per capita GDP, international trade	Fossil fuel energy consumption	Urbanisation
21	Cosmas et al. (2019)	1981–2016	Nigeria	1	Developing	ARDL & NARDL	GDP per capita, financial development, oil price, trade openness, financial development and share of manufacturing in GDP	Energy consumption	Population
22	Dogan and Seker (2016)		OECD countries	16	Developed	Pesaran CD test, the Pesaran–Yamagata's homogeneity test, the CADF and the CIPS unit root tests, the LM bootstrap cointegration test, the DSUR estimator, and the Emirmahmutoglu–Kose Granger causality test	Energy consumption, financial development and trade openness, real income		

Sustainability Pillars Variables

No	Study	Period	Country	Type	N	Methodology	Independent variables	Dependent/other variables	
23	Dogan and Turkekul (2016)	1960–2010	USA	Developed	1	Pesaran CD test, the Pesaran–Yamagata's homogeneity test, the CADF and the CIPS unit root tests, the LM bootstrap cointegration test, the DSUR estimator, Emirmahmutoglu–Kose Granger causality test	GDP, real output (GDP), the square of real output (GDP2), trade openness, financial development	Energy consumption, urbanisation	
24	Friedl and Getzner (2003)	1960–1999	Austria	Developed	1	Dickey–Fuller test (ADF test), Chow breakpoint test, OLS	GDP, import share, share of tertiary service sector of total GDP	Energy consumption	
25	Gill et al. (2018)	1970–2011	Malaysia	Developing	1	Autoregressive distributed lag (ARDL), Bounds test (to test the presence of long-run equilibrium relation among the time series variables)	GDP	CO_2 emission	
26	Gozgor (2017)	1960–2013	OECD countries	Developed	35	Pesaran CD test, second generation Panel Unit Root (PUR) tests, panel unit root test (CIPS) of Pesaran, PMG estimations of Pesaran	Trade openness, per capita income		
27	Ivanovski and Churchill (2020)	1990–2017	Australia	Developed	1	Club convergence algorithm (log-t-test)	State income per capita, international trade		
28	Iwata et al. (2010)	1960–2003	France	Developed	1	Autoregressive distributed lag (ARDL) approach	Electricity production from nuclear energy	Urbanisation	

Table 1. (*Continued*)

No	Author	Period	Country/ Countries	No of Countries	Developed/ Developing/ Income Class	Methodology	Sustainability Pillars Variables		
							Economic	Environmental	Social
29	Jalil and Mahmud (2009)	1975–2005	China	1	Developed	ARDL	Per capita real income, square of per capita income, trade openness	Commercial energy use	
30	Kohler (2013)	1960–2009	South Africa	1	Developing	ARDL, Johansen cointegration, VECM Granger causality	Foreign trade, Per capita real income, square of per capita real income	Per capita energy use	
31	Lapinskienė et al. (2017)	1995–2014	EU countries	22	Developed	Panel data analysis – fixed effects	GDP, R&D, energy taxes	Energy consumption	
32	Lau et al. (2014)	1970–2008	Malaysia	1	Developing	ARDL, Granger causality	Foreign direct investment, trade openness, GDP, GDP2		
33	Le Quéré et al. (2019)	2005–2015	Various	13	Developed			Energy use, fossil share, fossil utilisation and fossil CO_2 intensity.	
34	Liobikienė et al. (2016)	1990–2012	Baltic states		Developing	Divisia IDA method	GDP	Final energy consumption from renewable resources, inverse coefficient of share of renewable resources, energy consumption and decarbonisation index, intensity of renewable resources, energy efficiency	

#	Author (year)	Period	Countries	No.	Developed/Developing	Methodology	Variables	Variables	Variables
35	Onafowora and Owoye (2014)	1970–2008	Brazil, China, Egypt, Japan, Mexico, Nigeria, South Korea, and South Africa	8	Developed/Developing	ARDL, VECM Granger causality	GDP, trade openness	Energy consumption	Population density
36	Ozcan (2013)	1990–2008	Middle East countries	12	Developing	Panel data model, Pedroni cointegration, FMOLS estimator, Granger causality	Real GDP per capita, GDP2	Energy consumption	
37	Ozturk and Al-Mulali (2015)	1996–2012	Cambodia	1	Developing	GMM, 2SLS	GDP, trade openness	Energy consumption	Urbanisation, corruption and governance
38	Pao and Tsai (2011)	1980–2007	Brazil	1	Developing	Error Correction Model (ECM), Unit root tests (LLC, Breitung, IPS, ADF and PP tests), Johansen Fisher, Kao and Pedroni methods, Granger causality, panel causality tests	FDI net inflows, GDP	Energy consumption	
39	Pata (2018)	1974–2014	Turkey	1	Developing	ARDL bounds testing approach, Gregory-Hansen, and Hatemi-J cointegration tests	Economic growth, financial development	Total renewable energy consumption, hydropower consumption, alternative energy consumption	Urbanisation
40	Puertas and Marti (2021)	2011–2018	OECD countries		Developed	DEA-bootstrap, Malmquist Index (MI), GMM		Environmental policies, Eco-innovation, CO_2 productivity, energy productivity, non-energy productivity, disposal, recovery, material footprint	

Table 1. (*Continued*)

No	Author	Period	Country/Countries	No of Countries	Developed/Developing/Income Class	Methodology	Economic	Environmental	Social
								Sustainability Pillars Variables	
41	Saboori and Sulaiman (2013)	1971–2009	ASEAN countries		Developing	ARDL, Johansen–Juselius maximum likelihood approach, VECM Granger causality	Per capita real income	Energy consumption	
42	Saboori et al. (2012)	1980–2009	Malaysia	1	Developing	ARDL, Johansen cointegration, VECM Granger causality	GDP		
43	Shahbaz et al. (2013)	1980–2010	Romania	1	Developing	ARDL	GDP2	Energy consumption	
44	Shahbaz et al. (2012)	1971–2009	Pakistan	1	Developing	ARDL, Gregory–Hansen cointegration, VECM Granger causality	GDP, GDP2, trade openness	Energy consumption	
45	Tan et al. (2014)	1975–2011	Singapore		Developing	Unit root tests (ADF methodology), Johansen–Juselius cointegration test, Granger causality	GDP	Energy consumption	
46	Tang and Tan (2015)	1976–2009	Vietnam	1	Developing	Johansen cointegration, VECM Granger causality	GDP, GDP2, FDI (foreign direct investment)	Energy consumption	
47	Tiwari et al. (2013)	1966–2011	India	1	Developing	ARDL, Johansen cointegration, VECM Granger causality	GDP, GDP2, trade openness	Coal consumption	
48	Wang et al. (2011)	1995–2007	China	1	Developing	Pedroni cointegration test, VECM Granger causality	GDP, GDP2	Energy consumption	

No.	Author	Period	Country			Method		
49	Yildirim and Yildirim (2021)		Turkey	1	Developing	Dynamic ordinary least square (DOLS), the fully modified ordinary least square (FMOLS), and the canonical cointegrating regression (CCR) methods	GDP, trade, financial development, construction sector	Energy usage
50	Zmami and Ben-Salha (2020)	1980–2017	Gulf Cooperation Council countries	6	Developing	Stochastic Impacts by Regression on Population, Affluence, and Technology (STIRPAT) model, PMG-ARDL approach	Foreign direct investments, per capita GDP, international trade	Energy consumption
51	Zhu et al. (2021)	2004–2015	China	1	Developed	Panel fixed effect regression; panel quantile regression	GDP	Higher education Development. Higher education scale Higher education quality	Urbanisation

Hypotheses Development

Human activities have been linked to GHG emission, with increasing social activities contributing to the surge in GHG emission. Studies have, thus, examined how various social indicators such as population growth, literacy level, labour force, corruption index, urbanisation, migration, international tourism, institutional quality and globalisation, among others, affect GHG emission (Akadiri, Alola, et al., 2019; Akadiri, Bekun, & Sarkodie, 2019; Akadiri, Lasisi, et al., 2019; Alola, 2019b; Cosmas et al., 2019; Ozturk & Al-Mulali, 2015; Rosa & Dietz, 2012). These are discussed as follows:

Urbanisation

Arguments can be made for a positive and negative relationship between urbanisation and GHG emissions. Regarding the positive association arguments, it has been suggested that increasing human activities in terms of migration from rural areas to urban locations may increase the level of GHG emissions (Rosa & Dietz, 2012). One reason for this is that urbanisation has been linked to deforestation (as housing units and facilities must be created to accommodate the increasing population in urban locations), habitat loss, decreased biodiversity and environmental pollution (Zmami & Ben-Salha, 2020). Population increases in urban centres, thus, contribute to the emission rate of GHGs (Puertas & Marti, 2021). However, there may be countervailing effects which may lead to a negative association with suburban growth increasing emissions and core urban growth reducing emissions (Rosa & Dietz, 2012). For example, Glaeser and Kahn (2010) suggest that cities have significantly lower emissions than suburban areas. Despite the conflicting arguments about the nature of the relationship, empirical evidence so far points to a positive relationship. For example, Amin et al. (2020) found that increasing urbanisation has exacerbated the challenges of managing GHG emission. Azam and Khan (2016) equally concur. Similarly, Coskuner et al. (2020), Ivanovski and Churchill's (2020), and Pata's (2018) found a positive association between urbanisation and GHG emission. Owing to the conflicting arguments on the nature of the relationship, this discussion leads to a non-directional hypothesis that:

   H1a. Urbanisation has a significant association with GHG emissions in all countries.

   H1b. Urbanisation has a significant association with GHG emissions in developed countries.

   H1c. Urbanisation has a significant association with GHG emissions in developing countries.

Population

The number of people living in a particular location may affect the level of GHG emission, with densely populated areas recording high emission rate and sparsely populated locations witnessing low GHG emission rate because of a diminished level of human activities (Pata, 2018; Rosa & Dietz, 2012). However, this is not always the case. For example, Rosa and Dietz (2012) argue that many analysts uncritically assume that the changes in the scale of the human population produce proportional changes in stress on the environment by dividing population size into aggregate measures of stress such as GHG to yield per capita stress. However, it is possible that there are economies or diseconomies of scale associated with larger populations that may make more effective use of mass transit systems and other infrastructure, reducing per capita impact at a higher level of population. On the other hand, a larger population may produce 'frictional' problems such as traffic congestion, resulting in increased impacts such as carbon emissions (Rosa & Dietz, 2012). Existing studies have mostly produced results consistent with a positive association. For example, Cosmas et al. (2019), in Nigeria, conclude that population growth has contributed to GHG emissions. Onafowora and Owoye (2014) report that the increase in population contributes to GHG emissions. Alola (2019b) concludes from the study of United States that population growth through a high migration rate has contributed to GHG emissions. Despite the finding of positive association, our hypothesis is non-directional given the counterarguments. Therefore, we hypothesise that:

H2a. Population growth has a significant association with GHG emissions in all countries.

H2b. Population growth has a significant association with GHG emissions in developed countries.

H2c. Population growth has a significant association with GHG emission in developing countries.

Literacy

Literacy level in terms of education has been noted to facilitate reduction of GHG emission (Al-Mulali, Saboori, et al., 2015; Allard et al., 2018; Zhu et al., 2021). This is because being knowledgeable about the dangers of GHG emissions to the environment and society may influence attitudes towards taking measures to minimise carbon emissions. Higher education institutions are now integrating knowledge of environmental pollution and climate change in their curriculums as strategy to raise awareness on the dangers of GHG emissions (Ramos et al., 2015). Literacy on environmental pollution and climate change also promotes production and consumption habits that minimise negative externalities in form of GHG emissions. From the analysis of empirical evidence, most studies confirmed the reasoning for a positive relationship. For example, Al-Mulali, Saboori, et al. (2015) conclude that literacy level among labour force plays a critical role in minimising GHG emission. Allard et al. (2018) conclude that institutional quality (which is crucial for driving literacy level on GHG emission among the people of a nation) is critical in controlling and minimising negative production externalities in relation to GHG emission. Zhu et al.'s (2021) study in China also provide evidence that higher education development facilitate carbon emissions reduction. This informs the next hypothesis that:

H3a. High literacy level is negatively associated with GHG emission in all countries.

H3b. High literacy level is negatively associated with GHG emission in developed countries.

H3c. High literacy level is negatively associated with GHG emission in developing countries.

Corruption

Environmental pollution and climate change control measures may be bypassed by engaging in corrupt practices that hide the negative production externalities generated by organisations in the eyes of the public (Lisciandra & Migliardo, 2017). Thus, high corruption level may be positively associated with high GHG emissions. However, according to Akhbari and Nejati (2019), high corruption levels, through flawing the performance of the economic system, maim the development process in such a way that they delay the process of achieving proper levels of development and consequently lower levels of CO_2 emissions and higher environmental quality. The slowdown in investment and production may, therefore, result in lower GHG emissions in highly corrupt countries. This will result in a negative association between corruption and GHG emissions. However, empirical studies so far mainly report a positive association. For example, Ozturk and Al-Mulali's (2015) investigation in Cambodia conclude that corruption contributes to GHG emission. Similarly, Lisciandra and Migliardo (2017) found evidence that corruption deteriorates the overall environmental quality. Cole (2007) also reported that corruption is positively associated with the level of environmental pollution. Leitão (2010) observed that the degree of corruption in a country affects level of environmental pollution, with high level of corruption contributing to the level of GHG emission. Given these counterarguments, we, thus, hypothesise that:

H4a. Corruption level is significantly associated with GHG emission in all countries.

H4b. Corruption level is significantly associated with GHG emission in developed countries.

H4c. Corruption level is significantly associated with GHG emission in developing countries.

Control Variables

The study included country-level factors as control variables in the analysis of determinants of CO_2 emissions. This study includes GDP, an economic indicator (Andrés & Padilla, 2018; De Alegría et al., 2016; Liobikienė & Butkus, 2017), and an environmental variable relating to primary energy consumption (Azam & Khan, 2016; Cho et al., 2014; Cosmas et al., 2019). The level of economic development in terms of GDP may affect GHG emission because economic prosperity of a country may affect the availability of resources available to combat environmental pollution (Al-Mulali, Saboori, et al., 2015; Al-Mulali, Weng-Wai, et al., 2015). Furthermore, since economic sustainability is an important indicator of the level of commercial activities in a country, such increased economic activities may contribute to the level of GHG emission (Cosmas et al., 2019). It is, thus, important to control for the effect of economic indicators to see a purer effect of social determinants on GHG emission.

Similarly, environmental activities also affect GHG emission, as a growing number of studies have linked environmental pollution to various environmental factors (Dogan & Turkekul, 2016; Gill et al., 2018).

METHODOLOGY

Data and Sample

We use a balanced panel dataset comprising of the top 100 emitting countries across the world according to data from *Our World in Data*. The data cover nine years from 2012 to 2020 to investigate the determinants of GHG emissions in the selected countries as shown in Appendix 1. These countries have the highest GHG emissions as of 2020 and represent different regions, income levels, legal systems and levels of development. The countries were classified into developed and developing countries using the World Bank income classification. The World Bank classifies economies for analytical purposes into four income groups of: low, lower-middle, upper-middle and high income (The World Bank, 2021). Whilst the low and lower-middle groups are classified as developing countries, countries in the upper-middle, and high income strata are classified as developed countries (Gbadamosi, 2022). This basis was used to split countries into developed and developing countries as provided in Appendix 1. We use country-level data on social determinants such as urbanisation, population, literacy, corruption and economic indicators such as GDP and primary energy use. The data for the economic and social indicators of urbanisation, population and literacy were retrieved from the *World Bank Open Data*. We also use data on the Corruption Perceptions Index from the *Transparency International* database.

Empirical Model and Variables

To explore the determinants of GHG emissions in the top 100 emitting countries worldwide, we use univariate analysis to determine the correlation between variables, and multivariate analysis to determine the relationships and the statistical significance between the total CO_2 emissions and the determinants for emissions in the selected countries. The study utilises panel data; therefore, the multivariate analysis is conducted using the ordinary least squares regression model. Results of the Hausman test confirm that the fixed effects panel data model is appropriate. The panel data model is used because they (i) are able to attain more accurate inferences as a result of the larger number of observations, increased degrees of efficiency and enhanced efficacy of the model, (ii) can control omitted variables that are either missing or unobservable as well as capture unobserved heterogeneity among the individual units or overtime and (iii) are able to derive more accurate predictions for individual outcomes. The panel data model is proposed as below.

$$CO_2 = B_0 + BX_{i,t} + BZ_{i,t} + e_{i,t}$$
$$i = 1, \ldots, N, \qquad t = 1 \ldots, t$$

where CO_2 represents the level of CO_2 emissions of country i, at time t. X represents the explanatory variables of the social indicators examined such as urbanisation, population, literacy and corruption. Z is a vector for the country-level control variables of GDP and primary energy consumption. Based on results of the Hausman test, we adopt fixed effect estimations to establish the relationships between the variables in the panel data model. To allow for correlation within groups in the panel dataset, and to lessen the requirement for independent observations, we apply the robust standard errors in making deductions from the results. According to Pachauri and Meyer (2014) and Ritchie et al. (2020), the primary drivers of global climate change are the fossil fuel CO_2 emissions, and the responsibility of reducing emissions is shared between regions, countries and individuals. Basing on this, total CO_2 emissions for each of the top 100 emitting countries are, therefore, our dependent variable. We use several country-level determinants of CO_2 emissions in the top emitting countries as the independent variables in this chapter. The following determinants have been explored in previous studies; urbanisation (Amin et al., 2020; Azam & Khan, 2016), population (Cosmas et al., 2019; Onafowora & Owoye, 2014), literacy and corruption (Ozturk & Al-Mulali, 2015) as the social drivers of CO_2 emissions in a cross-country analysis. An environmental determinant (primary energy use) and economic determinant (GDP) were, therefore, included as control variables. In sum, taking out the impact of economic and environmental determinants of GHG emission by including them as control variables enhance the internal validity of the study by limiting their influence as confounding variables. A summary of variable measurement is presented in Table 2.

RESULTS AND DISCUSSION

Descriptive Statistics

The summary of descriptive statistics is reported in Table 3. The average population stands at 68 million people with urbanisation rate at 66% of the total population. The literacy rate is at 90% of the adult people above 15 years in the top 100 countries (Table 3, Panel A). For the corruption perception index, the average rate is 45 out of a scale of 100, with 100 as very clean and 0 for highly corrupt. The reported average GDP of the top 100 emitting countries is USD 1 trillion (Table 3, Panel A).

For the developed countries, the average population stands at 30 million people with urbanisation rate at 80% of the total population (Table 3, Panel B). The literacy rate is at 96% of the adult people above 15 years in the top 100 countries. For the corruption perception index, the average rate is 68 out of a scale of 100. The reported average GDP of the top 100 emitting countries is USD 1.2 trillion (Table 3, Panel B).

Table 2. Measurement of Variables.

S/N	Variable	Measurement	Literature Source
1	GHG emission	Total CO_2 emissions	Pachauri and Meyer (2014), Ritchie et al. (2020)
	Independent variables		
2	Urbanisation	Urbanisation rate	Amin et al. (2020), Azam and Khan (2016)
3	Population	Number of people	Cosmas et al. (2019), Onafowora and Owoye (2014)
4	Literacy	Number of educated adults above 15 years	Ozturk and Al-Mulali (2015), Zhu et al. (2021)
5	Corruption	Corruption perception index, with negative polarity of 100 (low corruption level) and 0 (high corruption level	Ozturk and Al-Mulali (2015)
	Control variables		
6	Economic Development	GDP	De Alegría et al. (2016), Liobikienė and Butkus (2017)
7	Primary energy consumption	Primary energy consumption rate	Azam and Khan (2016), Cho et al. (2014)

For the developing countries, the reported average GDP stands at USD 8.82 Billion. The corruption perception index for the developing countries stands at 33 out of 100 (Table 3, Panel C). Out of the overall population of 97 million people, 88% of adults above 15 years of age are reported as literate with an urbanisation rate of 56% (Table 3, Panel C).

Multivariate Results

The multivariate results are reported in Table 4, Panels A, B and C, respectively, representing the 3 models, where the first model represents all top 100 emitting countries in the world, while the second model presents results for the developed countries and the third model represents the results for the developing countries. In Table 4, Panel A, urbanisation has a significant negative relationship with CO_2 emissions ($p = 0.075$) in the top 100 countries and in developing countries ($p = 0.002$). Therefore, *H1a* and *H1b* are accepted. Urbanisation has no significant impact on GHG emissions in developed countries, which leads to the rejection of hypothesis *H1c*. The results in Table 4 also show that population is not significantly associated with GHG emissions in the top 100 developed and developing countries which means that *H2a*, *H2b* and *H2c* are rejected. Literacy has a marginal significant positive impact ($p = 0.104$) in developing countries but not the top 100 and developed. Hypothesis *H3a* is, therefore, accepted, while hypotheses *H3b* and *H3c* are rejected. Additionally, corruption has a significant positive relationship with GHG emissions ($p = 0.008$), implying that a low corruption level is associated with a high GHG emission rate in the top 100 countries. *H4a* is, therefore, accepted. Corruption is also significantly associated with GHG emissions in developing countries ($p = 0.024$), and *H4b* is accepted. However, corruption is not significant in developed countries leading to the rejection of *H4c*. Finally, the results in Table 4, Panel A, B and C also show that primary energy consumption has a significant positive relationship with the level of CO_2 emissions ($p = 0.000$), but GDP is not significant.

Discussion

The results for the association between urbanisation and GHG emissions show that for all countries and developed countries, there is a significant negative relationship. However, the results for developed countries show no significant relationship. The high significance level for developing countries, low significance level for all countries and non-significant result for developed countries suggest that the results of the association between urbanisation and GHG are being driven by developing countries. The non-significant result for developed countries may be attributable to measures taken by developed countries to minimise carbon

Table 3. Descriptive Statistics of Variables.

	Obs	Mean	Median	Std. Dev.	Skewness	Kurtosis
Panel A: All 100 countries						
Urbanisation	774	66.14707	69.4525	21.09833	−0.5708071	2.476233
Population	900	68.39986	20.48573	194.3891	6.050777	40.55552
Literacy	193	90.22694	94.46057	11.37831	−1.683861	4.918143
Corruption	873	45.99084	40	20.70018	0.5973358	2.325867
GDP	693	1,043,068	326,100.3	2,506,657	5.208643	32.18546
Primary energy consumption	873	1569.189	384.81	4611.98	6.14594	43.45957
Panel B: Developed countries						
Urbanisation	315	80.25903	82.5	12.53121	−0.5129896	2.527308
Population	333	30.34564	9.8904	55.76447	4.055393	20.91959
Literacy	46	96.26118	96.50278	2.262241	−0.9676543	3.577534
Corruption	324	68.03704	70	14.90398	−0.3032371	1.950693
GDP	259	1,290,883	396,507.5	2,802,412	4.762589	26.61897
Primary energy consumption	332	1759.115	523.1505	4197.293	5.112553	29.38496
Panel C: Developing countries						
Urbanisation	459	56.46239	56.403	20.31426	−0.2318815	2.067291
Population	486	97.37594	30.86791	256.3248	4.541623	22.73609
Literacy	146	88.26065	93.81009	12.40061	−1.295638	3.613934
Corruption	486	33.05144	34	9.048975	−0.3097164	2.676564
GDP	371	882,463.4	175,524.7	2,451,545	5.366339	33.51715
Primary energy consumption	462	1367.427	215.9825	5141.319	6.424188	44.56889

Table 4. Regression Results for Top 100 Emitting Countries.

Variable	Coefficient	Std. Error	t-Statistic	Prob.
Panel A – All countries				
Urbanisation	−5.211842	2.872002	−1.81	**0.075**
Population	−21.30055	36.67904	−0.58	0.564
Literacy	0.7631084	0.59551	1.28	0.206
Corruption	1.80981	0.6567991	2.76	**0.008**
GDP	38.39988	26.22589	1.46	0.149
Primary energy consumption	0.214518	0.0371602	5.77	**0.000**
R-squared	**0.6265**			
Fixed effects	**Yes**			
Observations	**162**			
Panel B – Developed countries				
Urbanisation	0.490579	4.403988	0.11	0.913
Population	−16.22506	35.94203	−0.45	0.660
Literacy	3.593312	6.32765	0.57	0.581
Corruption	−0.0835961	0.3893715	−0.21	0.834
GDP	−196.8805	121.4613	−1.62	0.131
Primary energy consumption	0.2522702	0.0855927	2.95	**0.012**
R-squared	**0.5973**			
Fixed effects	**Yes**			
Observations	**39**			
Panel C – Developing countries				
Urbanisation	−9.556319	2.911187	−3.28	**0.002**
Population	34.32511	57.42242	0.60	0.553
Literacy	0.8161527	0.4905248	1.66	**0.104**
Corruption	1.881301	0.8002019	2.35	**0.024**
GDP	53.07458	35.26405	1.51	0.140
Primary energy consumption	0.255624	0.0230879	11.07	**0.000**
R-squared	**0.7428**			
Fixed effects	**Yes**			
Observations	**123**			

emissions in cosmopolitan areas (Dogan & Turkekul, 2016; Gozgor, 2017). Results for all countries and developing countries are consistent with the argument that growth in suburban areas may lead to a decrease in GHG emissions in urban areas (Rosa & Dietz, 2012). The results are also consistent with the findings by Glaeser and Kahn (2010) in the United States who found that urban had significantly lower emissions than suburban areas. However, the results are inconsistent with the argument by Rosa and Dietz (2012) for a positive relationship based on the reasoning that the movement of people from rural areas to urban areas may increase the level of GHG emissions. The logic for an increase in GHG as urbanisation increases is deforestation because of upsurge of building activities to house more people (Zmami & Ben-Salha, 2020). Our results are also contrary to the findings of several studies such as Pata (2018), Ivanovski and Churchill (2020), and Coskuner et al. (2020) who all reported a significant positive relationship between urbanisation and GHG emissions.

With respect to the impact of corruption on GHG emissions, the results show that there is a significant positive relationship. However, this implies a negative relationship between GHG emissions and corruption. This is because corruption is measured by the corruption perception index (CPI), which gives greater values to those countries that are the least corrupt. Our result means that less corrupt countries are those that pollute the most. The finding may be explained by the argument that corruption decreases the performance of the economic system and slows down the development process in such a way that they delay the process of achieving proper levels of development and, consequently, lower levels of CO_2 emissions (Akhbari & Nejati, 2019). As suggested before, the slowdown in investment and, therefore, production in such countries may, therefore, result in lower GHG emissions in highly corrupt countries. This result contradicts the argument for a positive relationship between corruption and GHG emissions that environmental pollution and climate change control measures may be bypassed by engaging in corrupt practices (Lisciandra & Migliardo, 2017). Empirically, our findings are inconsistent with some previous studies that high corruption level is positively associated with GHG emission. For example, Lisciandra and Migliardo's (2017), Ozturk and Al-Mulali's (2015), and Cole (2007) who reported that corruption is positively associated with the level of environmental pollution.

Literacy level has a significant impact only in developing countries and not in the top 100 and the developed countries. The non-significance for the developed countries is hardly surprising given that the literacy rates in these countries are very high, and there is little difference among these countries. A possible reason for the significant relationship in developing countries may be because the messages about the dangers of GHG emissions to the environment and society is getting through, given that many developing countries have been affected by the effects of climate change recently. Also, higher education institutions are now integrating knowledge of environmental pollution and climate change in their curriculums as strategy to raise awareness of the dangers of GHG emissions (Ramos et al., 2015). The factors may influence attitudes towards taking measures to minimise carbon emissions in developing countries. The findings in developing countries are consistent with Zhu et al. (2021), who found that higher education development facilitates carbon emissions reduction. Further, our findings are also consistent with Sarwar et al. (2021) who report that the relationship between education and carbon emissions is significant and positive in the long run.

The results of the relationship between population and GHG emissions are not significant for all countries, developed and developing countries. This finding means that neither argument for a positive or negative relationship is supported. For example, we suggested based on prior studies that densely populated areas may record high GHG emissions compared to low density areas because of a diminished level of human activities (Akadiri, Lasisi, et al., 2019; Pata, 2018).

Based on Rosa and Dietz (2012), we also suggested that the relationship could be negative because of economies of scale associated with larger populations that may make more effective use of mass transit systems and other infrastructure, thus reducing per capita impact at a higher level of population. Our findings of no significant relationship contradict studies which reported positive relationships. These studies include Onafowora and Owoye (2014), Alola (2019b), and Cosmas et al. (2019) which conclude that population has a positive impact on GHG emissions.

SUMMARY AND CONCLUSION

This study investigated the social determinants (urbanisation, population, literacy and corruption) of GHG emissions in the top 100 emitting countries in the world, which were divided into developing and developed countries. The data were collected from central repositories for the different variables explored for the period 2012–2020 in a cross-country analysis. Fixed effects ordinary least squares regression was used to analyse the data. The findings indicate that urbanisation is a significant negative determinant of GHG emissions in all top 100 emitting countries and developing countries but not in developed countries. Furthermore, the determinants of GHG emissions vary for the different income levels of countries. Population was found not to have any significant influence on GHG emissions in the top 100 developed and developing countries. Regarding literacy, our results show that this only has a marginally significant positive influence in developing countries. Our results also show that corruption has a significant influence in the top 100 and developing countries but not in developed countries. Finally, for our control variables, we found that primary energy consumption has a significant positive impact on GHG emissions when all top 100 emitting countries are analysed and also sub-samples of developed and developing countries. Population was not found to be significant with any of the samples of countries analysed.

Our study results should be considered in light of a number of limitations. First, our period of analysis of nine years is very short compared to other studies. However, the period of analysis was dictated by the availability of data for all social determinants of interest. The second limitation is that our findings may also have been affected by the outbreak of the pandemic in 2020 which necessitated countries around the world to close most businesses. This means that for that particular year, the GHG emissions may not be determined by the social determinants that we have chosen to focus on in our study. Finally, although we included economic, social and environmental determinants, the number of determinants is low. This means that there are other potential determinants that we did not include, which could possibly influence the amount of GHG emissions. However, the number of determinants is comparable to previous studies.

Despite the limitation, our study contributes to existing knowledge by providing new evidence on how social factors influence GHG emissions. This is against the backdrop that most studies have focussed on environmental determinants (using the EKC) and economic determinants, with less focus on the social determinants of GHG. Second, by dividing our sample of the top 100 emitting countries into developed and developing and separately analysing how our social factors impact GHG emissions, we contribute to evidence on whether the determinants of GHG emissions differ in developed and developing countries. Such knowledge is important for formulating policies to reduce GHG emissions. Third, the findings from this study could also inform policy formulation on addressing the challenges of GHG emission from the social sustainability standpoint. This is because policies should be robust enough to tackle the economic, environmental and social challenges of GHG emissions. Policy formulation and implementations that focus on only economic and environmental challenges without addressing the social solutions may be counter-productive considering the interrelationship between the economic, environmental and social dimensions of sustainable development. Finally, the study analysed evidence from the top 100 emitting countries in the world using international evidence, thus enhancing the generalisability of the results, considering that the top 100 emitting countries account for about 95% of GHG emissions all over the world.

REFERENCES

Akadiri, S. S., Alola, A. A., & Akadiri, A. C. (2019). The role of globalization, real income, tourism in environmental sustainability target. Evidence from Turkey. *Science of the Total Environment, 687*, 423–432.

Akadiri, S., Bekun, F. V., & Sarkodie, S. A. (2019). Contemporaneous interaction between energy consumption, economic growth, and environmental sustainability in South Africa: What drives what? *Science of the Total Environment, 686*, 468–475.

Akadiri, S. S., Bekun, F. V., Taheri, E., & Akadiri, A. C. (2019). Carbon emissions, energy consumption and economic growth: Causality evidence. *International Journal of Energy Technology and Policy, 15*(2–3), 320–336.

Akadiri, S. S., Lasisi, T. T., Uzuner, G., & Akadiri, A. C. (2019). Examining the impact of globalization in the environmental Kuznets curve hypothesis: The case of tourist destination states. *Environmental Science and Pollution Research, 26*(12), 12605–12615.

Akhbari, R., & Nejati, M. (2019). The effect of corruption on carbon emissions in developed and developing countries: Empirical investigation of a claim. *Heliyon, 5*(9), e02516.

Al-Mulali, U., Saboori, B., & Ozturk, I. (2015). Investigating the environmental Kuznets curve hypothesis in Vietnam. *Energy Policy, 76*, 123–131.

Al-Mulali, U., Weng-Wai, C., Sheau-Ting, L., & Mohammed, A. H. (2015). Investigating the environmental Kuznets curve (EKC) hypothesis by utilizing the ecological footprint as an indicator of environmental degradation. *Ecological Indicators, 48*, 315–323.

Allard, A., Takman, J., Uddin, G. S., & Ahmed, A. (2018). The N-shaped environmental Kuznets curve: An empirical evaluation using a panel quantile regression approach. *Environmental Science and Pollution Research, 25*(6), 5848–5861.

Alola, A. A. (2019a). Carbon emissions and the trilemma of trade policy, migration policy and health care in the US. *Carbon Management, 10*(2), 209–218.

Alola, A. A. (2019b). The trilemma of trade, monetary and immigration policies in the United States: Accounting for environmental sustainability. *Science of the Total Environment, 658*, 260–267.

Alola, A. A., Yalçiner, K., & Alola, U. V. (2019). Renewables, food (in) security, and inflation regimes in the coastline mediterranean countries (CMCs): The environmental pros and cons. *Environmental Science and Pollution Research, 26*(33), 34448–34458.

Amin, A., Altinoz, B., & Dogan, E. (2020). Analyzing the determinants of carbon emissions from transportation in European countries: The role of renewable energy and urbanisation. *Clean Technologies and Environmental Policy, 22*(8), 1725–1734.

Andrés, L., & Padilla, E. (2018). Driving factors of GHG emissions in the EU transport activity. *Transport Policy, 61*, 60–74.

Azam, M., & Khan, A. Q. (2016). Testing the environmental Kuznets curve hypothesis: A comparative empirical study for low, lower middle, upper middle- and high-income countries. *Renewable and Sustainable Energy Reviews, 63*, 556–567.

Baek, J. (2015). Environmental Kuznets curve for CO2 emissions: The case of Arctic countries. *Energy Economics, 50*, 13–17.

Balogh, J. M., & Jámbor, A. (2017). Determinants of CO_2 emission: A global evidence. *International Journal of Energy Economics and Policy, 7*(5), 217–226.

Bekun, F. V., Alola, A. A., & Sarkodie, S. A. (2019). Toward a sustainable environment: Nexus between CO2 emissions, resource rent, renewable and nonrenewable energy in 16-EU countries. *Science of the Total Environment, 657*, 1023–1029.

Calbick, K. S., & Gunton, T. (2014). Differences among OECD countries' GHG emissions: Causes and policy implications. *Energy Policy, 67*, 895–902.

Cho, C. H., Chu, Y. P., & Yang, H. Y. (2014). An environment Kuznets curve for GHG emissions: A panel cointegration analysis. *Energy Sources, Part B: Economics, Planning and Policy, 9*(2), 120–129.

Cole, M. A. (2007). Corruption, income and the environment: An empirical analysis. *Ecological Economics, 62*, 637–647.

Coskuner, C., Paskeh, M. K., Olasehinde-Williams, G., & Akadiri, S. S. (2020). Economic and social determinants of carbon emissions: Evidence from organization of petroleum exporting countries. *Journal of Public Affairs, 20*(3), e2092.

Cosmas, N. C., Chitedze, I., & Mourad, K. A. (2019). An econometric analysis of the macroeconomic determinants of carbon dioxide emissions in Nigeria. *Science of the Total Environment, 675*, 313–324.

De Alegría, I. M., Basañez, A., De Basurto, P. D., & Fernández-Sainz, A. (2016). Spains fulfillment of its Kyoto commitments and its fundamental greenhouse gas (GHG) emission reduction drivers. *Renewable and Sustainable Energy Reviews, 59*, 858–867.

Dogan, E., & Seker, F. (2016). An investigation on the determinants of carbon emissions for OECD countries: Empirical evidence from panel models robust to heterogeneity and cross-sectional dependence. *Environmental Science and Pollution Research, 23*(14), 14646–14655.

Dogan, E., & Turkekul, B. (2016). CO2 emissions, real output, energy consumption, trade, urbanisation and financial development: Testing the EKC hypothesis for the USA. *Environmental Science and Pollution Research, 23*(2), 1203–1213.

Friedl, B., & Getzner, M. (2003). Determinants of CO2 emissions in a small open economy. *Ecological Economics, 45*(1), 133–148.

Gbadamosi, A. (2022). Understanding the developed/developing country taxonomy. https://www.a4id.org/policy/understanding-the-developeddeveloping-country-taxonomy

Gill, A. R., Viswanathan, K. K., & Hassan, S. (2018). A test of environmental Kuznets curve (EKC) for carbon emission and potential of renewable energy to reduce green house gases (GHG) in Malaysia. *Environment, Development and Sustainability, 20*, 1103–1114.

Glaeser, E. L., & Kahn, M. E. (2010). The greenness of cities: Carbon dioxide emissions and urban development. *Journal of Urban Economics, 67*(3), 404–418.

Gozgor, G. (2017). Does trade matter for carbon emissions in OECD countries? Evidence from a new trade openness measure. *Environmental Science and Pollution Research, 24*(36), 27813–27821.

Hussein, A. (2005). *Principles of environmental economics.* Routledge.

IPCC. (2014). *Climate change 2014: Impacts, adaptation, and vulnerability. Part A: Global and sectoral aspects. Contribution of working group II to the fifth assessment report of the intergovernmental panel on climate change.* (C. B., Field, V. R., Barros, D. J., Dokken, K. J., Mach, M. D., Mastrandrea, T. E., Bilir, M., Chatterjee, K. L., Ebi, Y. O., Estrada, R. C., Genova, B., Girma, E. S., Kissel, A. N., Levy, S., MacCracken, P. R., Mastrandrea, & L. L., White (eds.)).

Cambridge University Press. papers2://publication/uuid/B8BF5043-C873-4AFD-97F9-A630782E590D

Ivanovski, K., & Churchill, S. A. (2020). Convergence and determinants of greenhouse gas emissions in Australia: A regional analysis. *Energy Economics, 92*, 104971.

Iwata, H., Okada, K., & Samreth, S. (2010). Empirical study on the environmental Kuznets curve for CO_2 in France: The role of nuclear energy. *Energy Policy, 38*(8), 4057–4063.

Jalil, A., & Mahmud, S. F. (2009). Environment Kuznets curve for CO_2 emissions: A cointegration analysis for China. *Energy Policy, 37*(12), 5167–5172.

Kohler, M. (2013). CO2 emissions, energy consumption, income and foreign trade: A South African perspective. *Energy Policy, 63*, 1042–1050.

Lapinskienė, G., Peleckis, K., & Slavinskaitė, N. (2017). Energy consumption, economic growth and greenhouse gas emissions in the European Union countries. *Journal of Business Economics and Management, 18*(6), 1082–1097.

Lau, L. S., Choong, C. K., & Eng, Y. K. (2014). Investigation of the environmental Kuznets curve for carbon emissions in Malaysia: Do foreign direct investment and trade matter? *Energy Policy, 68*, 490–497.

Le Quéré, C., Korsbakken, J. I., Wilson, C., Tosun, J., Andrew, R., Andres, R. J., Canadell, J. G., Jordan, A., Peters, G. P., & van Vuuren, D. P. (2019). Drivers of declining CO_2 emissions in 18 developed economies. *Nature Climate Change, 9*(3), 213–217.

Leitão, A. (2010). Corruption and the environmental Kuznets curve: Empirical evidence for sulfur. *Ecological Economics, 69*, 2191–2201.

Liobikienė, G., & Butkus, M. (2017). The European Union possibilities to achieve targets of Europe 2020 and Paris agreement climate policy. *Renewable Energy, 106*, 298–309.

Liobikienė, G., Butkus, M., & Bernatonienė, J. (2016). Drivers of greenhouse gas emissions in the Baltic states: Decomposition analysis related to the implementation of Europe 2020 strategy. *Renewable and Sustainable Energy Reviews, 54*, 309–317.

Lisciandra, M., & Migliardo, C. (2017). An empirical study of the impact of corruption on environmental performance: Evidence from panel data. *Environmental and Resource Economics, 68*, 297–318.

Moses, O., Michael, E. E., & Dabel-Moses, J. N. (2019). A review of environmental management and reporting regulations in Nigeria. In *Advances in environmental accounting and management* (Vol. 8, pp. 159–182). https://doi.org/10.1108/s1479-359820190000008007

Moses, O., Nnam, I. J., Olaniyan, J. D., & Tariquzzaman, A. T. M. (2022). Sustainable Development Goals (SDGS): Assessment of implementation progress in BRICS and MINT. In *Advances in environmental accounting and management* (Vol. 10, pp. 11–44). https://doi.org/10.1108/S1479-359820220000010002

Onafowora, O. A., & Owoye, O. (2014). Bounds testing approach to analysis of the environment Kuznets curve hypothesis. *Energy Economics, 44*, 47–62.

Ozcan, B. (2013). The nexus between carbon emissions, energy consumption and economic growth in Middle East countries: A panel data analysis. *Energy Policy, 62*, 1138–1147.

Ozturk, I., & Al-Mulali, U. (2015). Investigating the validity of the environmental Kuznets curve hypothesis in Cambodia. *Ecological Indicators, 57*, 324–330.

Pachauri, R., & Meyer, L. (2014). *Climate change 2014: Synthesis report*. Contribution. In Contribution of working groups I, II and III to the fifth assessment report of the intergovernmental panel on climate change.

Pao, H. T., & Tsai, C. M. (2011). Multivariate Granger causality between CO_2 emissions, energy consumption, FDI (foreign direct investment) and GDP (gross domestic product): Evidence from a panel of BRIC (Brazil, Russian federation, India, and China) countries. *Energy, 36*(1), 685–693.

Pata, U. K. (2018). Renewable energy consumption, urbanisation, financial development, income and CO_2 emissions in Turkey: Testing EKC hypothesis with structural breaks. *Journal of Cleaner Production, 187*, 770–779.

Puertas, R., & Marti, L. (2021). Eco-innovation and determinants of GHG emissions in OECD countries. *Journal of Cleaner Production, 319*, 128739.

Ramos, T. B., Caeiro, S., Van Hoof, B., Lozano, R., Huisingh, D., & Ceulemans, K. (2015). Experiences from the implementation of sustainable development in higher education institutions: Environmental management for sustainable universities. *Journal of Cleaner Production*, *106*, 3–10.

Ritchie, H., Roser, M., & Rosado, P. (2020). CO_2 and greenhouse gas emissions. Our world in data. https://ourworldindata.org/. Accessed on October 21, 2022.

Rosa, E. A., & Dietz, T. (2012). Human drivers of national greenhouse-gas emissions. *Nature Climate Change*, *2*, 581–586.

Saboori, B., & Sulaiman, J. (2013). Environmental degradation, economic growth and energy consumption: Evidence of the environmental Kuznets curve in Malaysia. *Energy Policy*, *60*, 892–905.

Saboori, B., Sulaiman, J., & Mohd, S. (2012). Economic growth and CO_2 emissions in Malaysia: A cointegration analysis of the environmental Kuznets curve. *Energy Policy*, *51*, 184–191.

Sarwar, S., Streimikiene, D., Waheed, R., & Mighri, Z. (2021). Revisiting the empirical relationship among the main targets of sustainable development: Growth, education, health and carbon emissions. *Sustainable Development*, *29*(2), 419–440.

Shahbaz, M., Lean, H. H., & Shabbir, M. S. (2012). Environmental Kuznets curve hypothesis in Pakistan: Cointegration and Granger causality. *Renewable and Sustainable Energy Reviews*, *16*(5), 2947–2953.

Shahbaz, M., Mutascu, M., & Azim, P. (2013). Environmental Kuznets curve in Romania and the role of energy consumption. *Renewable and Sustainable Energy Reviews*, *18*, 165–173.

Tang, C. F., & Tan, B. W. (2015). The impact of energy consumption, income and foreign direct investment on carbon dioxide emissions in Vietnam. *Energy*, *79*, 447–454.

Tan, F., Lean, H. H., & Khan, H. (2014). Growth and environmental quality in Singapore: Are there any trade-off? *Ecological Indicators*, *47*, 149–155.

The World Bank. (2021). The world by income and region. https://datatopics.worldbank.org/world-development-indicators/the-world-by-income-and-region.html

Tiwari, A. K., Shahbaz, M., & Hye, Q. M. A. (2013). The environmental Kuznets curve and the role of coal consumption in India: Cointegration and causality analysis in an open economy. *Renewable and Sustainable Energy Reviews*, *18*, 519–527.

Wang, S. S., Zhou, D. Q., Zhou, P., & Wang, Q. W. (2011). CO2 emissions, energy consumption and economic growth in China: A panel data analysis. *Energy Policy*, *39*(9), 4870–4875.

Yıldırım, A. E., & Yıldırım, M. O. (2021). Revisiting the determinants of carbon emissions for Turkey: The role of construction sector. *Environmental Science and Pollution Research*, *28*(31), 42325–42338.

Zhu, T., Peng, H., Zhang, Y., & Liu, J. (2021). Does higher education development facilitate carbon emissions reduction in China. *Applied Economics*, *53*(47), 5490–5502.

Zmami, M., & Ben-Salha, O. (2020). An empirical analysis of the determinants of CO2 emissions in GCC countries. *The International Journal of Sustainable Development and World Ecology*, *27*(5), 469–480.

APPENDIX 1: LIST OF TOP GHG EMITTING COUNTRIES

No.	Top 100 Countries	Developed Countries	Developing Countries
1	China	China	India
2	United States	United States	Iran
3	India	Japan	Indonesia
4	Russia	Germany	Brazil
5	Japan	South Korea	South Africa
6	Iran	Denmark	Mexico
7	Germany	Canada	Turkey
8	South Korea	Australia	Vietnam
9	Saudi Arabia	United Kingdom	Egypt
10	Indonesia	Italy	Kazakhstan
11	Canada	San Marino	Malaysia
12	Brazil	Vatican City	Thailand
13	South Africa	Taiwan	Pakistan
14	Mexico	France	Iraq
15	Turkey	Monaco	Ukraine
16	Australia	Spain	Argentina
17	Vietnam	Andorra	Algeria
18	United Kingdom	United Arab Emirates	Russia
19	Italy	Netherlands	Poland
20	San Marino	Czech Republic	Philippines
21	Vatican City	Austria	Nigeria
22	Poland	Israel	Bangladesh
23	Taiwan	Greece	Qatar
24	France	Hungary	Uzbekistan
25	Monaco	Sweden	Colombia
26	Egypt	Norway	Kuwait
27	Kazakhstan	Finland	Venezuela
28	Malaysia	Portugal	Oman
29	Thailand	Switzerland	Chile
30	Pakistan	New Zealand	Turkmenistan
31	Spain	Ireland	Serbia
32	Andorra	Hong Kong	Montenegro
33	United Arab Emirates	North Korea	Romania
34	Iraq	Slovakia	Morocco
35	Ukraine	Croatia	Belarus
36	Argentina	Liechtenstein	Singapore
37	Algeria		Libya
38	Kenya		Peru
39	Netherlands		Laos
40	Philippines		Mongolia
41	Nigeria		Bulgaria

(Continued)

No.	Top 100 Countries	Developed Countries	Developing Countries
42	Bangladesh		Myanmar
43	Qatar		Bahrain
44	Czech Republic		Azerbaijan
45	Uzbekistan		Ecuador
46	Colombia		Trinidad and Tobago
47	Kuwait		Dominican Republic
48	Venezuela		Tunisia
49	Oman		Lebanon
50	Chile		Jordan
51	Turkmenistan		Saudi Arabia
52	Serbia		Syria
53	Montenegro		Sri Lanka
54	Romania		Bosnia and Herzegovina
55	Morocco		Cuba
56	Austria		Angola
57	Israel		Bolivia
58	Belarus		Sudan
59	Greece		South Sudan
60	Singapore		Guatemala
61	Libya		Nepal
62	Hungary		Ethiopia
63	Peru		Ghana
64	Sweden		Kenya
65	Norway		
66	Laos		
67	Finland		
68	Portugal		
69	Mongolia		
70	Bulgaria		
71	Myanmar		
72	Bahrain		
73	Switzerland		
74	Azerbaijan		
75	Ecuador		
76	New Zealand		
77	Ireland		
78	Hong Kong		
79	North Korea		
80	Slovakia		
81	Trinidad and Tobago		
82	Dominican Republic		
83	Tunisia		
84	Lebanon		

(Continued)

No.	Top 100 Countries	Developed Countries	Developing Countries
85	Jordan		
86	Denmark		
87	Liechtenstein		
88	Syria		
89	Sri Lanka		
90	Bosnia and Herzegovina		
91	Cuba		
92	Angola		
93	Bolivia		
94	Sudan		
95	South Sudan		
96	Guatemala		
97	Nepal		
98	Croatia		
99	Ethiopia		
100	Ghana		

INDEX

ABS ranking scheme, 16
Advances in Environmental
    Accounting and
    Management (AEAM),
    6, 22
Agency theory, 32–33
Assessment of future risk, 113–114
Australian Business Dean Council
    (ABDC), 16
    A-ranked journals category, 18
    ranking classification scheme, 18
    basic panel fixed model, 62

Binary logistic regression analysis,
    44–45
    corporate governance variables, 45
    dependent variable, 44
Block ownership, 54–55
Board independence, 88
Board interlocks (*see also* Women
            board interlocks)
    CEO interlocks, 86–87
    control variables, 91–93
    correlation matrix and
            multicollinearity, 96
    data and sample selection, 89–90
    descriptive statistics, 93
    empirical results, 93–98
    hypotheses development, 86–89
    independent board interlocks, 88
    main results, 96–98
    measurement of variables, 90
    methodology, 89–93
    model specification, 90–91
    multiple directorships environment
            in India, 85
    resource dependency theory, 84–86
    sensitivity tests, 98
    theoretical framework and
            hypotheses, 85–89

total board interlocks, 88–89
Board size, 52–53, 56–57, 60
BoardIndenpendence (corporate
    governance control
    variables), 40
BoardSize (corporate governance
    control variables), 40
Bombay Stock Exchange (BSE), 5,
    89–90
Breusch–Godfrey Serial Correlation
    LM Test, 106
Breusch–Pagan–Godfrey Test, 106
Brundtland Commission, The, 12
*Business Strategy and the
    Environment*'s GHG
    publication, 22

Carbon dioxide (CO_2), 82, 128
Carbon Disclosure Leadership Index
    (CDLI), 52–53
Carbon Disclosure Project (CDP), 31,
    89–90, 108, 110–111
    disclosures, 109
    questionnaire, 115–116
    scores, 116
Carbon emissions, 5
Carbon emissions performance (CP),
    96–97
    CEO interlocks, 86–87
    control variables, 91–93
    correlation matrix and multi-
            collinearity, 96
    data and sample selection, 89–90
    descriptive statistics, 93
    empirical results, 93–98
    hypotheses development, 86–89
    independent board interlocks, 88
    main results, 96–98
    measurement of variables, 90
    methodology, 89–93

model specification, 90–91
multiple directorships environment
    in India, 85
resource dependency theory, 85–86
sensitivity tests, 98
theoretical framework and
    hypotheses, 85–89
total board interlocks, 88–89
women board interlocks, 87–88
Carbon management accounting
    (CMA), 14–15
CEOs' interlocks (CEIL), 98–99
Chartered Association of Business
    Schools (ABS), 16
Chief executive officers (CEOs), 56,
    82–83
    interlocks, 83–84, 86–87
China
    binary logistic regression analysis,
        44–45
    control variables, 40–41
    data collection and methodology,
        38–41
    dependent variable, 39
    descriptive statistics, 41
    empirical results, 41–45
    GHG emissions disclosures in,
        29–32
    government ownership in, 5
    hypotheses development, 36–38
    independent variables, 40
    literature review and hypotheses
        development, 32–38
    model specification, 38–39
    sample selection, 38
    SOE, 34, 36, 38
    theoretical framework, 32–34
China Stock Market & Accounting
    Research Database
    (CSMAR), 31
Chinese Communist Party (CCP),
    34–35
Chinese SOEs, 31, 35–38
Climate Accountability Institute, 3
Climate change, 82, 108
    control measures, 144

Companies Act, The (2013), 85, 89
Company-specific control variables,
    73
Conference of Parties (COP), 5–6
Continuous variables, 118
Control variables, 40–41, 61, 76, 91,
    93, 100–101, 144–145
Corporate environmental
    performance (CEP), 14
Corporate governance
    correlation of dependent and
        independent variables, 70
    dependent variable, 63–69
    econometric modelling, 60
    hypothesis development, 56–59
    independent variables, 70
    literature review, 55–56
    measurement of variables, 60–61
    mechanisms, 54
    methodology, 59–63
    multivariate results, 70–73
    results, 63–73
    review of prior studies, 56
    robustness check, 73
    study design and sample selection,
        59–60
    theoretical foundation, 55
    variables, 45, 52–53
Correlation matrix, 96
Correlation of Dependent and Inde-
    pendent Variables, 70
Corruption, 144
Corruption perception index (CPI),
    150
COVID-19 pandemic, 108
Cyclones, 2–3, 128

Decision-making process, 34–35
    in SOE, 34–35
Dependent variables (see also Inde-
    pendent variables), 39, 44,
    60, 63, 69, 116
    correlation of, 70
Developed countries, 128–129,
    132–133, 145–146

determinants of GHG emissions in,
        130
Developing countries, 128–129,
        132–133
    determinants of GHG emissions in,
        130, 145
Development process, 150
Droughts, 2–3, 128
Duality (corporate governance control
        variables), 40

Econometric modelling, 60
Economic sustainability, 144–145
Economics-oriented decision-making
        process, 37
Emission Industry, 40
Empirical model, 145–146
Environmental disclosure, 111
Environmental Kuznets curve (EKC),
        128–129
Environmental pollution, 144
Environmental responsibilities, 30–31
Explanatory research design, 59–60

Financial slack, 40, 61, 76
Financial-sector firms, 59–60
FirmSize, 40
Fixed–effects modelling technique, 62
Full Information Maximum Likeli-
        hood (FIML), 97
Future risk variable, 121

GenderDiversity (corporate gover-
        nance control variables), 40
Generalised method of moments
        (GMM), 97–98
Global Climate Risk Index 2020, 82
Global Reporting Initiative (GRI), 13
Global warming, 52
Greenhouse gas disclosures, 30–32, 60
    board size and, 56–57
    correlation of dependent and
        independent variables, 70
    dependent variable, 63–69
    econometric modelling, 60
    hypothesis development, 56–59

independent variables, 70
    insider ownership and, 59
    literature review, 55–56
    measurement of variables, 60–61
    methodology, 59–63
    multivariate results, 70–73
    ownership concentration and,
        58–59
    proportion of non-executive
        directors and, 57–58
    results, 63–73
    review of prior studies, 56
    robustness check, 73
    study design and sample selection,
        59–60
    theoretical foundation, 55
Greenhouse gas emissions, 2, 6, 23,
        30, 52, 56–57, 82, 108–109,
        128
    detrimental effect of, 30
    disclosures, 74–75
    GHG articles spread by continent,
        19
    GHG articles spread by country,
        17–19
    method and data, 16
    results, 16–20
    studies on GHG reporting and
        disclosure research, 13–16
Greenhouse gases (GHGs), 2, 12
    contributions to special issue, 4–6
    issue, 4
    literature, 14
    practices, 12–13
    reporting initiatives, 12–13
    studies on GHG reporting and
        disclosure research, 13–16
Gross domestic product (GDP), 6, 128
    GDP/CAPITA, 41
Gulf Cooperation Council, 132

Hausman's test, 116
Heckman's regression analysis, 98
Heteroscedasticity test, 70, 106
High-income countries, 128–129

Human-induced actions, 128

Incentives, 109
Income groups, 145
Income status, 128–129
Independent board interlocks (IBIL),
        88, 100
Independent variables (*see also*
        Dependent variables), 40,
        60, 70
    correlation of, 70
India, 82
    carbon emissions performance in, 5
    multiple directorships environment
        in, 85
Indian Companies Act (2013), 86,
        89–90
Indian public Ltd companies, 87
Industry variable, 73
Insider ownership (independent
        variable), 60, 75–76
    and GHG disclosures, 59
Institutional theory, 111, 113
Intergovernmental Panel on Climate
        Change (IPCC), 12
International Financial Reporting
        Standards (IFRS), 57
ISI-IF number, 18–19
Issue documents, 4

Jarque–Bera test for normality,
        106
Johannesburg Stock Exchange (JSE),
        109
Journals, 22

Key management personnel, 114
Kyoto Protocol, 82–84, 108, 112

Legitimacy theory, 32, 111
Leverage, 91, 93, 100–101
Literacy, 6, 129–130, 143–144, 150
Low-income countries, 128–129
Lower middle-income countries,
        128–129

Majoritarian electoral systems (MAJ),
        15–16
Management incentives, 113
MarketBookValue, 40
Meta–analysis of research in GHG
        practices, 13
Ministry of Environment, Forest and
        Climate Change (MoEF),
        82
Mixed-method approach, 19
Monetary incentives, 109, 113
Monetary rewards, 113
Multicollinearity, 70, 96
Multiple directorships environment in
        India, 85
Multivariate results, 70–73

National Association of Corporate
        Director's guideline, The,
        86
Neo-institutional theory, 32
Net-zero carbon emissions,
        12
Net-zero goal (2050), 22
New York Stock Exchange (NYSE),
        5, 54, 59–60
Non-executive directors (NEDs),
        52–53, 60, 73, 75
    and GHG disclosures, 57–58
    proportion of, 53
Non-monetary incentives, 109,
        119–120
Non-monetary rewards, 113

OECD, 30–31, 34–36
Ordinary least squares dummy
        variable model, 62
Organisation strategy, 86
Organization of Petroleum Exporting
        Countries (OPEC),
        131–132
Ownership concentration
        (independent variable), 60
    and GHG Disclosures,
        58–59

Panel data, 116
  model, 145–146
Paris Agreement, 108–109, 112
Paris Climate Agreement (PCA), 5–6,
  12–14, 22, 97
Paris climate change agreement
  assessment of future risk, 113–114
  CDP Questionnaire, 115–116
  descriptive statistics, 116–121
  key management personnel, 114
  literature review, 110–114
  management incentives, 113
  Paris Agreement, 112
  research approach, 116
  research methodology, 114–116
  results, 116–121
  prior studies and hypotheses
    development, 112–114
  theoretical framework, 110–112
Policy-oriented decision-making
  process, 37
Political self–interests, 31–32, 36–37
Population, 142–143
Power differentials, 33–34
  in SOEs, 37–38

Qualitative articles, 22
Quantitative articles, 22
Quantitative data, 69

Ramsey's RESET test for linearity,
  106
Recognition, 113, 119–120
Regression model, 73
Research approach, 116
Resource dependency theory, 84–86
ROA, 40

Sargan test, 97
SEBI Listing Obligations and
  Disclosure Requirements
  (SEBI LODR), 85
Second-order autocorrelation test, 97
Securities and Exchange Board of
  India (SEBI), 85
Sensitivity tests, 98

Social determinants of greenhouse gas
  emissions
  control variables, 144–145
  corruption, 144
  data and sample, 145
  descriptive statistics, 146–147
  empirical model and variables,
    145–146
  hypotheses development, 142–145
  literacy, 143–144
  literature review, 130–133
  methodology, 145–146
  multivariate results, 147–148
  population, 142–143
  results, 146–151
  urbanisation, 142
Sociopolitical theories of voluntary
  disclosure, 111
Sound corporate governance
  mechanisms, 55
South African Department of
  Environmental Affairs, The
  (South African DEA),
  110–111
Stakeholder theory, 32, 55–57, 111
Stakeholder–agency theory, 32–34,
  36–38
Stakeholders, 32–33, 53, 75–76
State-owned enterprises (SOEs),
  30–31, 34, 36, 38, 40
Static model of panel data, 62
Study models, 62–63
Sustainable Development Goal 13
  (SDG13), 13–14

Top emitters, 2–3
  environmental management
    practices of, 4
Top GHG emitting countries,
  156–158
Total board interlocks (TBIL), 88–89,
  100
Total disclosure index score, 60

United Arab Emirates (UAE), 19

United Nations Environmental
    Programme (UNEP), 12
United Nations Framework
    Convention on Climate
    Change, The (UNFCCC),
    82, 108
United Nations Global Compact
    (UNGC), 12
United States, 52, 54–55
  GHG disclosures in, 5
Upper-middle income countries,
    128–129
Urbanisation, 131–133, 142

Variables, 39, 62–63, 145–146
  control variables, 61
  dependent variable, 60

independent variables, 60
  measurement of, 60–61, 90
Variance inflation factors (VIFs),
    96
Voluntary disclosure, 110
  practices, 111
  sociopolitical theories of, 111

Wald test, 97
Women board interlocks (WEIL),
    83–84, 87–88, 99–100
World Bank, The, 145
World Commission on Environment
    and Development, 12
World Health Organisation, 30
World Meteorological Organisation,
    12

Printed and bound by CPI Group (UK) Ltd, Croydon, CR0 4YY

01/07/2024

14521975-0001